Preparing Literature Reviews

Qualitative and Quantitative Approaches

Second Edition

M. Ling Pan

Pyrczak Publishing
P.O. Box 250430 • Glendale, CA 91225

"Pyrczak Publishing" is an imprint of Fred Pyrczak, Publisher, A California Corporation.

Project Director: Monica Lopez.

Cover design by Robert Kibler and Larry Nichols.

Editorial assistance provided by Sharon Young, Brenda Koplin, Kenneth Ornburn, Randall R. Bruce, Cheryl Alcorn, and Erica Simmons.

Printed in the United States of America by Malloy, Inc.

ISBN 1-884585-56-6

Contents

Continued →

Table

Introduction to the Second Edition

A literature review is an original work based on a critical examination of the literature on a topic. The reviewer should evaluate the available evidence as well as relevant theories (while noting gaps in the literature) and create a synthesis that points readers in the direction of what seems likely to be true about the topic. Reviewers deal with likelihoods because all methods of inquiry are subject to error.

Preparing an adequate literature review is far from being a mechanical process. Instead, it is part science and part art. "Science" comes into play because there are usually a considerable number of original research reports to be evaluated when preparing a review on a given topic. Knowing the basics of the scientific method, many of which are covered in this book, is important to making proper evaluations of relevant research. "Art" (i.e., the subjective part) comes into play because the reviewer needs to make sense of the body of literature, which may require subjective judgments regarding which sources to emphasize, how to combine various sources, and how to account for gaps in knowledge on a topic so that a cohesive synthesis of the literature results.

Qualitatively Oriented Versus Quantitatively Oriented Reviews

As you know from the subtitle of this book, you will learn the basics for preparing both qualitative (i.e., narrative) and quantitative reviews. These do not constitute a dichotomy. Rather, literature reviews exist on a continuum from very highly qualitative (with little mention of statistics or the research methods used to obtain them) to very highly quantitative (with the final synthesis based on the mathematical averaging of results across various studies reported by different researchers). Most beginning students should consider writing a qualitative review in which statistical material is very judiciously selected for inclusion in the review. This book shows you how to select and interpret such statistical material and how to present it without overwhelming your readers.

As you will learn in this book, qualitative reviews and quantitative reviews have a great deal in common, so almost all of this book (Chapters 1 through 10 and Chapters 13 through 15) will be relevant regardless of the reviewer's orientation to the issue of quantification. Even Chapters 11 and 12, which cover the highly quantitative technique called "meta-analysis," contain suggestions for those who write qualitative reviews.

About the End-of-Chapter Exercises

The end-of-chapter exercises are designed to be used as homework assignments. They will help you review the material you have read and also help you consider how to use what you have learned from each chapter while you are preparing your literature review.

About the Appendices

Appendix A presents a checklist of the guidelines presented throughout this book. It can be used in several ways. First, it can be used as an index to help you quickly locate material that you read earlier and want to locate in order to reread and review it. Second, you can use it as a checklist of reminders to reconsider as you revise each draft of your review. Third, instructors can use it for easy reference when commenting on students' literature reviews. For instance, instead of writing out a criticism (either positive or negative), an instructor can refer to the checklist to quickly locate appropriate guidelines in order to write statements such as "Please improve this section. See Guideline 8.5." or "Good application of Guideline 9.2."

Appendix B provides an overview of the differences between qualitative and quantitative *research*. In the body of this book, you will find extensive discussions of the differences between qualitative and quantitative *literature reviews*. It is important to note that *research* can also be qualitatively or quantitatively oriented. Appendix B will help you understand the strengths and weaknesses of both orientations to research, which will help you evaluate each type properly when you prepare a literature review.

About the Model Literature Reviews

Seven model literature reviews are presented near the end of this book. They are "models" in the sense that they are well-written examples that illustrate various ways to evaluate, discuss, and synthesize literature. Note, however, that no one model fits all purposes. For instance, a literature review written for inclusion in a doctoral dissertation normally would be more extensive and detailed than one written as a senior project by an undergraduate.

Model Literature Reviews 1 through 5 are qualitatively oriented, while Reviews 6 and 7 are meta-analyses, which is a quantitative approach to synthesizing literature.

A common set of questions appears at the end of all the model literature reviews. These are designed to help you consider the strengths of each review and will be useful as classroom discussion items.

About the Second Edition

The treatment of meta-analysis has been expanded and now constitutes two chapters. In addition, three new chapters have been added: Chapter 13 (A Closer Look at Creating a Synthesis), Chapter 14 (Writing Titles and Abstracts), and Chapter 15 (Citing References).

Acknowledgments

Dr. Gene Glass of Arizona State University, Tempe, and Dr. Deborah M. Oh of California State University, Los Angeles, provided many helpful comments to this book. Although these individuals made important contributions to the development of this book, errors and omissions, of course, remain the responsibility of the author.

Concluding Notes

I wish you success in preparing your literature review, and I hope that the guidelines and examples in this book will prove helpful. The guidelines are based on my extensive reading of literature reviews in a variety of fields for more than three decades.

Note that I have included a large number of examples to illustrate the guidelines in this book. The examples that have references, of course, are quoted from published sources. The remaining examples were written by me. These were written to parallel types of material I have frequently encountered in literature reviews. In many of these cases, the examples illustrate undesirable techniques that should be avoided. Instead of quoting such examples (and potentially embarrassing the authors), I created ones similar to those that I have seen in recent literature reviews.

I encourage you to share with me your criticisms of this book. You can communicate with me via my publisher. The mailing address is shown on the title page of this book. Also, you can send e-mails to me in care of the publisher at info@pyrczak.com.

M. Ling Pan
Los Angeles, California

Notes:

Chapter 1

Qualitative Versus Quantitative Reviews

A literature review is a *synthesis* of the literature on a topic. To create the synthesis, one must first interpret and evaluate individual pieces of literature. Then, the ideas and information they contain must be integrated and restated in order to create a new, original written work. Box 1A contains the definition of "synthesis" given in the on-line version of the *Merriam-Webster Unabridged Dictionary* (2003).

Box 1A *Dictionary definition of "synthesis."*

> *Synthesis*: "The combining of often varied and diverse ideas, forces, or factors into one coherent or consistent complex."

In light of the definition of the term "synthesis," it is clear that a literature review is *not* a simple string of summaries of the works of others. Instead, it is a complex, coherent work based on the diverse material found in the literature on a topic.

Brief Overview of Steps in Preparing a Literature Review

The first step is to select a topic. In most cases, this is an interactive process in which the initial search of the literature reveals how much exists on a topic. Based on this information, the initial topic may need to be narrowed if there is too much literature or broadened if there is too little. At the same time, the needs of the audience for whom the review is being written will influence the selection of a topic.

The second step is to read the literature and make notes, with an eye toward getting a broad overview of which issues have been thoroughly covered, which ones need more investigation, which principles seem most firmly established and/or most widely accepted as being valid, and, perhaps most important, which theories have a bearing on the topic being reviewed.

While conducting the second step, establish specific purposes for your literature review. For instance, Box 1B shows some possible purposes for a review. Note that establishing purposes is an interactive process (i.e., as you initially read the literature, you modify the purposes in light of what you read). For instance, if there are no experiments on a treatment (see Purpose 3 in Box 1B), you cannot include synthesizing the results of them as one of the purposes.

Note that the purposes should be put in writing. These can then be incorporated into the introduction to your literature review. In addition, if you are preparing a literature review for a class, you might share your purposes with your instructor in order to get feedback on their appropriateness before you begin to write your review.

Box 1B *Sample purposes for a literature review on Treatment X.*

The purposes of this literature review are to:

1. trace the history of scientific developments, including relevant theories, that resulted in the development of Treatment X,
2. summarize and evaluate the legal and ethical issues involving the implementation of the treatment,
3. estimate the overall degree of effectiveness of the treatment by evaluating the experiments in which the treatment was compared with a placebo, and
4. describe possible fruitful areas for future research based on the research conducted to date.

The next steps are to evaluate and interpret the literature. Many authors of literature reviews give high evaluations to sources that present the results of rigorous scientific studies. (Often, these authors tend to be quantitatively oriented.) Others give high evaluations to studies that provide crucial insights even if the underlying methods for collecting data are mildly, or even seriously, flawed. (Often, these authors tend to be qualitatively oriented.) Regardless of their orientations, all authors of literature reviews should pay special attention to literature that presents, tests, and/or builds on the theories related to their topics.

Next, the literature needs to be synthesized. This is done by first grouping various sources according to their similarities and differences while considering possible explanations for differences (and contradictions) in the literature. Note that a synthesis very often will not consist of a single, straightforward conclusion. Instead, it might consist of speculation on how the pieces of evidence found in the literature fit together along with some tentative conclusions and a discussion of their implications. This often leads to ideas for future research that might produce a more definitive understanding of the topic.

Finally, the first draft of a literature review should be reviewed by others. Of course, a review by an expert is highly desirable. However, note that a well-written review should be comprehensible to even nonexperts such as other students who can often provide valuable feedback. Revising (and, in some cases, entirely rewriting) a review in light of this feedback is a crucial step in producing a literature review of high quality.

One of the biggest mistakes novice writers make is to be defensive when receiving feedback, which dilutes its role in improving a review. It is especially important to pay careful attention to any portion of the review that a reviewer says is unclear. Even if it is perfectly clear to you (perhaps, because you have more context from your reading of the literature), you should consider rewriting it in order to make it clearer for your readers. Box 1C summarizes the major steps in preparing a literature review.

Box 1C *Summary of major steps in preparing a literature review.*

The major steps in preparing a literature review are:
1. Select a topic, and modify it in light of the amount of available literature and your audience's needs.
2. Read the selected literature carefully in order to get a broad overview, with attention to the relationship of the literature to theory or theories, and establish specific purposes for your literature review.
3. Evaluate and interpret the literature on the topic.
4. Create a synthesis by reconciling similarities and differences in the literature. Consider the implications of possible conclusions, and identify fruitful areas for future research.
5. Write a first draft, get feedback on it from others, and revise or rewrite your review.

In this book, we will consider the preparation of both qualitatively oriented and quantitatively oriented reviews. The following guidelines will help you distinguish between the two types of reviews.

✤ Guideline 1.1

In quantitatively oriented literature reviews, precise statistical results from the literature are presented and sometimes mathematically combined.

Authors of both quantitative and qualitative reviews should write narratives that describe the importance of their topics, provide overviews of the types of literature that exist on their topics (including gaps in the literature), and make overall evaluations of the bodies of literature on their topics. The main distinction between the quantitatively oriented and qualitatively oriented reviews lies in the extent to which specific statistics are used in creating a synthesis. Those who write quantitatively oriented reviews base their synthesis and conclusions more closely on specific statistical values than those who write qualitatively oriented reviews. Compare the statement in Example 1.1.1 below with the one in Example 1.3.1 (under Guideline 1.3) to get a better understanding of this distinction. Both statements refer to the same three studies.

Example 1.1.1

Sample statement that might appear in a quantitatively oriented review:

The three experiments in which Drug A was compared with a placebo yielded mean reductions on the Pain Relief Scale of 2.1, 3.3, and 4.0 points on a scale from 0 (no pain) to 20 (extreme pain). All three were statistically significant at the $p < .05$ level. The mean (i.e., arithmetic average) of these three means is 3.1, which is the best estimate of the effectiveness of Drug A. Hence, Drug A appears to produce a small but significant reduction in pain.[1]

✎ Guideline 1.2

If the main thrust of a review is the mathematical combination of results of studies by various researchers, the result is called a meta-analysis or meta-analytic review.

The prefix "meta-" means *going beyond* or *transcending*. Thus, meta-analysis refers to a statistical analysis that goes beyond or transcends previous statistical analyses. For example, the author of Example 1.1.1 used a meta-analytic technique by going beyond the original analyses and averaging results across three studies.

The use of meta-analytic techniques (such as averaging means or correlation coefficients across studies) is most likely to be found in quantitatively oriented reviews. There is no reason, however, why the author of a primarily qualitatively oriented review could not occasionally use such a technique to make his or her review more quantitatively oriented than it otherwise would be.

When the main thrust of a review is to identify and include only those studies that lend themselves to statistical averaging and when the synthesis and conclusions are based primarily on this mathematical combination of the statistical results, the entire document is called a "meta-analysis" or "meta-analytic review."[2]

Chapter 11 describes some straightforward meta-analytic techniques that can be used by those who write *both* quantitatively oriented and qualitatively oriented reviews. In addition, that chapter along with Chapter 12 provide enough information so that one could produce a basic meta-analytic review.

✎ Guideline 1.3

In qualitatively oriented reviews, statistical studies are often described in general terms, but precise statistical values are de-emphasized.

Authors of qualitatively oriented reviews typically present evidence found in the literature with little emphasis on the precise statistical results. Nevertheless, relevant

---

[1] As you probably know, the *mean* is the most popular average. When different studies have different numbers of participants (or subjects), a weighting procedure should be employed in computing the mean of the means. This procedure is covered in Chapter 12. For the purposes of this example, we will assume that all three experiments had the same number of participants. Combining statistical results across experiments, as illustrated in Example 1.1.1, is called *meta-analysis*, which is the topic of Chapters 11 and 12.

[2] Note that while some researchers regard a meta-analysis as a mathematical literature review, others regard it as original research. Hence, it is not uncommon to find meta-analyses published as original research in journals that have editorial policies that do not permit publication of qualitatively oriented reviews. Also note that if your ultimate goal is publication of your literature review in a journal that publishes reviews, you should examine a number of reviews in those journals in order to learn how they are written. While some prestigious journals such as *Psychological Bulletin* publish only literature reviews, others mainly publish reports in which literature reviews are the preface to reports of original empirical research (see Guideline 1.6 for a definition of "empirical research").

statistical evidence is referred to and even interpreted in a general sense, as illustrated in Example 1.3.1 in which no statistics are reported.

Example 1.3.1

Sample statement that might appear in a qualitatively oriented review:

In each of the three experiments in which Drug A was compared with a placebo, there was a very small but significant reduction in pain reported by those who took the drug. The failure to obtain a large reduction in pain points to the need to investigate other drugs that may be more beneficial in reducing pain.

Note that both Examples 1.1.1 and 1.3.1 refer to the same three studies in the literature. However, 1.1.1 is much more quantitative than 1.3.1.

In summary, authors of highly qualitatively oriented reviews often make general references to statistical findings but typically report few statistical values.

ꙮ Guideline 1.4

Qualitative and quantitative reviews have many common features.

The authors of both qualitatively oriented and quantitatively oriented reviews have an obligation to cover certain common ground, including the following:

a. introducing the topic and defining key terms,
b. establishing the importance of the topic,
c. providing an overview of the amount of available literature and its types (e.g., theoretical, statistical, speculative),
d. describing how they searched for relevant literature,
e. discussing their selection of literature to include in their review (especially if there is much literature on the topic and not all of it could be covered),
f. pointing out gaps in the literature (i.e., areas that are not covered by the literature),
g. describing and, if possible, reconciling discrepancies in the literature,
h. arriving at a synthesis, and
i. discussing possible implications and directions for future research.

These and many other important issues in the preparation of both qualitatively oriented and quantitatively oriented literature reviews are covered in Chapters 2 through 10 along with Chapters 13 through 15. Chapters 11 and 12 present meta-analytic techniques, some of which might also be used by those who are preparing qualitatively oriented reviews.

ꙮ Guideline 1.5

Many literature reviews are a blend of qualitatively oriented and quantitatively oriented approaches.

Many literature reviews employ a blend of techniques. That is why the term "oriented" is used throughout this book. It would be difficult to find in print a purely qualitative review (one without even some general references to statistical results) or to find a purely quantitative review (one without a qualitative narrative component that helps readers interpret the statistical aspects of the literature being cited).

✤ Guideline 1.6
Distinguish between qualitative versus quantitative *literature reviews* and qualitative versus quantitative *empirical research.*

As you know, a literature review is a narrative essay in which the literature on a topic is evaluated, described, and synthesized. The synthesis may be based on ordering and comparing pieces of literature and using logic (and sometimes, just plain common sense) to arrive at conclusions. Such a review is a *qualitatively oriented review.* If the synthesis is based primarily on statistics reported in the literature, it is a *quantitatively oriented review.* In the most highly quantitative review (called a "meta-analysis"), statistics from various studies are mathematically combined to create new statistics on which the synthesis is primarily based.

The term *empirical* refers to making observations. When it is combined with the term *research*, it refers to a research process in which direct, original observations are made in order to create new data or information. For example, if you select a sample of students enrolled in a college and ask them a series of questions about their satisfaction with the abilities of their instructors, you are generating new data. The data can be in the form of statistics (such as the percentage who answered each yes–no question in a certain way), which is called *quantitative empirical research.* The data for such a study can also be in the form of words that describe students' extended verbal responses to interview questions. These results are often expressed as themes that are typically illustrated with quotations from the participants. This type of empirical research is called *qualitative empirical research.* For more information on the distinctions between qualitative and quantitative empirical research, see Appendix B.

Note that conducting *library research*, which needs to be done in order to locate information generated by others, is *not* equivalent to conducting *empirical research*, in which researchers make original observations to create new information or data.

An important implication of this guideline is that the type of literature that exists on a topic may influence the type of review that is written. If most of the literature on a topic consists of reports of qualitative research, a qualitatively oriented review (or at least a blend with an emphasis on qualitative aspects) would be in order. The opposite is true for areas in which most of the research is quantitative.

✎ Guideline 1.7
Read both qualitatively oriented and quantitatively oriented reviews in preparation for writing a new review.

One of the best ways to learn how to write in any genre is to read many examples of it. Whether you plan to write a qualitatively oriented or a quantitatively oriented review, make a point of reading at least several examples of each very early in your planning stages. Those of you who feel secure in your knowledge of statistics and prefer a *quantitative* approach to acquiring knowledge might be impressed with how informative and helpful a *qualitative* review can be. On the other hand, those who are *qualitatively* oriented might find useful techniques to use in a qualitative review by reading *quantitative* reviews. In this book, we will consider some simple techniques for introducing quantitative information into qualitative reviews, in effect, creating a blend of orientations.

A good place to start is to read Model Literature Review 1, which is an example of a short, qualitatively oriented review. Note that Model Literature Reviews 5 and 6 are examples of highly quantitative reviews. (The model literature reviews are near the end of this book.)

Note that these model reviews are, in my opinion, good, solid examples, even though they may have characteristics that might be criticized. Also note that a review might be a model of excellence for one purpose and/or audience while it might be considered quite inadequate for another purpose and/or audience. For instance, a review that is part of a doctoral thesis or one that is written for possible publication in a top-flight journal normally would be more comprehensive and insightful than one written in a single semester as a term paper for a course. If your primary audience is your professor (or a committee of professors), you should seek their guidance on their expectations for your review—including the issue of whether they would prefer a qualitatively oriented or quantitatively oriented review.

Timeline Considerations

Determine how much time is available before the final draft of your literature review is due, and prepare a *written* timeline. Begin by allocating about one-fifth of your available time to each of the five steps in Box 1C on page 3. For example, in a ten-week quarter, allocate two weeks for the first step, two weeks for the second, and so on. If a step takes more or less time than initially allocated, revise and *rewrite* your timeline. Putting it in writing will encourage you to start early and pace yourself.

Exercise for Chapter 1

1. A classmate asks you to critique the first draft of a literature review she has written for a class assignment. While reading the draft, you realize that she has, for the most part, simply summarized one study after another—each summarized in its own paragraph. Based on the information in this chapter, what advice would you give her?

2. In this chapter, you learned that a literature review synthesizes the literature on a topic. In your own words, how would you define a "synthesis"?

3. In this chapter, the process of establishing specific purposes for a review is referred to as "interactive." What does this mean?

4. While some reviewers give high evaluations to literature that reports the results of scientific studies, others may give high evaluations to literature that provides crucial insights even if the scientific methodology is flawed. According to this chapter, to what should all authors of literature reviews pay special attention?

5. In this chapter, what is referred to as a "crucial step" in producing a literature review of high quality?

6. An entire review is called a meta-analysis (i.e., meta-analytic review) when the *main thrust* of the review is to do what?

7. Why is the term "oriented" used throughout this chapter?

8. Briefly define the term "empirical research."

9. Initially, about how much time should be allocated to each of the five steps listed in Box 1C? What is your timeline?

10. *A question for students who have previously written a literature review and/or those who have read reviews extensively*: Do you think that it is possible for a reviewer to be entirely objective? To be very close to being entirely objective? To what extent do statistics help reviewers be objective? Explain.

Chapter 2

Selecting a Topic for Review

The selection of a topic is the single most important step in preparing a literature review. This chapter will help you select topics you might want to review. In the next chapter, you will learn how to refine your topic selections.

✍ Guideline 2.1
Consider carefully your audience's expectations and/or requirements when selecting a topic.

If your primary audience is your professor (or a committee of professors), read carefully any handouts on the literature review assignment, and make careful notes of oral directions that are given.

Some professors will indicate a fairly short maximum page length and number of references to be cited. For such an assignment, a rather narrow topic is usually desirable so that the literature review will be more than just a superficial overview of a broad area. Other professors expect students to write as many pages and cite as many references as needed to provide comprehensive reviews of their topics. In this case, a narrow topic will produce a short paper, and a broader topic will provide you with the opportunity to write a long review. In all cases, you should consult with your professor regarding your topic selection very early in the process.

If you are writing for possible publication in a journal, study examples of reviews in the journals to which you might submit your review. Often, journals print guidelines for potential authors in each issue.

✍ Guideline 2.2
When selecting a topic, emphasize your audience's expectations and requirements instead of your personal interests.

Whenever possible, you should write on a topic of interest to you. Some of you may already have a very strong desire to write a review on a particular topic. This is acceptable as long as you can approach the topic with an open mind and evaluate fairly any literature that is inconsistent with your theories or opinions on the topic.

It is usually highly undesirable to "force a topic to fit" an assignment. For instance, if you are writing a literature review for a history of sociology course but you have a strong interest in a new topic that has a very short history, you should put your topic idea aside (for possible use in another course) and select one that is appropriate for the course in which you are currently enrolled.

One reason that submissions to journals are often rejected is that they are "off topic." If the editor sees that the topic of your literature review is not within the content domain to which the journal is devoted, your literature review will be returned to you without consideration by the editor's editorial board, which provides advice on which submissions to accept for publication. Journals vary greatly in the types of content they cover. If your goal is publication, make sure that your topic is appropriate for publication in at least two or three journals. Also, note that many academic journals have a policy of not publishing (or seldom publishing) stand-alone literature reviews. Instead, they publish exclusively original reports of empirical research that begin with a literature review and are followed by a description of the research methods and the findings. For sample reviews of this type, examine Model Literature Reviews 1 and 3 in this book.

↬ Guideline 2.3

Put possible topics *in writing*. If your professor is your audience, ask him or her to examine your written topic ideas.

Your topic ideas might be single words, or they may be expressed in short phrases, sentences, or paragraphs. In any case, your ideas should be put in writing. It is often helpful to put your written topic ideas away for a day or two and then reconsider them.

Unless your professor asks you to do otherwise, keep your initial written list of topics simple. Avoid the temptation to write essays about your experiences relating to your potential topics and why you want to learn more about them. Your professor will let you know if and when this type of material should be written.

Presenting topic ideas in writing to your professor will help you avoid miscommunication. The feedback you get from a professor (or a committee of professors) on your topic ideas should *not* be construed to be a contract. Like you, your professor may have second thoughts during the early stages of topic selection. Instead, think of presenting ideas in writing to a professor as a way to begin a concrete, specific dialogue on possible topics.

↬ Guideline 2.4

Consider brainstorming a list of possible topics.

The basic premise of brainstorming is to produce (usually tape-record or write down) ideas uncritically. Brainstorming usually works best when conducted by a small group, so you might want to form a group of fellow students for this activity. Group members generate ideas (often in response to ideas suggested by others in a back-and-forth oral dialogue) without criticizing each other's ideas. The reason for not criticizing them is that criticism can inhibit spontaneity and creativity.

At some later point, of course, you and/or your group will need to critically evaluate the ideas generated by a brainstorming session. Sometimes, you will find that combining ideas generated during brainstorming will produce a creative, useful topic for a literature review.

↳ Guideline 2.5
Consider starting by initially selecting broad topics and then narrowing them by adding delimitations.

A delimitation is a restriction on a topic. For instance, a broad topic such as "compliance with physicians' directions by patients" could be delimited in a number of ways. Examples 2.5.1 through 2.5.4 show some possibilities. Note that by adding delimitations, you are making your topic narrower. Avoid the temptation to add so many delimitations that your topic becomes too narrow.

Example 2.5.1
Sample topic delimited by age of patients:

Compliance with physicians' directions by elderly patients.

Example 2.5.2
Sample topic delimited by type of compliance:

Compliance with physicians' directions regarding medications.

Example 2.5.3
Sample topic delimited by type of disease:

Compliance with physicians' directions by patients with diabetes.

Example 2.5.4
Sample topic with two delimitations (type of compliance and type of disease):

Compliance with physicians' directions regarding medications by patients with diabetes.

A common way to delimit a topic is to restrict it by using one or more demographic variables. A demographic variable is a background variable with two or more categories. By selecting one or more of the categories and using them as delimitations, you can narrow your topic. The first column in Box 2A shows some demographic variables widely examined in research. The second column gives samples of categories that might be used when delimiting a topic.[1] The first demographic variable in the box is "age"; its use was illustrated in Example 2.5.1 above. The second one is "education, classification." You might, for example, delimit your topic to "gifted."

---

[1] Not all demographics are appropriate for all topics. Example: It would be inappropriate to use political affiliation as a delimiting variable in a literature review of the emotional status of people who have recently been diagnosed with breast cancer (e.g., it would be inappropriate to plan to review literature on the emotional status of only Republicans who have recently had the diagnosis). When a demographic is highly inappropriate to a topic, there will be little, if any, literature on the topic.

Box 2A *Sample demographic variables and categories.*

Sample demographic variables for delimiting topics:	*Sample categories that might be used to delimit topics:*
age	elderly
education, classification	gifted
education, highest level of	college graduate
education, type of	vocational
employment, length of	newly hired
employment status	employed part-time
ethnicity/race	Caucasian
extracurricular activities	competitive sports
gender	male
group membership	union member
health, mental disorder	depressed
health, overall status	poor health
health, physical disease	diabetes
hobbies	gardening
household composition	intact family with children
income, household	$20,000 to $35,000
income, personal	high income
language preference	Spanish
marital status	divorced
nationality, current	Canadian
national origin	Mexico
occupation	nurse
place of birth	Korea
political activism	votes regularly
political affiliation	Independent
relationship status	divorced
religion, affiliation	Greek Orthodox
religiosity	attends religious services often
residence, place of	New York City metropolitan area
residence, type of	homeless
sexual orientation	heterosexual
size of city/town/area	large urban area
socioeconomic status (SES)	middle SES

Note that you should have a rationale for the selection of delimiters. For instance, cognitive factors associated with medical compliance might be quite different for those with low levels of education than for those with more education, which would be a rationale for delimiting the topic in Example 2.5.5 on the next page.

Of course, you can use more than one category to delimit a topic, as illustrated in Example 2.5.5, in which two categories of "level of education" (high school and college) are used.

Example 2.5.5

Sample topic with three delimitations (type of compliance, type of disease, and level of education [with two categories for level of education]):

Compliance with physicians' directions regarding medications by high school and college graduates with diabetes.

If you add too many delimitations (e.g., including only certain categories of age, gender, and socioeconomic status in addition to the three delimiters in Example 2.5.5) or select inappropriate delimiters (e.g., including certain hobbies and only certain political affiliations in the example), you may not find enough literature on your topic to meet the requirements for your literature review. Errors such as these will become obvious when you search the literature because you will find very little, if any, literature on topics with either too many or highly inappropriate delimiters. Techniques for searching for literature are covered in the next two chapters.

᭒ Guideline 2.6
Scan titles and abstracts of articles in your topic area early in the process of selecting a topic.

Scan the titles of journal articles and their abstracts (i.e., summaries of articles that are usually published near the beginning of articles) in your general area of interest. For example, if you are writing a literature review for a social psychology class, scan the titles of articles in journals such as the *Journal of Personality and Social Psychology*. While an introductory social psychology textbook covers broad, major issues, journal articles tend to deal with very specific issues. Scanning titles may help you identify a reasonably narrow issue on which to write a literature review.

Many of my students have been surprised at the wide variety of interesting topics covered in academic journals. The titles shown in Example 2.6.1 piqued my interest. (Of course, what is "interesting" is in the eye of the beholder.) Each title can provide ideas for possible literature review topics. For example, the first title suggests the possibility of examining the literature on various types of commitment in intimate relationships.

Example 2.6.1

Five "interesting" journal titles identified by a quick scan of various journals:

1. Approach Versus Avoidance: Different Types of Commitment in Intimate Relationships[2]

2. Portrayals of Overweight and Obese Individuals on Commercial Television[3]

3. Black Single Custodial Fathers: Factors Influencing the Decision to Parent[4]

---

[2] Frank & Brandstaetter (2002, p. 208).
[3] Greenberg, Eastın, Hofschıre, Lachlan, & Brownell (2003, p. 1342).
[4] Coles (2003, p. 247).

4. Why Do We Punish? Deterrence and Just Deserts as Motives for Punishment[5]

5. Victim and Offender Accounts of Interpersonal Conflict: Autobiographical Narratives of Forgiveness and Unforgiveness[6]

Note that all the articles for which the titles are given in Example 2.6.1 contain numerous references to related literature you might use in refining your topic or cite in your literature review. For instance, the article with the first title in Example 2.6.1 (on types of commitment in intimate relationships) has many references, including the ones in Example 2.6.2. From the titles, these references seem to be "direct hits" for the topic at hand. Each of them will undoubtedly contain additional references to literature on the topic.

Example 2.6.2

Three closely related articles on intimate relationships identified by examining the references in the first article in Example 2.6.1:

1. Level of Commitment, Mutuality of Commitment, and Couple Well-Being[7]

2. Willingness to Sacrifice in Close Relationships[8]

3. Toward a Theory of Commitment[9]

Note that the last title in Example 2.6.2 contains the word "theory," which leads us to the next guideline.

✎ Guideline 2.7
Consider selecting a topic on which there is theoretical literature.

Theories help advance science by providing principles that explain the dynamics of a variety of findings. For instance, one published review of literature examined 70 empirical studies on perceived organizational support (POS) theory.[10] In brief, the theory suggests that "...employees develop *global beliefs* concerning the extent to which [an] organization values their contributions and cares about their well-being" (p. 698). [Emphasis added.] Also, according to POS theory, employees tend to assign humanlike characteristics to the organizations that employ them (i.e., the characteristics personify the organizations). Finally, note the word "perceived" in the name of the theory. According to the theory, employees' *perceptions* of organizations' commitment to them are the key—*not* the perceptions of management or others such as employees of governmental agencies that regulate businesses. As the authors of the review article point out, POS theory leads to a number of predictions about the behavior of employees, some of which are shown in Example 2.7.1.

---

[5] Carlsmith, Darley, & Robinson (2002, p. 284).
[6] Zechmeister & Romero (2002, p. 675).
[7] Drigotas, Rusbult, & Verette (1999, p. 389).
[8] Van Lange, Rusbult, Drigotas, Arriaga, Witcher, & Cox (1997, p. 1373).
[9] Lydon (1996, p. 191).
[10] Rhoades & Eisenberger (2002, p. 698).

Example 2.7.1

A sample of important predictions from perceived organizational support (POS) theory:

Employees who perceive strong organizational support within a given organization (in contrast with those who perceive weak organizational support) should:

1. report greater job satisfaction,
2. have stronger feelings of competence and worth,
3. be more productive in their standard job activities,
4. take actions (beyond their standard ones) that help the organization, and
5. have fewer incidences of tardiness and absenteeism.

To the extent that theories are true, they can often help in practical problem solving. For instance, many employers try to reduce tardiness by imposing penalties (see Point 5 in Example 2.7.1). However, creating an atmosphere in which employees perceive the personified organization is committed to them might not only help reduce tardiness but might also have other beneficial effects, such as taking actions beyond the standard ones to help the organization (see Point 4 in Example 2.7.1). Put another way, theories often provide solutions that have multiple benefits because each accounts for a number of variables.

Because theories help to unify our thinking about problem areas, often lead to important predictions, and often help in practical problem solving, consider whether there is theoretical literature on the topics you are considering for review. Other things being equal, select a topic with one or more theoretical bases instead of a topic that has not been tied to theory.

✤ Guideline 2.8
Consider selecting a theory as the topic for a literature review.

The previous guideline suggests that you consider selecting a topic (such as types of commitment in intimate relationships) on which there is theoretical literature. In contrast, this guideline suggests that you review the literature on a theory, regardless of the topics to which the theory is applied. Textbooks in content areas usually describe major theories, which you might consider as topics. Less well-known and emerging theories, which might be of more interest to you, can be identified through a literature search, which we will consider in the next chapter. At this point, however, note you can locate literature on theories by searching databases using the term "theory."

Because the consideration of theories is important in this chapter as well as in later ones, consider the formal definition of the term "theory" shown in Box 2B. As you know, a *set* is a group or collection of items. A set is *coherent* when its items are both related to each other logically and are consistent with each other.

Box 2B *Definition of "theory."*

> *Theory*: "A *theory* is a *coherent set* of hypothetical, conceptual, and pragmatic principles forming the general frame of reference for a field of inquiry (as for deducing principles, formulating hypotheses for testing, undertaking actions)." [Emphasis added.][11]

Note that writers sometimes use the term *models* interchangeably with the term *theories*. Strictly speaking, the term *model* should be reserved for reference to how a *particular* set of operations works and interacts. For example, one might develop a model of how faculty on college/university campuses communicate by studying the particular lines of communication that are typical on campuses and the types of content typically communicated. In contrast, a *theory* is less restrictive and has the potential for use in many situations. For instance, social exchange theory is a communication theory that suggests that people assess communications in terms of payoffs (the "what's in it for me?" approach). It also suggests that the accuracy of the assessment of payoffs is dependent on the accuracy of the content that is being exchanged. As you can see, such a *theory* is not specific to communication in a particular setting or for a particular group. Instead, it can be applied to a wide variety of communication situations such as communications among religious groups, large corporations, neighborhood associations, and so on. Thus, it is a theory—and not a model—because of its wide applicability to many communication situations.

In terms of selecting a topic, a corollary to the guideline we are considering is that you may want to consider reviewing the literature on a model (such as models of communication processes on campuses) *or* on a theory (such as social exchange theory).[12]

✑ Guideline 2.9
Consider preliminary definitions of the terms in the topics you are considering.

Suppose you are considering "power sharing among couples" as a possible topic on which to write a literature review. You will, of course, need to define both "power sharing" and "couples." For example, your definition of power sharing could include financial power sharing, child-rearing power sharing, recreational power sharing, and so on. If you find little literature on one type of power sharing, you might want to use a broad definition and include several types. If you find much, you might want to restrict it to just one or two types of power sharing. We will consider searching the literature in the next chapter.

Looking up topic terms in a standard dictionary is often useful. Consider the term "couples" in the previous paragraph. Example 2.9.1 shows just a small part of the definition of the term "couple" (when used as a noun) in an unabridged dictionary. Compare definitions

---

[11] *Merriam-Webster Unabridged Dictionary* accessed at http://unabridged.merriam-webster.com/cgi-bin/unabridged? va=coherent on October 20, 2003.
[12] For more information on social exchange theory, see Griffin (1994).

a and **d** in the example. Would you be interested in reviewing literature on power sharing among married couples *or* power sharing among unmarried couples who work together cooperatively in their occupations?

Example 2.9.1

Dictionary definition of a seemingly simple-to-define term ("couple"):

1. a: a man and his wife: a man and woman married or engaged <she and John would make a lovely *couple*—John Galsworthy> **b:** a man and woman paired as partners in any work, recreation, or other activity **c:** a man and wife employed together to perform usually related jobs in a single establishment (as butler and cook in a household) **d:** any two persons paired together in some work, enterprise, or activity[13]

✥ Guideline 2.10
If your literature review will introduce your original empirical research, strive for a close fit between the topic(s) reviewed and the variables studied in your research.

Most reports of original research begin with an introduction that includes a literature review.[14] Unless your audience (such as your professor) indicates otherwise, the topic reviewed should closely match the variables studied. For instance, if you will be conducting a study on a specific technique for teaching reading using phonics, it would usually be inappropriate to select a topic as broad as "teaching reading" for your literature review. In fact, there is so much literature just on phonics, you would probably want to delimit your topic to some aspect of the use of phonics in teaching reading. By delimiting it, your literature review will help to introduce the report of your specific empirical study without diverting your readers with a discussion of literature on extraneous issues.

✥ Guideline 2.11
Consider your orientation and whether a topic you are considering lends itself more to qualitative or quantitative analysis.

Many issues naturally lend themselves to quantitative studies. For example, suppose you want to review the literature on the unemployment rate in rural areas of the United States. Because unemployment rates are statistical, your review will cover much quantitative material. In addition to economics, other examples of areas in which studies tend to be quantitative are many areas of geography (such as demographic studies), many areas of

---

[13] *Merriam-Webster Unabridged Dictionary* accessed at http://unabridged.merriam-webster.com/cgi-bin/unabridged on September 21, 2003. (Note: Access to the unabridged version requires a subscription.)

[14] For a thesis or dissertation, you may be required to write a chapter that introduces the topic and a separate chapter that reviews the literature. For journal articles, the introduction and literature review are typically integrated with each other.

health (such as survival rates and the outcomes of prescription drug trials), and many areas of criminology (such as statistical studies of prison populations). If you are not quantitatively oriented, you might want to avoid these types of topics to the extent permitted by your audience's needs and expectations.

New areas of investigation are often examined with qualitative studies. Many others are examined in both quantitative and qualitative studies. Determining the orientation of the majority of the research on a topic will be discussed in the next chapter.

↳ Guideline 2.12
Consider reviewing the literature on instrument(s) or assessment procedure(s).

When empirical research (i.e., research in which original research is conducted through observation) is conducted, researchers use instruments such as tests, personality scales, questionnaires, and interview schedules. Almost without exception, instruments in the social and behavioral sciences have many limitations. The most important considerations in evaluating instruments are validity and reliability, which, arguably, are not perfect for any instrument. (These considerations are discussed in Chapter 7.)

Suppose, for example, you are interested in the construct called "anxiety." You might review the literature on the Beck Anxiety Inventory (BAI), which has been widely used to study anxiety in a variety of populations and situational contexts. Your review might cover (a) the history of attempts to measure anxiety (and its historical as well as current definitions), (b) the development of the BAI, which was designed to measure anxiety as a trait separate from depression (an important issue because the two variables tend to vary together), and (c) the types of research in which the BAI has recently been used. Those who read such a review will obtain an understanding of the nature of anxiety (as we currently understand it, at least from the point of view used to develop the BAI) and the limitations of research on anxiety in general (because the quality of the published research is limited by the quality of the instruments used to measure it).

↳ Guideline 2.13
Select a topic with an eye toward your future goals and activities.

This guideline was alluded to earlier in this chapter. However, it is important enough to deserve to be stated as its own guideline. The most common future goals and activities are your career aspirations and your future academic pursuits. Note that when applying for admission to an advanced degree program, you may be asked to provide a sample of your writing. If your literature review is on a topic related to the program, it might be an excellent paper to submit as a writing sample.

Exercise for Chapter 2

1. Write very brief descriptions of at least two preliminary topic ideas in which you have a personal interest.

2. Evaluate each idea you wrote down for Question 1 on a scale from 5 (highly appropriate for the intended audience that will be reading your review) to 1 (highly inappropriate).

3. If your audience is your professor (or a committee of professors), how clear are his or her expectations at this point in time? Write down any questions about expectations that you want to ask at the next class meeting.

4. Have you examined any model literature reviews? If so, which ones or which types (e.g., the ones at the end of this book *or* sample reviews written by students in previous semesters *or* ones in other sources such as academic journals)? If yes, did examining them help you? Why? Why not?

5. Name a broad topic in which you are interested. Delimit it by using one category of one of the sample demographic variables in Box 2A in this chapter.

6. Further delimit the topic you wrote for Question 5 by using one or more additional categories for one or more of the demographic variables in Box 2A.

7. Can you think of demographic variables that are not included in Box 2A but which might be important in your field? If so, name them.

8. At this point, would you be interested in reviewing the literature on a theory (or model)? Explain. (See Guideline 2.8.)

9. At this point, would you be interested in reviewing the literature on a topic on which the research is probably highly quantitative? Explain. (See Guideline 2.11.)

10. At this point, would you be interested in reviewing the literature on instrument(s) or assessment procedure(s)? Explain. (See Guideline 2.12.)

11. Do you have any specific future goals and/or activities that might influence your selection of a topic? If so, describe them.

Notes:

Chapter 3

Searching for Literature and Refining the Topic

The processes of searching for literature and refining your topic are intertwined because the amount of literature you find on a topic of interest to you will determine whether you need to broaden it (to find more literature) or narrow it (to retrieve less literature). In addition, as you sample the literature on a topic, you may discover related topics that are of even greater interest to you than your original topic.

This chapter is based on the assumption that you will be conducting an electronic search for literature. Note that almost all databases designed to assist in the location of literature have been computerized and are available in electronic form.

Many of the examples in this chapter are from the *PsycARTICLES* database, which is published electronically by the American Psychological Association (APA).[1] At the time of this writing, it contains more than 25,000 searchable full-text articles (i.e., the complete articles, not just summaries) from 42 journals published by APA and allied organizations. Psychology students will also want to examine *PsycINFO*, which contains abstracts (i.e., summaries only) of more than 1.5 million references to both APA and non-APA journal articles and books. You should be able to access these databases free of charge at your college or university library. If you do not have access via your library, you can purchase a personal subscription. Visit www.apa.org for more information.

Almost all academic fields have one or more major electronic databases that assist in the search for literature on a topic. In education, the major one is Educational Resources Information Center (*ERIC*), which, at the time of this writing, contains references to more than one million records that provide citations for journal articles, books, conference papers, and so on. Some of the examples in this chapter are from searches of the *ERIC* database.[2] At the time of this writing, the *ERIC* Web site was about to undergo extensive changes as the Department of Education began the process of developing a new model for its database of educational materials. The Department of Education is streamlining *ERIC* to include only the database; other components, such as *AskERIC*, were to be discontinued in December 2003. Although the *ERIC* Web site will be in a transition period beginning in 2004, when the development of the new model begins, all information in this chapter about *ERIC* searches

---

[1] Unless otherwise specified, *PsycARTICLES* searches for this chapter were conducted using "all fields" (as opposed to just the "title field," the "abstract field," or some other restrictive field).

[2] Unless otherwise specified, all *ERIC* searches were restricted to journal articles that were searched using terms typed into the "key words" field on the search screen.

and the references obtained from these searches applies until the new model is adopted sometime in 2004.[3]

ERIC defines "education" in its broadest sense (i.e., *not* as a field devoted only to classroom and curriculum issues). For instance, a sociology student interested in reviewing literature on the homeless could do a "simple search" (with no restrictions to the search) in *ERIC*, which, at the time of this writing, retrieved references to 1,585 documents on the homeless. Restricted to only journal articles (i.e., a "restricted search," not a "simple search"), 591 journal articles were retrieved. Likewise, a business student using the term "advertising" would find 5,795 documents by conducting a "simple search." Restricting the search to only journal articles, the search retrieved 1,613.[4] As you can see by these examples, an *ERIC* search will probably be fruitful for students interested in almost any topic that deals with human behavior.

Box 3A shows the output for one of the articles identified in the *ERIC* search using the term "advertising." Note that on the first line, the *ERIC* number (i.e., ERIC_NO) is EJ638975. When the six-digit number begins with EJ, it is a journal article. (EJ stands for "educational journal." However, note that *ERIC* searches a wide variety of journals, not just ones with "education" in their titles.) When the six-digit number begins with ED, it is an unpublished document, such as a conference paper or government report. (ED stands for "educational document.")

Box 3A *Main portion of an* ERIC *entry for an article on advertising.*

> **ERIC_NO:** EJ638975
>
> **TITLE:** Looking for Meaning in All the Wrong Places: Why Negative *Advertising* Is a Suspect Category.
>
> **AUTHOR:** Richardson, Glenn W., Jr.
>
> **PUBLICATION_DATE:** 2001
>
> **JOURNAL_CITATION:** Journal of Communication; v51 n4 p775-800 Dec 2001
>
> **ABSTRACT:** Presents a critical review of academic work on negativity in political *advertising* that shows that the concept has been defined in ways that are too broad, insufficiently holistic, and too pejorative. Suggests exploratory data indicate that the component parts of negativity are: misleading claims, emotional appeals, one-sided attacks, and a "generally loathsome view of politicians." (SG)
>
> **Continued on next page.**

---

[3] The *ERIC* Web site, at www.eric.ed.gov, has information and will provide updates concerning the transition to the new database model.

[4] Journal articles tend to be of better quality than other *ERIC* documents because journal articles are typically reviewed (and often modified to improve them) before being accepted for publication. However, unpublished documents in the *ERIC* database often provide information on specialized topics and educational programs that are not described in journals.

> **MAJOR_DESCRIPTORS:** *Advertising*; Discourse Analysis; Negative
> Attitudes; Political Campaigns;
> **MINOR_DESCRIPTORS:** Communication Research; Higher Education;
> **IDENTIFIERS:** *Advertising* Effectiveness; *Political *Advertising*
> **PUBLICATION_TYPE:** *080*; 143

Note that access to the *ERIC* system is free. Its home page can be accessed by visiting www.eric.ed.gov, where you will find information about its services, history, and how to conduct effective searches for relevant literature.

Other major databases include *Sociological Abstracts* (formerly *SocioFile*), *Linguistics and Language Behavior Abstracts*, *Social Work Abstracts*, *Business Source Plus*, *Health Source Plus*, *MEDLINE/PubMed*, as well as *Astronomy and Astrophysics Abstracts*. Academic libraries typically maintain subscriptions to the on-line versions of these databases (as well as to the APA indices and *ERIC*). These library subscriptions allow free access to the databases for faculty and students. Check for handouts in your library on its database subscriptions, and/or consult with a reference librarian to determine which databases are available. Also, note that there are highly specialized databases (not listed here) that you might be able to access through your library. You can identify these through library handouts and/or consultation with a reference librarian.

✤ Guideline 3.1
Invest time in learning how to conduct advanced searches of a database.

Databases will allow you to conduct very basic searches to locate literature relating to a topic of interest to you. For instance, in *ERIC* a basic search is called a "simple search"; in *PsycARTICLES* and *PsycLIT*, it is called a "quick search." It is desirable to conduct a basic search to get an overview of the amount and types of literature available on your topic. However, before spending much time reviewing what you have retrieved from a basic search, read the introductory material for the database, which tells you how the database is structured, what its features are, and how to conduct an advanced search. If the database has a thesaurus of keywords on which it is structured, review the thesaurus for relevant terms to use in your search. These steps will typically make your search much more efficient and save you time in the long run. A number of the advanced search techniques that are available on major databases are described in some of the following guidelines.

✤ Guideline 3.2
Familiarize yourself with the Boolean operators NOT, AND, and OR.

By using the Boolean logical operators (NOT, AND, and OR), you can broaden or narrow a search.[5] For instance, consider the results of four searches shown in Example 3.2.1,

---

[5] The term "Boolean" is based on the name of the British mathematician, George Boole, who developed Boolean logic.

which were conducted in the *PsycARTICLES* database. The example makes it clear that the operators NOT as well as AND *reduce* the number of references found while OR *increases* the number.

Notice that when we add the number of articles identified for "depression NOT treatment" to the number for "depression AND treatment," we get the total number for the term "depression" (816 + 246 = 1,062). In other words, by using NOT and AND, we have partitioned the 1,062 articles on depression into two distinct groups: those that include "treatment" and those that do not. Using OR, on the other hand, greatly increases the number of articles identified because it yields citations to all articles dealing with depression as well as all articles dealing with "treatment," regardless of whether the treatment is for depression, which would not be an appropriate way to search if your main topic is "depression."

Example 3.2.1
Number of journal articles identified using NOT, AND, and OR:

Term entered in database restricted to the years 1995 to the time this was written:	Number of journal articles identified:
depression	1,062
depression NOT treatment	816
depression AND treatment	246
depression OR treatment	2,654

Suppose you want to write a literature review on the treatment of depression. For most purposes and audiences, a review that referred to 246 articles would be excessive. Some of the following guidelines will illustrate techniques for making a search narrower so that it yields fewer references.

✍ Guideline 3.3
Consider using demographics to delimit your search.

Box 2A in Chapter 2 lists a number of widely used demographics. Staying with the same topic (treatment of depression) and adding the demographic "elderly" (i.e., treatment AND depression AND elderly), the *PsycARTICLES* database yields only 12 documents, which might not be sufficient for some purposes, depending on the nature of your assignment. Examining the on-line information on how to use the *PsycARTICLES* database (which should have been done earlier by following Guideline 3.1), we find that the database uses the specific terms shown in Example 3.3.1 to refer to various age groups.

Example 3.3.1
Terms used by PsycARTICLES *to refer to age groups*:

Childhood (birth to 12 yrs)	Adulthood (18 yrs & older)
Neonatal (birth to 1 mo)	Young Adulthood (18 to 29 yrs)
Infancy (2 to 23 mo)	Thirties (30 to 39 yrs)

Preschool Age (2 to 5 yrs)   Middle Age (40 to 64 yrs)

School Age (6 to 12 yrs)   Aged (65 yrs & older)

Adolescence (13 to 17 yrs)   Very Old (85 yrs & older)

Conducting the search again using "treatment" AND "depression" AND "aged" (the term used by *PsycARTICLES* instead of *elderly*), the database yields 60 articles. Assuming that some of them will not be useful for one reason or another and that some will overlap with each other and can be referred to jointly, 60 references is a good number to start with for most literature review purposes.[6]

Note that most databases have guides to the terms they use (often called a thesaurus of terms). You should refer to these in order to identify terms to use to make your searches of the literature more efficient and comprehensive. For instance, *ERIC* publishes the *Thesaurus of ERIC Descriptors*, which shows the terms the *ERIC* system uses. An important feature of the *Thesaurus* is that for a given term you look up, there are suggested broader terms (identified as "BT") and narrower terms (identified as "NT") that will help you widen or narrow your search as needed.

✜ Guideline 3.4
Search for theoretical literature on your topic.

In the previous chapter, we explored the desirability of selecting a topic that is related to a theory. Adding the keyword "theory" in the search we have been considering (i.e., "treatment" AND "depression" AND "aged" AND "theory") yields only two articles. At first, this may seem to be a disappointingly small number. However, we have already identified 60 articles (see the discussion under the previous guideline). The two articles on theory, which in this case are "cognitive theory of personality disorders" and "developmental therapy theory," will help you zero in on possible theoretical bases that you might discuss in your literature review.

✜ Guideline 3.5
Examine the references cited in the literature that you locate.

Under the discussion of the previous guideline, only two theoretical articles were located. However, each article has a fairly lengthy discussion of the theories in question, which would provide you with an overview of each theory as it applies to the specific topic. Perhaps more important is the fact that each has numerous references to other literature, including a book on each of the theories, which are shown in Example 3.5.1. Even though the titles do not suggest that they deal with the aged, they are clearly on-target in terms of the

---

[6] Often, some references are not useful because their content is not on-target. For instance, an article on depression among the aged who are prison inmates might be beyond the scope of the review you are planning to write. Other references may not be useful because they are so fundamentally weak that they do not contribute to our understanding of your topic. Evaluating articles to determine their strengths and weaknesses is covered in Chapters 6 and 7 of this book.

two theories, providing you with sources that are probably more comprehensive than journal articles for obtaining information for creating theoretical perspective(s) in your literature review.

Example 3.5.1

Two books on theory identified in the references of the two articles:

Clark, D. A., Beck, A. T., & Alford, B. A. (1999). *Scientific foundations of cognitive theory and therapy of depression.* New York: Wiley.

Ivey, A. E. (1986). *Developmental therapy: Theory into practice.* San Francisco: Jossey-Bass.

✥ Guideline 3.6

Search databases for the names of prominent individuals who have written on your topic.

Suppose your tentative topic is "teaching mathematics." An *ERIC* search using "teaching AND mathematics" yields 7,865 journal articles, which is obviously an overwhelming number. If you add Piaget's name (a famous developmental theorist) to the search (i.e., "teaching AND mathematics AND Piaget"), you will obtain a manageable 30 journal articles.

✥ Guideline 3.7

Consider using the term "history" as a keyword in a database search.

Suppose one topic you are considering is "the effects of television on children." Using "children AND television AND history" in an *ERIC* search, you would find 30 journal articles such as the one in Example 3.7.1, which contains information on an important aspect of the history of the topic. This reference and the other 29 would provide material for presenting a historical context in your literature review. Learning the history of a topic can help you develop a broad understanding of how scholars' thoughts on an issue (in reaction to new research findings and emerging theories) evolved over time, including paths in thinking that were abandoned because they were not fruitful in advancing understanding of the topic. The 30 articles might also become the sole topic for a literature review with a title such as "The History of Research on the Effects of Television on Children."

Example 3.7.1

A reference on children and television using "AND history" in an ERIC *search*:

EJ445162. Kunkel, Dale. Crafting Media Policy: The Genesis and Implications of the Children's Television Act of 1990. *American Behavioral Scientist*; v35 n2 p181-202 Nov-Dec 1991.[7]

---

[7] This reference is shown as it appears in the database. It was *not* formatted to conform to any particular style manual.

↳ Guideline 3.8

Consider using "definition" as a keyword in a database search.

In Chapter 2, Guideline 2.9 suggests that you consider how you will define the terms in the topics you are considering. To locate definitions of the terms you are interested in, use the word "definition" as a keyword in your database search. Often, this will not be fruitful. However, sometimes an especially useful reference that discusses definitions will be retrieved. For instance, a *PsycARTICLES* search using "panic attacks AND definition" as keywords retrieved the reference shown in Example 3.8.1. This could be a keystone article for a reviewer because it is a relatively long article that spells out definitions *and* their implications for research, which would be quite useful when reviewing research literature on panic attacks.

> **Example 3.8.1**
> *The reference retrieved using "panic attacks AND definition":*
>
> Definitions of panic attacks and panic disorder in the DSM-IV: Implications for research. By Barlow, David H.; Brown, Timothy A.; Craske, Michelle G. *Journal of Abnormal Psychology*. 1994 Aug Vol 103(3) 553–564[8]

↳ Guideline 3.9

Consider using an exact phrase match.

Using an exact phrase match will identify only literature that has the exact words of a phrase in the exact same order. Many databases allow you to do this by putting the phrase in either double or single quotation marks. In *PsycARTICLES*, using the phrase *school achievement* retrieved 653 journal articles. Using the phrase 'school achievement' (with single quotation marks for an exact phrase match) retrieved only those 26 journal articles that contained the exact phrase "school achievement." Thus, an exact phrase match reduces the number of citations to relevant literature. In this case, it reduced the unmanageable 653 articles to only 26 articles.

↳ Guideline 3.10

Consider using truncated terms or wildcards.

Suppose you wanted to review literature on a topic with reference to people whose national origin is Mexico. Searching *PsycARTICLES* using the term "Mexico" yields 107 journal articles. Searching using "Mexican" yields 68 articles. If we truncate the term by using an asterisk, which is the symbol for truncation in *PsycARTICLES* (i.e., using Mexic*), we retrieve 168 articles.

---

[8] This reference is shown as it appears in the database. It was *not* formatted to conform to any particular style manual.

The advantage of truncation is that it identifies literature on all articles that contain terms starting with "Mexic" *while eliminating duplicates*. In other words, there are 107 articles with the word "Mexican" and 68 with the word "Mexico," which gives us a total of 175 articles (107 + 68 = 175). However, we know that some of these contain both "Mexican" and "Mexico" because the search conducted with the truncated term "Mexic" (i.e., a search for both "Mexico" and "Mexican" to yield a single list of citations) retrieved only 168. Thus, conducting a truncated search, you will obtain one list with no duplicates.

A wildcard allows you to leave out a letter or string of letters when you search. In *ERIC*, a question mark is a wildcard for a single letter. Entering "poet?" as a search term yields articles with words such as "poet" and "poets."

♯ Guideline 3.11

Consider using the term "review" as a keyword in a database search.

When they locate previous reviews on their topic, some students naively abandon the topic, thinking that the work of creating a review has already been done. However, each review is an original creative synthesis, so that another review on the same topic may be substantially different from the first one. If you locate a previous literature review on your topic, not only will you learn more about your topic from such a review, you can critique and reinterpret the information and ideas in the review as well as bring it up-to-date in your new literature review.[9] Because authors of reviews often use the phrases "A Literature Review" or "A Review of the Research" in the titles of their articles, it can be fruitful to use the keyword "review" in your database search. For instance, a search in *ERIC* using "cheating AND review" as keywords (restricted to having the keywords in the titles) retrieved the reference to the literature review shown in Example 3.11.1, in which the word "review" is in the subtitle of the article.

Example 3.11.1

The reference retrieved using "cheating AND review":

EJ567552. Whitley, Bernard E., Jr.. Factors Associated with Cheating Among College Students: A Review. *Research in Higher Education*; v39 n3 p235–74 Jun 1998.[10]

♯ Guideline 3.12

Consider using the term "qualitative" as a keyword in a database search.

In the previous chapter, you were advised to consider whether the literature on the topics you are considering tends to be quantitatively or qualitatively oriented. Traditionally, if

---

[9] Of course, if you cite and critique a prior review, you are ethically bound to read the original sources that were cited in that review.

[10] Note that this reference is shown as it appears in the database. It was not formatted to conform to any particular style manual.

a research article is quantitatively oriented, its title and abstract will *not* indicate that fact. However, the fact that a study is qualitatively oriented is sometimes mentioned in the title and/or abstract of the article.[11] If you are interested in finding out if qualitative research has been conducted on your topic, use the term "qualitative" as a keyword in your search. For example, a search of the *PsycARTICLES* database for the keyword "qualitative" in the title of articles and "spinal cord injury" retrieved the two articles shown in Example 3.12.1, in which the word qualitative has been italicized.

Example 3.12.1

Titles of references retrieved by searching using the keywords "qualitative AND spinal cord injury":

Quality of Life after Spinal Cord Injury: A *Qualitative* Study[12]

Factors Affecting Employment Following Spinal Cord Injury: A *Qualitative* Study.[13]

↳ Guideline 3.13
Consider restricting your search to the title and/or abstract fields.

Suppose your topic includes the word "discipline." A search of *PsycARTICLES* yields 301 articles that contain the word in one or more fields.[14] If, at its core, an article is focused on "discipline," the keyword is very likely to be used in the title and/or abstract (i.e., summary). Searching for "discipline" in just the titles of articles retrieved 27 articles (a much more manageable number than the original 301). Searching for it in just the abstracts retrieved 280 articles, which is still quite large, but this search probably weeded out some of the 301 that were less clearly focused on the topic of discipline. Requiring that the articles have the word "discipline" in *both* the title AND the abstract is more stringent and retrieved only 21 articles, which are probably highly relevant because the author chose to use the term "discipline" in both the title and abstract.

↳ Guideline 3.14
Consider restricting your search to the author field.

Many prolific researchers conduct research on a selected topic over a period of decades. For instance, the insights on a topic gained from one study often leads to the development of

---

[11] For much of the previous century, quantitative research dominated the research literature in the social and behavioral sciences. Hence, readers assumed that an article in a research journal was quantitative. During the last quarter of the previous century, qualitative research became much more common. To distinguish their research from the more dominant quantitative research, qualitative researchers often include the word "qualitative" in the titles of their research articles.

[12] Duggan & Dijkers (2001, p. 3).

[13] Chapin & Kewman (2001, p. 400).

[14] The default in a *PsycARTICLES* search is "all fields." Using this produces a search for the keyword(s) in any and all fields. However, by using the dropdown menu, you can restrict the search to just selected fields such as titles, abstracts, authors, and language.

new hypotheses on the same topic that the same researchers investigate in subsequent studies. To locate the literature authored by such a researcher, restrict a search to the author field (i.e., from the drop down menu in *PsycARTICLES*, select "author" and type in the author's name). For instance, Albert Bandura has conducted research for years on self-efficacy. By selecting the "author" field from the pull down menu in a *PsycARTICLES* search and typing in "Bandura," 26 journal articles that Bandura authored or coauthored from 1988 through 2003 are identified.

Note that Guideline 3.6 suggests that you use a combination of topic keywords (e.g., "teaching AND mathematics") and an author's name (e.g., "Piaget"). This guideline, in contrast, suggests that you restrict your search to just an author's name, which will yield articles on all topics on which the author has written. This gives you a broader basis for understanding what the author has accomplished. In addition, you may find articles that do not have the topic keywords but have a bearing on the topic because the author has written other articles on it (e.g., an article describing a theory—without mentioning your topic—that may have applications to your topic).

♄ Guideline 3.15
Consider searching a citation index.

Using some of the suggestions for searching literature described above, suppose you found a pivotal journal article written by Smith that was published several years ago. By using a citation index, you can identify other literature in which Smith's article has since been cited. This literature might provide alternative perspectives on Smith's article; some might critique it, others might report successful and unsuccessful attempts to replicate Smith's research, while still others might provide evidence for and against Smith's theory, and so on. Obviously, there is great potential for obtaining very valuable information by using a citation index.

When searching a citation index, do not be surprised to find that the author of the pivotal article (such as Brenda Smith) had cited herself in a number of other articles she had published since the time that she published the one you consider pivotal. This is not uncommon because a researcher (or theorist) will often pursue a given line of research (or theory development) over a period of years or even decades. You will want to read Smith's subsequent work because she may have obtained results in later studies that shed new light on the earlier findings that led her to a reinterpretation or expansion of (or even rejection of) the interpretation of the findings in the pivotal article that you had identified earlier.

Most academic libraries maintain subscriptions to major citation indices such as the *Social Science Citation Index*, the *Science Citation Index*, and the *Arts and Humanities Citation Index*. These can be searched electronically if your library maintains an appropriate subscription. Print versions are also available.

✤ Guideline 3.16
Maintain a written record of how you conducted your literature search.

Suppose you come to the conclusion that "few experimental studies have been published on the XYZ phenomenon." Such a statement might be challenged by a professor, committee of professors, or journal editors who are familiar with relevant experimental studies that you have failed to cite. By being able to state specifically which databases you searched *and* how you searched them, you can deflect criticism that you have been careless in your search. Also, by providing this information to them, they might be able to refer you to resources or suggest literature search techniques that might help you improve your search.[15]

It is important to make *written notes* of your search techniques from the very beginning of your literature search. It may be months (or perhaps even years in the case of a dissertation) before you are asked to describe the literature search techniques you used. Relying on just your distant memory may cause you to give an embarrassingly fuzzy answer to the question.

Concluding Comments

Although only two databases were used for the examples in this chapter, most databases have the same features. You will be able to conduct an efficient and comprehensive search of the literature only by studying the instructions and examples provided on-line for each database you use. Pay special attention to any "advanced search" capabilities provided by a database.

As you examine the titles of the literature you have retrieved, you will see whether you need to take steps to limit your search (so that you will have a smaller number of references to deal with) or broaden your search (so that you will have a larger number of references). Trying various search techniques such as those described in this chapter will pay you back many times over by providing you with a highly suitable list of articles, books, and other documents on the topic on which you will be writing a literature review.

Exercise for Chapter 3

1. Have you identified one or more databases that you plan to search for literature on your preliminary topic ideas? Have you previously used the database(s)? If yes, do you have any suggestions for other students who might use them?

---

[15] With the exception of reports on meta-analyses, a topic that is covered in Chapter 11 of this book, authors of journal articles seldom describe their literature search techniques. Students who are writing term papers, theses, or dissertations, however, might consider describing these either in their literature review or in an appendix to it. Do this only after consulting with the chair of your thesis or dissertation committee.

2. Which of the following should retrieve more articles from an electronic database?

   A. discipline OR punishment
   B. discipline AND punishment
   C. discipline NOT punishment

3. Suppose for a moment that a topic you are considering is "career counseling." At the time of this writing, 2,038 journal articles were retrieved via a basic *ERIC* keyword search. Name a demographic variable that could be used to delimit the topic and, hence, retrieve a more manageable number of references.

4. At this point, do you know of any theories you want to cover in your literature review? Will you search for relevant theories when you search for literature? Explain.

5. Do you know the name of a prominent researcher and/or theorist who has published on a topic of interest to you? If so, name the topic, and name him or her.

6. According to this chapter, is using the keyword "definition" in a search often very fruitful? Is it recommended that you do this? Explain.

7. Will using an "exact phrase match" increase *or* decrease the amount of literature retrieved?

8. According to this chapter, should you abandon a topic if your literature search identifies a previously published review on the same topic? Explain.

9. According to this chapter, under what circumstances should you restrict your database search to the title and abstract fields?

10. Very briefly explain what a "citation index" does.

11. Has the material in this chapter convinced you of the need to make detailed written notes on how you search for literature on a topic? Explain.

12. Have you tried to use a database since reading this chapter? Did you examine the description of how to conduct an advanced search (if it is available)? Did you learn of any useful techniques not described in this chapter? If so, briefly describe them.

Chapter 4

Retrieving and Evaluating Information from the Web

When writing literature reviews, writers often need up-to-date information. Because of the ease of electronic publishing, the Web is more likely to have such information than conventionally printed materials. Note that it is not uncommon for a printed journal article or book to be published a year or more after it was written.

Sometimes literature reviews begin with current statistics on how many people (and/or the percentage of people) have a certain characteristic or a particular problem. Suppose, for instance, that your general topic for a literature review is cigarette smoking by pregnant women. Examine Box 4A, which shows two possible beginnings for a first paragraph for a review. The second one, which cites current statistics found on the Web, is stronger and more compelling than the first one.[1]

Box 4A *The beginning of two possible first paragraphs for a literature review. The second one cites recent statistics found on the Web.*

> 1. Many pregnant women continue to smoke despite warnings from the medical community. This makes it important to review literature to identify effective programs that...
>
> 2. Approximately 17 percent of pregnant women smoked cigarettes within the last month, according to a recent national survey (NHSDA, 1999).[2] This makes it important to review literature to identify...effective programs that....

Note that many sources on the Web post the latest available information, which may not be completely up-to-date. For instance, the information in Box 4A was the most current available (for 1999) when retrieved in 2003 for use in this book. Nevertheless, a journal article or book published in 1999 would probably contain even older statistics given the publication lag in conventional, hard-copy publishing.

Note that Web addresses (i.e., URLs) frequently change, Web sites often are discontinued, and access that might be free at the time of this writing might not be free by the time you try to access them. If you have difficulties locating Web sites given in this book, use a general search engine such as www.Google.com to locate newer sites, free sites, and sites that may contain specific information regarding your topic.

---

[1] Using simple, compelling statistics is appropriate in both qualitative and quantitative reviews.
[2] Retrieved September 19, 2002, from http://www.samhsa.gov/oas/2k2/PregAlcTob/PregAlcTob.htm

↳ Guideline 4.1

FedStats is a very important source of statistical information.

At www.FedStats.gov, you will be able to access statistics from more than 100 Federal agencies.[3] Prior to establishment of this Web site, writers needed to search for statistics agency-by-agency. While the FedStats site still allows you to do this, you can also search by *topic* and the FedStats search engine will automatically search all agencies for relevant links to federal statistics. This is important for two reasons: (1) you do not have to search each agency separately and (2) an agency that you are not aware of may have statistics relevant to your topic.

For example, conducting a search by first clicking on <u>Topic links – A to Z</u> produced a screen with the letters of the alphabet underlined. (As you know, Web links to other sites are usually underlined and/or are sometimes identifiable by other means such as the use of a different color, such as blue, for a link.) By clicking on the letter <u>C</u>, the extensive set of links shown in Box 4B was obtained. By clicking on the <u>Breast</u> link (the second link from the top), the links in Box 4C were obtained.

Box 4B *FedStats links for the letter C.*

Cancer:	Consumer Credit
-- *Atlas of Cancer Mortality in the United States*	Consumer product safety
-- Breast	Consumer Price Indexes
-- Cervical	Consumption, energy
-- Lung	Corporations
-- Mortality maps	Country profiles
-- Prostate	Crime (See also *Law enforcement*):
Charitable trusts	-- Characteristics of crime
Children:	-- Children
-- Administration for Children programs and services	-- Crime in schools
-- Adoption	-- Crimes reported to the police
-- *America's Children* (ChildStats)	-- Criminal offenders
-- Behavior and social environment indicators	-- Drugs
-- Child care	-- Firearms
-- Child support enforcement	-- Hate
-- Cigarette smoking	-- Homicide
-- Delinquency and victimization	-- Prison inmates
-- Delinquency case records (data and analysis software package)	-- Terrorism
	-- Victims
-- Juvenile arrests	-- Violent
-- Juveniles as offenders	**Criminal justice:**
-- Juveniles as victims	-- Corrections
-- Juveniles in court	-- Capital punishment
-- Juveniles in detention and corrections	-- Inmates
-- Drug use	-- Jails
-- Economic security indicators	-- Prisons
-- Education indicators	-- Probation and parole statistics
-- Foster care	-- Courts and sentencing
-- HeadStart	-- Court organization
-- Temporary Assistance for Needy Families	-- Criminal case processing
Health:	-- Pretrial release and detention
-- Child and infant	-- Sentencing
-- Indicators	**Continued on next page.**

---

[3] Be sure to go to www FedStats.*gov* and *not* www.FedStats.*com*. The latter is *not* a government site.

-- Insurance
-- Population and family characteristics
-- Nutrition
-- WIC
Civil justice statistics
Coal
Commodity flow
Common cold
Communications:
-- Broadcast radio and television
-- Cable television providers by community served (size 9M)
-- Telephone industry and telephone usage
-- Wireless communications services
Computer and Internet use
Construction
Industry tax statistics:
-- Corporations
-- Exempt organizations' unrelated business
-- Partnerships
-- Sole proprietorship

-- Criminal record systems
-- Employment and expenditure
-- Federal justice statistics
-- Indigent defense statistics
-- Law enforcement
   -- Campus law enforcement
   -- Federal law enforcement
   -- State and local law enforcement
-- Prosecution
Crops:
-- Crop progress and weather, weekly
-- Data by county
-- Data by state, historic
-- Field
-- Fruits and nuts
-- Vegetables

Box 4C *A large sample of the links obtained by clicking on* Breast, *which is the second link in Box 4B (under the main heading "Cancer").*

Treatment
Information about treatment, including surgery, chemotherapy, radiation therapy, immunotherapy, and vaccine therapy
• Breast Cancer Treatment
[patients] [health professionals]
• Male Breast Cancer Treatment
[patients] [health professionals]
• Breast Cancer and Pregnancy
[patients] [health professionals]
• More Information

Prevention, Genetics, Causes
Information related to prevention, genetics, risk factors
• Breast Cancer Prevention
[patients] [health professionals]
• Genetics of Breast and Ovarian Cancer
• Digest Page: Menopausal Hormone Use
• More Information

Screening and Testing
Information about methods of cancer detection including new imaging technologies, tumor markers, and biopsy procedures
• Breast Cancer Screening
[patients] [health professionals]
• NCI Statement on Mammography Screening
• HHS Affirms Value of Mammography
• Get a Mammogram
• More Information

Clinical Trials
Information on clinical trials and current news on trials and trial-related data
• Breast Cancer Trial Results
• Search for Clinical Trials

Cancer Literature
Resources available from the PubMed database
• Cancer Topic Searches: Breast Cancer
• Cancer Topic Searches: Cancer Genetics
• Cancer Literature in PubMed

Related Information
Other information, including reports about NCI priorities for cancer research and initiatives
• Breast Cancer Progress Review Group
• Early Reproductive Events and Breast Cancer

Statistics
Information related to cancer incidence, mortality, and survival
• Probability of Breast Cancer in American Women
• Breast: U.S. Racial/Ethnic Cancer Patterns
• Finding Cancer Statistics

↳ Guideline 4.2
State and local governments and their agencies often post very current statistics on the Web.

While you can obtain information at the local level at FedStats.gov, you can sometimes obtain more current statistical information from nonfederal governmental sources. Example 4.2.1 shows the latest statistics on property crimes in Buffalo, New York, posted on FedStats at the time of this writing as well as the latest ones obtained by going directly to the City of Buffalo Web site.[4] Note that the federal statistics are current as of 1999, while the City's statistics are two years more current than the federal ones.

Example 4.2.1

Property-crime statistics for Buffalo, New York, from federal and local sources:

Year	FedStats Web Site	City of Buffalo Web Site
2001	not available	16,185
2000	not available	16,591
1999	17,436	17,436

↳ Guideline 4.3
Use the raw statistics from governmental agencies, not statistics filtered by individuals or groups with special interests.

Government statistics are usually collected by civil service employees (not political appointees). While there may be errors in their work, there is no more reason to suspect them of deliberately biasing their data collection procedures than to suspect any other type of researcher of doing so. However, some individuals (such as politicians and others with special interests) may understandably be selective (and perhaps misleading) in choosing which statistics to report. Hence, it is usually best to obtain the original government reports either in print or via the Web. However, as you will see in Guideline 4.5, those with vested interests in statistical information sometimes provide useful links or primary-source information (via the Web), which can be helpful when writing a literature review.

Note that in some cases, it is appropriate to present original government statistics in a literature review *and* discuss how they are interpreted by individuals and organizations with varying special interests.

---

[4] Retrieved September 19, 2002, from www.city-buffalo.com/Files/1_2_1/Police/Crime%20Statistics.htm

✍ Guideline 4.4

Consider consulting the Library of Congress's Virtual Reference Shelf on the Web.

The Library of Congress maintains a Web site titled the Virtual Reference Shelf. It is an excellent site for general references such as dictionaries, general history, abbreviations, genealogy, and so on. It can be found at www.loc.gov/rr/askalib/virtualref.html.[5] Box 4D shows the main links at that site. At the bottom of the home page (not shown in the box but clearly visible on the Web site) is a link for "Ask a Librarian," which can be a very useful service if you are struggling to find specialized information to use in your literature review.

Box 4D *Links on the home page of the Library of Congress's Virtual Reference Shelf.*

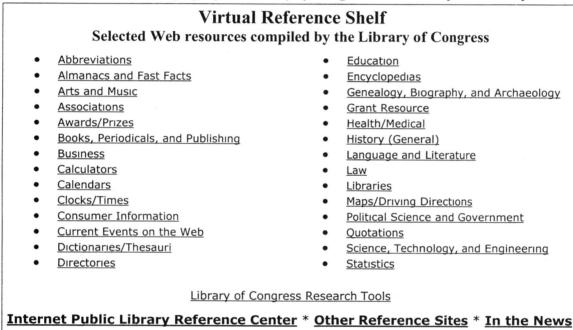

✍ Guideline 4.5

Consider accessing information posted on the Web by associations and businesses.

A wide variety of associations post information (and statistics) on the Web. Following the link called "Associations" in the Virtual Reference Shelf (see the fourth link in Box 4D), you can identify hundreds of associations, many of which are quite specialized. For instance, there are employee associations such as the Southern California Association of Fingerprint Officers at www.scafo.org, which publishes an on-line journal titled *The Print* in which there

---

[5] Rather than typing (and risk mistyping) long URLs, it is sometimes faster to do a quick search on a major search engine such as www.Google.com using a term such as "Virtual Reference Shelf." Use the quotation marks around the terms (e.g., "Virtual Reference Shelf") to conduct an exact phrase match and exclude other Web sites that might have only one of the words such as "virtual."

are original articles as well as reprints of articles from other sources. In addition, there are Web sites maintained by political lobbying and advocacy associations such as the American Civil Liberties Union at www.aclu.org, which publishes a newsletter and sells inexpensive special reports such as *Unequal, Unfair, and Irreversible: The Death Penalty in Virginia.*

You should also consider accessing information posted on the Web by businesses. Suppose you are writing a literature review on allergies for a health education class. Going to the home page for the drug Flonase® will provide you with a reference to an article in an academic journal.

You should be cautious when citing information found on Web sites maintained by associations and businesses. On the other hand, because of their special interest in certain topics, they may have more information (and newer information) than other sources.

Keep in mind that complete objectivity in research cannot be achieved. All associations and businesses that sponsor research have points of view that might influence what is researched, how questions are worded, how the sample is drawn, how the information is presented, and so on. Your job is to try to understand their points of view and identify which information on the Web is reliable and useful for the purposes of your literature review. The evaluation of research literature is discussed in Chapter 7.

✎ Guideline 4.6
Major search engines used by the public at large often provide helpful information for use in academic literature reviews.

At the time of this writing, www.Google.com is a popular search engine. Box 4E shows the main portion of the advanced search page. Assuming you want to review literature on the "gender gap" in voting (but do not want to trace it back to the suffrage movement), you could enter "gender gap" for the *exact phrase*, enter "voting, vote, and voter" for *with at least one of the words*, and "suffrage" for *without the words* (see Box 4E on the next page).

This search retrieved an overwhelming 9,440 Web sites. By changing *Occurrences* (third line up from the bottom of Box 4E) from "anywhere in the page" to "in the title of the page," a list of only nine Web sites was obtained. These nine are probably the most relevant Web sites because the words were important enough to be in their titles. Scanning the URLs at the bottom of the listings, you will find that some were posted by associations, several were posted by government agencies, and one was posted by a university. Example 4.6.1 shows the beginning of one, which discusses some statistical matters regarding the gender gap.[6] Note that the statistics in this example are secondary source material, which you should confirm independently by referring to the original sources. However, you should also note that the *interpretations* of the statistics are *primary sources* of information. Thus, you can cite an interpretation of statistics (and even discuss varying interpretations posted by various

---

[6] Retrieved November 2, 2003, from www.equityfeminism.com/articles/2000/000089.html

associations and individuals) as primary source material after confirming the accuracy of the statistics they are interpreting by referring to the original source(s) of them.

Box 4E   *An advanced search for "gender gap" in voting without coverage of the issue of "suffrage."*

Google™ **Advanced Search**

Advanced Search Tips | All About Google

Find results	with **all** of the words		10 results	Google search
	with the **exact phrase**	gender gap	
	with **at least one** of the words	voting vote voter	
	without the words	suffrage	

Language	Return pages written in	any language
File Format	Only	return results of the file format	any format
Date	Return web pages updated in the	anytime
Occurrences	Return results where my terms occur	anywhere in the page
Domain	Only	return results from the site or domain	
		e g google.com, .org More info
SafeSearch	⦿ No filtering ○ Filter using SafeSearch	

Example 4.6.1

An article on the Web retrieved by searching for "gender gap" in the title:

NOW and the Voting Gender Gap

By Brian Carnell

Tuesday, December 12, 2000

The National Organization for Women keeps making a claim in its press releases about the recently concluded election that, while technically true, completely glosses over the reality of the election. Here's a random sample by Tanya Melich:

Unlike Florida, the proof of our power is not sullied with statistical probabilities. Nationally, women gave Gore their vote by an 11 percent margin while Bush won men by 11 percent. In Florida, the margins mirror this national vote with women backing Gore and men Bush. Whether by age, education, or economic status, the pattern holds....

This paragraph is disingenuous. Yes, the pattern holds by age, education, or economic status—unfortunately, it *does not* hold by race and by marital status. The so-called gender gap is in fact largely a racial gap. Black and Hispanic women broke overwhelmingly toward Gore, while depending on which polling data you rely on, Bush barely won or barely lost the white female vote. If, in fact,...

Example 4.6.1 reveals a problem frequently encountered when gathering information on the Web: The material that is referenced is undated. In this particular case, the quotation from Tanya Melich is from an undated Web source. Without dates, it is hard to follow the history or line of discussion on a topic. Note that some Web sites prominently display the date on which the site was last updated. This can be very helpful in determining whether you are reading current information.

ꙮ Guideline 4.7
Pay attention to the extension (gov, edu, org, com, and net) in the results of Web searches.

As you probably know, the extension "gov" in a URL stands for "government," "edu" stands for "education," "org" stands for "organization," "com" stands for "commercial," and "net" stands for "network." These extensions can be helpful if you are sorting through a large listing of Web sites retrieved by a search engine. For instance, you might want to start with those with the extensions of "gov" and "edu" because they may be more likely to be nonpartisan and noncommercial than other Web sites.

As an illustration of the importance of paying attention to the extensions, consider this example: A search using the term "depression" on a major search engine produced links to a large number of Web sites. The sixth one in the list was titled "NIMH-Depression." If someone was not familiar with the acronym "NIMH," he or she might have passed it over unless the individual notices "gov" in the URL for the site. Going to the site, the individual would find a home page on depression maintained by the National Institute of Mental Health, a prestigious federal agency. This site contains a large number of fact sheets, summaries, booklets, and an important link that leads to other links to information on depression maintained on the Web by other organizations such as the Mayo Foundation for Medical Education and Research, and the American Academy of Family Physicians. In general, highly reliable sources such as NIMH tend to link only to other reliable sources.

✍ Guideline 4.8

Consider clicking on "cached" when opening a Web site from a search engine.

Search engines often list the Web sites with their titles underlined or in a different color to indicate that they are links. However, when the option is available (such as in Google), it is usually more desirable to click on "cached" near the end of the description of the link than to click on the title of a Web site. By clicking on "cached," you will go to the Web site, but the words you used in your search will be highlighted in different colors from the other words at the Web site, which makes it easier for you to locate your topic(s) within a Web site, especially if much material is presented at the site.

✍ Guideline 4.9

When you find a Web site that is very useful, consider following the links, if any, that it provides.

While this guideline is alluded to in the discussion under Guideline 4.7, it is important enough to be stated as its own guideline. At commercial sites, the links provided typically lead to other commercial sites. However, at noncommercial sites, the links often lead to other noncommercial sources of information that are relevant to the topic(s) they cover. Highly reliable and/or prestigious Web sites tend to provide links only to similar Web sites.

Concluding Comments

In the previous chapter, we explored techniques for locating published literature— typically academic material published in hard-copy form (and, sometimes, also published on the Web). In this chapter, we concentrated on using Web sources to obtain information directly—not just to identify hard-copy literature published somewhere else.

The mercurial nature of the Web is the source of both a major strength and a major weakness. The strength is that its quick "changeability" allows individuals and organizations to promptly post detailed, current information. Prior to development of the Web, the dissemination of information often had a publication lag of up to a year (or sometimes more) in traditional, hard-copy publishing. A major weakness of publishing on the Web is that almost anyone can post information (whether it is correct or not) without the scrutiny that the material would typically undergo if it were being published in hard copy. This is true because, unlike publishing on the Web, hard-copy publishing is expensive and risky to a publisher's financial status if too many of its publications are not successful in the marketplace. Hence, most traditional publishers take great care in the editorial process to check and cross-check the accuracy of content and the clarity of its presentation.

As the Web becomes an increasingly important source of information for those who review literature, it is important to establish criteria to consider when evaluating a Web-based source of information. In developing criteria, some of the considerations are:

1. Who sponsors the Web site in question? A government agency? A professional association? An advocacy group? A for-profit corporation?

2. Does the Web site present primary source material (i.e., original) or just secondary source material?

3. If secondary material provides the "factual" underpinnings of the content of a Web site, is the material analyzed thoughtfully and logically, hence, making an original contribution by presenting original interpretation(s)?

4. Does the Web site indicate when it was published on the Web and/or when it was last updated?

5. Are complete references to cited material given?

6. Does traditional, hard-copy literature that is more thorough and complete than the material published on a Web site exist? (For instance, does the Web site contain only summaries of more extensive hard-copy publications?)

7. Is the purpose of the site merely to persuade readers to take a position (such as a political position or a position that is favorable to a commercial product) rather than to provide information and well-rounded, logical interpretations? If the answer to this question is "yes," this does not necessarily mean that the site does not contain valuable information, but it does suggest that a reviewer would want to exercise considerable care and good judgment when using information from such a site.

Enjoy using the Web while searching for material to use in literature reviews. Explore it using search engines in various ways, and follow potentially interesting links. Taking time to thoroughly explore your topic on the Web may give you new perspectives and information that you might incorporate into your literature review, it may help you refine your topic, or it might even lead you to change to an entirely different topic that you find more interesting or important. These beneficial outcomes can result only when you allot sufficient time to explore the many strands of the Web.

Exercise for Chapter 4

1. Examine the two beginnings in Box 4A at the beginning of this chapter. Do you agree that the use of recent statistics from the Web makes the second one stronger than the first? Why? Why not?

2. Go to www.FedStats.gov and look up a topic on which you are considering writing a review. Make notes on how you conducted the search (e.g., by alphabetical topics, by clicking on a map, by searching press releases, and so on). Write down a few relevant statistics, if any, that you found.

3. Look up the Web site for the state or local government where you live. (You can usually find it by using a general search engine.) Explore the site. Does it contain any information on a topic that you are considering reviewing? Explain.

4. Google.com is mentioned throughout this chapter as a general search engine. Can you name others? (If not, search for others by going to www.Google.com and conducting a search for other search engines.) Do you have a favorite one? Explain.

5. In the discussion of Guideline 4.5, you read this statement: "Complete objectivity in research cannot be achieved." At this point, do you agree? Why? Why not?

6. As a general rule, what happens to the number of Web sites retrieved when you search for a term only in the titles instead of "anywhere on the Web pages"?

7. If you conducted a search on the Web and retrieved many more sites than you wanted, would you be tempted to skip over the ones with a "com" extension in their URLs? Why? Why not?

8. Seven questions that might assist in evaluating a Web-based source of information are provided in the Concluding Comments near the end of this chapter. Do you agree that all are important? Can you add any to the list? Explain.

Notes:

Chapter 5

Taking Notes and Avoiding Unintentional Plagiarism

If you have selected a topic of interest to you, you will understandably want to start reading (or at least scanning) the literature as you collect it. It is important to start taking notes as soon as you start reading, especially if you are locating a large amount of literature on your review topic. Few things in academic writing are as frustrating as remembering an interesting fact, opinion, or other important material and being unable to relocate it because you failed to note it when it was first encountered.

In this chapter, the term "taking notes" is defined very broadly to include not only writing notes on paper (or cards), but also underlining or highlighting on a photocopy (or the original, if it belongs to you), using Post-It® flags, and making notes using a word processor.

Failure to take good notes from the very beginning can lead to a case of unintentional plagiarism such as the one described in Box 5A.

Box 5A *A case of unintentional plagiarism.*

> A student has read extensively on her topic and has given it considerable thought. As she begins to write, she recalls an especially interesting point of view she saw somewhere in the literature she collected and now wants to use it in her literature review. However, she did not make note of it and is having trouble locating its source. She believes that the point of view in question is quite logical, makes common sense, and, thus, is "obvious." Because of this, she decides that incorporating the point of view in her literature review without citing its source will not constitute plagiarism.

Failure to cite a source for an original idea constitutes plagiarism even if the idea (or point of view) is logical and makes common sense. Keep in mind that ideas that are *not* logical and do *not* make common sense probably would not be published in the first place. Even "obvious ideas" belong to the person who first uttered or wrote them. The citation decision chart in Box 5B on the next page should be helpful in determining whether or not to cite material.

Box 5B *Citation decision chart.*[1]

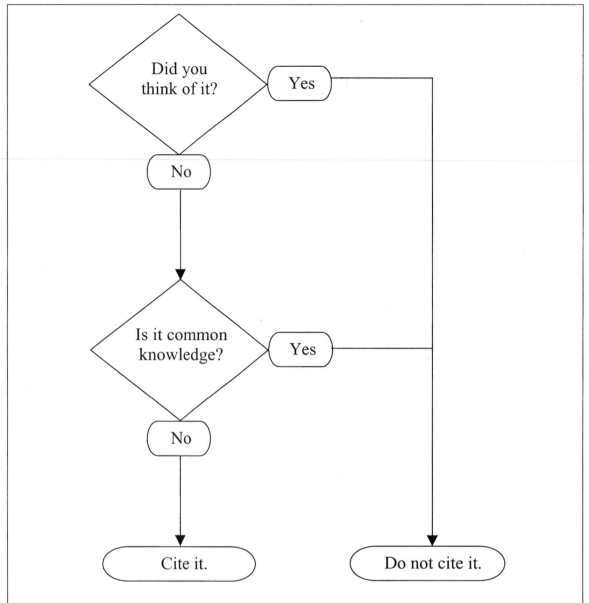

✍ Guideline 5.1

Common knowledge does not need to be cited, but original expressions of it should be cited.

To understand this guideline, consider the meaning of the term *statistically significant difference*: "a difference larger than would be expected on the basis of random error." This concept is common knowledge among those trained in statistics. If you provide a routine definition in your own words in your literature review, you do not need to cite a source.

---

[1] From Harris (2001, p. 155). Copyright © 2001 by Pyrczak Publishing. All rights reserved. No duplication permitted without written permission from the publisher. Reprinted with permission.

However, if you locate and use an original expression of the definition or an example that illustrates the meaning of the definition, you should cite its source.

❧ Guideline 5.2

If you rephrase someone else's idea in your own words, the original source should be cited.

The definition of plagiarism in Box 5C makes this guideline clear. Italics have been added for emphasis.

Box 5C *A definition of plagiarism.*[2]

> "Plagiarism is the failure to distinguish the student's own words and ideas from those of a source the student has consulted. *Ideas derived from another, whether presented as exact words, a paraphrase, a summary, or quoted phrase, must always be appropriately referenced to the source,* whether the source is printed, electronic, or spoken. Whenever exact words are used, quotation marks or an indented block indicator of a quotation must be used, together with the proper citation in a style required by the professor [or other audience such as a journal editor]."

❧ Guideline 5.3

Failure to indicate clearly the beginning *and* end of summarized literature may lead to charges of plagiarism.

As you know, when you copy exact words, you should put quotation marks around short quotations and indent longer quotations. Doing this clearly indicates where the quotation begins and ends. You also know that if you summarize literature written by others, you need to attribute it to them.

A special problem arises when another person's ideas are summarized in more than one paragraph, which is common in literature reviews—especially when discussing crucial pieces of literature. Compare Example 5.3.1 with Example 5.3.2. In both cases, all three paragraphs are summaries from a single source. Note that in Example 5.3.1, the second and third paragraphs might be mistaken to be original contributions of the person writing the literature review because there is no reference to the author (i.e., Wright). In contrast, Example 5.3.2 makes it clear that Wright's report is the source of the material in all three paragraphs because the source is mentioned in all three.

---

[2] From Harris (2001, p. 132). Copyright © 2001 by Pyrczak Publishing. All rights reserved. No duplication permitted without written permission from the publisher. Reprinted with permission.

Example 5.3.1

*Three paragraphs that summarize a single source. (**Unacceptable**)*:

With the development of new telescopic methods, **Wright** (2002) was able to show that the coloration of the moon is....

Knowing the correct coloration of the moon helps scientists in three important ways....

Earlier studies failed to identify the correct coloration because of two serious flaws in their methodology. First, they....

Example 5.3.2

*Three paragraphs that summarize a single source. (**Acceptable**)*:

With the development of new telescopic methods, **Wright** (2002) was able to show that the coloration of the moon is....

Wright also pointed out that knowing the correct coloration of the moon helps scientists in three important ways....

Earlier studies failed to identify the correct coloration because of two serious flaws in their methodology, according to **Wright**. First, they....

Notice that "Wright" is used three times in Example 5.3.2. In English composition courses, you may have been taught to avoid redundancy. However, in scientific writing, redundancy is not only acceptable but is desirable if it assists readers in understanding research reports and helps to identify clearly the sources of all ideas.

Keeping accurate notes on the sources of all ideas and clearly indicating the sources in your writing will help you avoid charges of plagiarism.

✤ Guideline 5.4

Establish criteria for the inclusion of literature in your review.

This guideline will help to keep your review focused on the key aspects of your topic. However, it is difficult to finalize selection criteria until you have started to read and make notes on the literature you have collected. This is true for three reasons. First, the body of literature that you have collected may have special characteristics that lead to the development of criteria that you could not anticipate in advance. Second, you may find that your criteria are so restrictive that very little literature can pass muster to be included in your review. Finally, your criteria may not be stringent enough, and you may find that you have an overwhelmingly large amount of literature to review.[3]

---

[3] As you know from earlier chapters, you can reduce the amount of literature to be reviewed by delimiting it to literature that deals with people who have only certain demographics. In this guideline, we are discussing criteria, such as methodological issues in research, that go beyond demographics.

Consider the work of Akinbami, Cheng, and Kornfeld (2001). They established criteria for selecting literature on teen-tot programs[4] to discuss in their literature review. Some of the criteria are shown in Example 5.4.1. As a result of applying their criteria, the initial 46 published evaluations identified by the authors were reduced to just four. In their literature review, the authors provided a thorough review of these four evaluations. Of course, if your audience (such as your professor) requires more references, you might need to adjust your criteria so that they are less restrictive.

Example 5.4.1

A sample of the criteria for selection of literature on teen-tot programs:

1. Must describe a *comprehensive* program (e.g., clinical health supervision, assistance with staying in school…).
2. Must clearly describe the clinical component.
3. Must have statistical results—not just results described in narrative form.

↳ Guideline 5.5

Give each piece of literature a unique identifier such as the surname of the first author.

The identifiers could also be numbers such as 1, 2, and 3. Using identifiers can make your note taking more efficient and effective, which we will explore in the next guideline.

↳ Guideline 5.6

While taking notes, consider building a table that summarizes key points in the literature you are reviewing.

One way to organize your material initially is to build a table in which you list the identifiers (such as the surnames of the first authors mentioned in the previous guideline) in the first column and special characteristics of each study in the other columns (with "descriptors" as headings.)[5] Example 5.6.1 shows a simple table of this type with descriptors such as number of participants, level of education, etc. Other descriptors could be added such as location of the study, methodology used (e.g., qualitative versus quantitative and/or experimental versus nonexperimental), socioeconomic status of the participants, and so on. Such a table will help you get an overview of the literature you are reading. If it is carefully constructed, you might want to include the table in your literature review to provide your readers with an overview. In the narrative portion of your review, you will want to point out

---

[4] Teen-tot programs provide one-stop service centers to assist teenage parents and their children. A major goal is to help teenagers avoid additional pregnancies until they are financially and psychologically ready for them.

[5] Tables are easy to build with modern word processing programs. For example, when using Microsoft® Word, click on "Table" at the top of the screen, then click on "Insert." From that point on, building a table will be obvious. If you want to use a large number of columns, switch from "portrait" to "landscape" (which will turn the page on its side so that it is wider than it is long) by clicking on "File," then "Page Setup," then "Landscape," and then "OK."

the highlights of such a table, but it is not necessary to repeat all the tabled information in your narrative.

Because such tables provide only summary material regarding selected characteristics of the literature you are reviewing, your narrative should go beyond the contents of the table to discuss additional issues, relationships among various studies that are not obvious from the table, possible conclusions based on all the literature sources, and so on.

Example 5.6.1

A sample "notes table," which helps organize literature and provide an overview:

Identifier	Level of Education	Type of Measure	Number of Participants	Type of Assignment	Outcome
Applegate (2004)	College	Questionnaire	25 E, 20 C	Random	Sig. in favor of E
Brown (2001)	College	Interview	10 E, 10 C	Intact Groups (Nonrandom)	Diff. not sig.
Jones (2003)	General Adult Population	Observation	30 E only	(No control group)	Diff. not sig.
Chang (2002)	High School	Questionnaire	50 E, 50 C	Random	Sig. in favor of E
Solis (2004)	College	Questionnaire	110 E, 115 C	Random	Sig. in favor of E
Note. E = Experimental Group; C = Control Group; Diff. = difference; Sig. = statistically significant.					

An important advantage of a table like the one in Example 5.6.1 is that patterns you might otherwise overlook may become obvious. For instance, from the table it is clear that the three studies that had significant differences (all in favor of the experimental group) were conducted with random assignment, which is highly desirable in an experimental study. Note that experiments are almost always quantitative.

Tables can also be built for nonexperimental quantitative studies (such as surveys, which do not have control groups) as well as qualitative studies that do not report statistics in the results sections. Regardless of the types of studies you are summarizing in a table, it is recommended that the first column contain identifiers and that the remaining columns contain information on characteristics of participants, the types of measures used, and the outcomes of the studies.

Box 5D shows a summary table that was included in the published literature review by Akinbami, Cheng, and Kornfeld (2001), which was briefly discussed under Guideline 5.4. Because only four published evaluations were reviewed, it was possible for the authors to provide a considerable amount of information on each evaluation in fewer than two pages. If you are reviewing larger amounts of literature, consider including less information on each source to keep the table from becoming too large.

Box 5D *Sample summary table.*

Table 1

Teen-Tot Program Characteristics, Interventions, and Outcomes

Program	Intervention	Evaluated Outcomes	Strengths and Weaknesses
TEEN-TOT CLINIC Nelson, Key, Fletcher, Kırkpatrıck, & Feınsteın (1982) • Duration. 18 mos postpartum. • Participants (*n* = 35)· age < 17 yrs, race 91% black. Referred from urban hospitals • Control group (*n* = 70): matched for maternal and child characterıstıcs. Receıved care at public clınıcs	1. Well-chıld health vısıts, developmental assessment, nutrıtıon counselıng, WIC, referral to communıty services. 2 Group sessıons on child development and parentıng skılls. 3. Contraceptıve counselıng and services 4. Assıstance with education, employment, living arrangements, goals, and relatıonshıps	1. 91% vs. 46% controls fully ımmunızed (6 mos). * 97% vs 83% controls between 5th–95th growth percentıles (6 mos).* 2. [None reported] 3. Contraceptıve use (6 mos): 91% vs. 63% controls.* Repeat pregnancy (18 mos): 16% vs. 38% controls * 4. School enrollment (6 mos): 86% vs 66% controls *	↑ Matched control group. No difference between partıcıpant and control group characteristics. ↓ No analysis of attrition ↓ Many outcomes reported only at 6 mos. ↓ Small number of partıcıpants.
QUEENS HOSPITAL CENTER. Rabın, Seltzer, & Pollack (1991) • Duration· until mother 20 yrs old. • Partıcıpants (*n* = 498): age < 20 yrs, race not specified. Recruıted from clınıcal adolescent program • Control group (*n* = 91). from adult obstetrıc clinic. Received care ın pediatric and adult famıly planning clınıc	1 24-hour "on-call" system, each teen-ınfant paır assigned to one interdisciplinary team. 2. Famıly lıfe education program wıth bi-weekly classes for partıcıpants, theır partners and famılıes. 3 Comprehensıve services available on-site (mental health center, WIC, housing office, high school equivalency program, day care center).	1. Clınıc attendance: 75% vs 18% of controls.* Maternal morbıdıty† and ınfant morbıdıty‡ lower among partıcıpants.* 2. Contraceptıve use: 85% partıcıpants vs. 22% of controls * Repeat pregnancy. 9% partıcıpants vs. 70% controls.* 3. School attendance: 77% partıcıpants vs. 38% controls.* School completıon: 95% partıcıpants graduated from high school Employment: 48% partıcıpants vs. 22% controls.*	↑ No difference between partıcıpant and control group characteristics. ↓ Length of participation not specified. ↓ No discussıon of attrıbutıon or dropout characteristics. ↓ Intervals of outcome evaluation not specified.
TEEN MOTHER AND CHILD PROGRAM. Elster, Lamb, Tavare, & Ralston (1987) • Duration. 2 yrs postpartum • Partıcıpants (*n* = 125): age < 18 yrs, race > 80% whıte. 35% from hıgh socioeconomic group. Self-referral, community referral • Control group (*n* = 135): Recruıted from WIC sıte Received care from community providers	1 Prenatal care, education, psychosocıal and nutrıtıonal assessments 2 Health care for ınfants and teen mothers Staff on call. WIC referral. 3. Individual counseling about financial management, school, and work Referrals for vocational traınıng, education 4. Contraceptıve education. 5. Infant health and development education 6 Counseling on parenting, ınterpersonal relationships, and stress Outreach to fathers.	1. Partıcıpants had more prenatal visits.* No difference in preterm or low bırthweıght. 2–6. Participants had better composite scores at 12 and 26 mos postpartum* (repeat pregnancy, school/job attendance, receıpt of entitlements, ER vısıts, hospıtalızatıons, ımmunızatıons, maternal preventive health efforts, chıld developmental knowledge, and General Well-Being Schedule scores). Greater ımmunızatıon completion among participants.* No significant difference ın ınfant growth and development or repeat pregnancy rates.	↔ Participants more lıkely to have hıgher ıncome, attend school, graduate, or be working at tıme of enrollment. Multiple regression used to control for differences ↓ Hıgh attrıtıon rate.
			Continued on next page.→

SPECIAL CARE PROGRAM. O'Sullivan & Jacobsen (1992) • Duration. 18 mos. • Participants (*n* = 120): age < 18 yrs, race 100% black. Recruited from urban teaching hospital. • Random assignment to control group (*n* = 123). Received routine care	1. Well-baby visits Participants received reminders if appointment missed.	1 Clinic attendance (18 mos): 40% vs. 22% of controls Immunizations (18 mos): 33% vs. 18% of controls.*	↑ Randomized study ↑ Outcomes analyzed among dropouts ↔ High attrition rate, but 91% of original participants and controls interviewed at 18 mos
	2. Social worker reviewed family planning methods, made referrals to birth control clinic.	2. Repeat pregnancy (18 mos): 12% vs. 28% of controls *	
	3 Health care provider asked about mother's plan to return to school	3. Return to school: > 50% of both participants and controls (no significant statistical difference)	
	4. Health teaching in the waiting room. Infant care and appropriate ER use education	4. ER use: 75% vs. 80% for controls (no significant statistical difference).	

* Statistically significant difference using chi-square test (95% confidence level).
† Disease state of pelvic organs, upper respiratory, hematologic, or gastrointestinal systems requiring multiple doctor visits or hospitalizations
‡ Includes maternal morbidity definition plus any accident in a child under 2 years of age.
ER· emergency room
WIC: Women Infant Children program

♄ Guideline 5.7

Consider using color-coding while reading and making notes.

Color-coding while you are reading can help you quickly locate material as needed while you are writing your literature review. You might use one color for references to relevant theories, another for definitions of terms, another for results sections, and so on.

♄ Guideline 5.8

Pay special attention to definitions while taking notes.

If different authors use different definitions of the variables you are reviewing, you will need to take the differences into account in your literature review. One possibility is to consider whether studies with one type of definition tend to have one type of result while those with another definition tend to have a different type.

Note that definitions sometimes change over time, making it difficult to identify trends in findings from earlier to later studies. For instance, "physical child abuse" tends to be more broadly defined today than it was by previous generations. Forms of physical punishment administered by parents and teachers that were considered acceptable at one time are now considered harsh and sometimes abusive. This change in definitions makes it difficult to make valid generalizations about whether such abuse has been increasing or decreasing across time periods from the research on the incidence of child abuse conducted over a long period of time.

As you know, the previous guideline suggests you use a special color to code definitions for easy reference when you begin to write your review. After color-coding definitions in a particular color, you will be able to quickly locate definitions to reread them and compare them with each other. If there are major differences among them, this fact should be discussed in your literature review.

ᕮ Guideline 5.9
Pay special attention to researchers' descriptions of the limitations of their research methodology.

Authors of research articles often describe the limitations of their studies. While this may be done anywhere in their articles, they typically discuss them in the Discussion section near the end of their articles. Making notes on the limitations that are discussed (and perhaps color-coding them) may save you time when you consider the strengths and weaknesses of the various studies you are reviewing. Some researchers will provide extensive discussions of their study limitations, which you can then use when evaluating studies conducted by others who do not recognize or discuss their limitations. Example 5.9.1 shows some short excerpts from a lengthy statement of limitations that appears near the end of a research article.[6]

Example 5.9.1
Brief excerpts from researchers' self-critique mentioning limitations:

The study has three limitations. First, the investigation was conducted at a single site and we cannot generalize....

Second, the sample size limited the number of variables we could include in the analysis.... For example, client and clinician race or ethnicity...may play a role.... However, given the sample size, it would not have been statistically prudent to include a set of client and clinician characteristics....

Third, because the same individuals did the ratings [two sets of ratings]..., there could have been a response bias—that is, a rater's judgment on one scale could have influenced his or her judgment on the other scale. However....

ᕮ Guideline 5.10
It is misleading to read and make notes only on the abstracts of articles without disclosing the fact that you have done so.

Most journal articles begin with abstracts that summarize the articles. Many journals put severe restrictions on the length of abstracts. For example, the *Publication Manual of the American Psychological Association* suggests that they contain 120 words or less.[7] Thus, researchers can cover only the most salient details in their abstracts, and reading only the abstracts and not the entire articles will provide you with only limited information on the contents of the literature you have collected. Example 5.10.1 shows an abstract of typical length for research articles in the social and behavioral sciences.

---

[6] Loneck, Banks, Way, & Bonaparte (2002, p. 141).
[7] American Psychological Association (2001, p. 15).

Example 5.10.1

An abstract for a journal article of typical length:

This study examined the effects of a relapse prevention program (RP) and a 12-step continuing care program (for two years) on both depressed and nondepressed patients. Patients were randomly assigned to programs. Depressed patients attended more treatment sessions and had more cocaine-free urines during treatment than participants without depression, but they drank alcohol more frequently before treatment and during the 18-month posttreatment follow-up. Cocaine outcomes in depressed patients deteriorated to a greater degree after treatment than did cocaine outcomes in patients without depression, particularly in patients in RP who had a current depressive disorder at baseline. The best alcohol outcomes were obtained in nondepressed patients who received RP. The results suggest that extended continuing care treatment may be warranted for cocaine-dependent patients with co-occurring depressive disorders.[8]

Reading only the abstract in Example 5.10.1, a reviewer might make a note such as *Relapse prevention therapy is superior to 12-step focused group intervention (McKay et al., 2002)* and include the note in a literature review. Unless the reviewer starts the statement with a phrase such as *According to the abstract…*, readers will assume that the review was prepared with care and, of course, the entire research article was read. Thus, reading and making notes on only abstracts without acknowledging that this was done is misleading and unethical. Note that most professors prohibit such a practice.

Not reading the entire article and relying on only the abstract shown in Example 5.10.1 would leave the reviewer without knowledge of a vast array of important facts and issues that would have bearing on the evaluation of the research and how it should be treated in the literature review. Some of these are shown in Example 5.10.2.

Example 5.10.2

A sample of important facts and issues that would be missed if a reviewer relied on only the abstract shown in Example 5.10.1 instead of reading the entire article summarized by the abstract:

1. All participants were male veterans who were referred to the continuing care program at Philadelphia Veterans Affairs Medical Center. [Note: This is a highly specialized group.]
2. Most of the participants had already participated in a four-week intensive outpatient program at the medical center. [Note: This prior treatment may have interacted with the treatments in this study.]
3. Self-reports on cocaine use were validated with urine toxicology tests. [Note: The use of urine tests is an important strength of this study.]

---

[8] McKay et al. (2002, p. 225). For instructional purposes, this abstract was modified slightly.

4. The study had a very high follow-up rate. [Note: This is an important strength of the study.]

5. The study did not include biochemical tests to collaborate alcohol use. [Note: This is a weakness of the study.]

✑ Guideline 5.11

Make notes on how other writers have organized the literature on your topic.

Before you write your review, you should develop an organizational scheme. For instance, you might start with how many people are affected by a problem, followed by a definition of a problem, followed by a discussion of relevant theories, and so on. Briefly examine Model Literature Review 6 on religion-accommodative counseling. It begins with some statistics on religious beliefs in the United States. Flipping through the pages of the review, you will see major headings that are centered in bold as well as second- and third-level headings that are in italics. These headings and subheadings indicate the organizational structure of the review.

Example 5.11.1 shows the organizational scheme for a recently published literature review. The first-level headings (i.e., main headings) are centered and in a larger font than the other headings, the second level (i.e., next lower level) is shown centered and in italics, and the third level is in italics at the beginnings of the paragraphs. Noting these helps you understand what the writer thinks are the major issues (as indicated by the first-level headings) and what other issues are subsumed under each other (as indicated by the second- and third-level headings).

Example 5.11.1[9]

Three levels of headings, which indicate the organization of a literature review:

Title: Medical Decision-Making and Minors: Issues of Consent and Assent

The review begins with two paragraphs that introduce the general topic. These paragraphs appear below the title without a heading:

In recent years, the physician-patient relationship has transformed from one of paternalism into an egalitarian and participatory partnership in which patients and physicians work together to make healthcare decisions (Committee on Bioethics, 1995). Today, there is general societal acceptance that "patients have a right to know about....

Although adults receive considerable encouragement to become active participants in healthcare decisions, children and adolescents often have little voice in decisions about their....

---

[9] Kuther (2003, pp. 343–355).

Informed Consent: The Cornerstone of Healthcare

In its simplest form, informed consent is the treatment authorization given by a patient to a physician. Legally, it is....[followed by an additional paragraph]

Ambiguities in Consent: Minors

The process of informed consent becomes more complicated when considering minors because these is only limited direct application of the doctrine of informed consent in pediatrics....[one paragraph total]

Minors and Consent: Legal Perspectives

In the United States, state legislation requiring parental consent for medical treatment reflects the conception that minors....[followed by three additional paragraphs]

Minors' capacity to provide voluntary consent. Voluntary consent reflects a deliberate choice that is made freely and is not....[followed by two additional paragraphs]

Minors' capacity to make rational decisions. A rational decision demonstrates an understanding and appreciation of the relevant information....[followed by six additional paragraphs]

Minor Assent: Developmentally Appropriate Decision-Making

Given the increasing recognition that most adolescents have the capacity to participate in decisions about their healthcare.... [one paragraph total]

Ethical Perspectives on Assent

Assent is a means of involving minors in treatment decisions. It is an interactive process between....[followed by one additional paragraph]

Benefits of Assent

Solicitation of assent from minors engages them in graduated levels of decision-making, in which they participate in....[followed by three additional paragraphs]

Assent and Consent: Unresolved Questions

When may a minor give consent, and when assent? Legally, unless he or she is an emancipated minor, mature minor, or.... [one paragraph total]

Decision-Making Capacity and Consent

Physicians are given great responsibilities in that it is largely their judgment that determines a minor's decision-making....[followed by one additional paragraph]

Minors and Treatment Refusal

The paucity of ethical guidelines on how to proceed should a minor refuse treatment, or when there are disagreements....[followed by one additional paragraph]

Disagreements Between Minors and Parents

    Although guidelines for physicians recommend that they respect adolescents' autonomy by encouraging.…[followed by two additional paragraphs]

Conclusion

    Despite empirical research suggesting that.…[followed by one additional paragraph]

    There is no single organizational scheme that is suitable for all topics and audiences. As you read the literature on your topic, consider making notes on how others have organized their discussions of the topic. Note that even journal articles that present original empirical research on a topic often begin with brief literature reviews. It is a good idea to note how these are organized even if they do not have subheadings within the review.

    As you begin reading and making notes, develop a tentative organizational scheme, and then modify it as you get ideas by reading additional literature. In the end, you should have an original scheme for organizing the particular body of literature that you are reviewing.

Exercise for Chapter 5

1. Have you ever written a paper and had an ethical dilemma about citing a source for an idea (such as not being able to recall the source but wanting to use the idea anyway)? If yes, how did you resolve it?

2. According to this chapter, if an author presents original ideas that are logical and make common sense, should that author's work be cited?

3. State several facts, concepts, or ideas you believe are "common knowledge" whose sources do not need to be cited. Discuss them with your classmates to see if they agree with you.

4. Authors of a literature review wrote this statement: "Providing for defense and security is a singular and defining purpose of national government."[10] The context in which this sentence appears makes it clear that the authors are referring to the national government of the United States. The authors do not cite a reference for the sentence. Do you think that they should have cited a reference, *or* do you think the sentence makes a statement that is common knowledge? Explain.

5. Authors of a literature review wrote that "approximately 5 of every 100 high-school-age students drop out of school each year. This figure has remained constant for the past 10

---

[10] Torres-Reyna & Shapiro (2002, p. 279).

years."[11] Do you think that the authors should have cited a reference, *or* do you think the sentence makes a statement that is common knowledge? Explain.

6. According to this chapter, does rephrasing the expression of the ideas of others relieve you of the responsibility to cite their sources?

7. According to this chapter, what might happen if you fail to indicate clearly the beginning *and* end of material that you summarize in a literature review?

8. Consider one of the topics on which you might write a literature review. At this point, can you think of any criteria that you might use for the inclusion (and/or exclusion) of literature? Explain. See Guideline 5.4.

9. At this point, do you plan to build a table to summarize key points while you take notes on the literature you collect? Why? Why not? See Guideline 5.6.

10. Name at least three characteristics that you might color-code when reading and making notes on the literature you collect. Name characteristics other than those mentioned in this chapter. See Guideline 5.7.

11. Briefly explain why it is important to pay special attention to definitions while taking notes.

12. According to this chapter, where do authors of research articles typically discuss the limitations of their studies?

13. Do you agree that it is misleading to read and make notes only on the abstracts of articles unless you disclose this to your readers? Do you think it is unethical? Explain.

14. Read the abstract for Model Literature Review 5 on predicting school violence. (Note that abstracts appear at the beginning of articles.) Then briefly scan the review for at least three important facts or ideas that would be missed by someone who read only the abstract. Write them here.

---

[11] Wood, Murdock, & Cronin (2002, p. 605).

Chapter 6

Guidelines for Evaluating Sources of Literature

In this chapter, we will consider guidelines for evaluating *sources* of literature, with special attention to academic journals. In the next chapter, you will find guidelines for evaluating individual research reports, which are typically published in academic journals.

✍ Guideline 6.1
Even the most prestigious sources publish reports of flawed research.

In every professional field, some journals are considered more prestigious than others. Often, those published by large professional associations or by universities are considered prestigious. For example, the American Psychological Association (APA) publishes a large number of journals, all of which receive a large number of submissions for possible publication. Because the number of articles published per journal is quite limited (sometimes as small as a dozen or so each year), the vast majority of submissions are rejected for one or more reasons, resulting in the publication of only the better research in APA journals. Examples of university-based, prestigious journals are *Teachers' College Record* (published by Teachers College of Columbia University) and the *Journal of Asian American Studies* (published by the Johns Hopkins University Press).

Despite their prestige, even these journals publish research that is flawed because conducting research typically involves studying only the individuals who are willing to be studied (and not necessarily the ones who should be studied), making compromises due to limited resources (such as using paper-and-pencil questionnaires instead of expensive one-on-one interviews), and using flawed designs and procedures (such as conducting a poll by telephone, which biases the sample against those who do not have phones). These types of research problems and compromises are discussed in detail in the next chapter. At this point, note that even the best research reported in the most respected journals typically has one or more flaws.

As a general rule, more-prestigious journals (or Web sites) are more reliable sources of information than less-prestigious ones. However, the strengths and weaknesses of an individual article published in any journal (even prestigious ones) should be evaluated carefully by someone preparing a literature review. Guidelines for doing this are described in the next chapter.

Box 6A shows three reasons why an editor of a highly respected journal (with the assistance of his or her reviewers) might decide to publish a report on seriously flawed research.

Box 6A   *Three reasons why methodologically weak articles are published.*

1. The topic of the article might be very *timely*. For instance, a methodologically weak manuscript on an infectious disease that is being covered widely in the mass media might be selected for publication in a medical journal over a methodologically stronger manuscript on a disease that is not of current general interest. This is especially true if there is little or no previously published research on the "timely disease" (or timely topics in fields other than medicine).

2. The article might have important *theoretical implications*. As you know from earlier material in this book, theory development is a major function of science because theories help us explain diverse observations and assist us in making predictions. An article that presents strong, logically constructed theoretical arguments (even if the underlying research methodology is weak or questionable) has a better chance of publication than one that does not have important theoretical implications.

3. The editors may be striving for *balance*. For instance, a journal devoted to family issues has published many articles on spousal abuse—almost all of which were on husbands abusing their wives. A methodologically weak research article on wives abusing their husbands might be published despite its weaknesses to provide balance in the overall coverage of the journal and to help fill in the gap in the literature.

Note that the results of methodologically flawed research (even in nonprestigious journals) are not necessarily wrong. Instead, the results are *questionable*. As a result, an individual writing a review needs to consider how the flaws might have affected the results. Often researchers will discuss this issue in the Discussion and Conclusions sections of their research reports. In addition, the material in the next chapter will help you in evaluating and interpreting research.

✎ Guideline 6.2
Consider who sponsors a publication. Professional associations, foundations, government agencies, and for-profit companies are major sponsors.

As mentioned under Guideline 6.1, professional associations publish journals, and sometimes publish books and pamphlets. Associations such as the American Association for

Public Opinion Research, the Library Administration and Management Association, and the Society of Pediatric Nurses have large memberships. Consequently, they receive large numbers of submissions of manuscripts to be considered for publication in their journals. From these submissions, journal editors are able to select those that most closely meet their editorial policies and seem likely to make important contributions to the field.[1]

Foundations, government agencies, nonprofit agencies, and for-profit companies also publish journals and books in professional fields. Many of these have high standards and publish excellent material. However, it is possible that some journals published by for-profit companies are less selective than other sources in deciding what to publish.

✎ Guideline 6.3

Check to see whether a journal (or publisher) has an independent editorial board.

Editorial boards establish guidelines and policies for journals. Members of the boards usually serve as reviewers of manuscripts that are submitted for possible publication (see the next guideline). The names of editorial board members are usually published near the beginning of each issue of a journal. The independence of the board from the publisher is indicated by institutional affiliations that are listed with their names. Most editorial board members are affiliated with colleges and universities and are *not* employees of the publisher of the journals.

✎ Guideline 6.4

Check to see whether a journal uses a "blind" peer-review process when selecting manuscripts for publication. (This is also called a "juried process.")

Typically, the editor of a journal checks to see that a manuscript submitted for consideration for publication covers a topic within the field covered by the journal. If so, he or she submits it to several knowledgeable professionals (the jury of peers, who are often members of the editorial board) for critical review. Note that information regarding authorship of the submissions is almost always removed, which makes the reviewers "blind" to the authorship. The reviewers critique the manuscript and make overall recommendations regarding whether it should be published. Often, they recommend that a manuscript be published contingent on the author making certain changes that the reviewers believe will improve the research report.

Almost invariably, journals published by professional associations are peer-reviewed because the editors are accountable to the members of the associations. All members, and especially those whose manuscripts have been rejected, want the process for selecting

---

[1] This does not mean, however, that they are free of flaws. Instead, it means that the content is appropriate for the journal and the manuscript meets at least minimal standards for the expression of ideas, originality, methodological soundness, relationship to theory, and other criteria established by the journal's editors.

manuscripts for publication in their associations' journals to be done in a fair and objective manner, which is accomplished by using a blind peer-review process.

It is not always easy to determine whether a journal is peer-reviewed. A major tip-off is if the "instructions to authors" states that all information indicating authorship or sponsorship should be submitted on a piece of paper that is separate from the manuscript. This usually indicates that there will be a "blind" peer-review (i.e., a review without the reviewer knowing the authorship).[2]

Approval through a peer-review process does not guarantee that the manuscripts selected for publication as articles will be strong from a research methodology point of view. (See Box 6A.) It does mean, however, that peers have judged them to contain information that will be useful to the professionals who read the journals despite any flaws.

Note that major publishers of textbooks also use a peer-review process in deciding which manuscripts to publish as books. Much of the material in textbooks, however, is considered "secondary" because it is usually based on original works written by others (i.e., textbook authors summarize the state-of-the-art in a particular field based on the writings of others in the field). When writing a literature review, aim to cite only primary sources whenever possible.

✤ Guideline 6.5
Consider the institutional affiliation of the author.

Articles in academic journals and books on academic topics understandably tend to be written by professors. Government employees and employees of private, for-profit, and nonprofit companies also write manuscripts for publication in journals. Sometimes, authorship will give you hints as to quality and objectivity. For instance, be cautious when the authors' affiliations (and perhaps the journals' sponsorships) are special-interest groups that lobby for a particular point of view within the political system (e.g., gun control, abortion laws, and so on). While they may have solid data in which they firmly believe, you will want to evaluate such articles with extra care since the authors may have "blind spots."

✤ Guideline 6.6
Consider the overall quality of a journal in which an article is published.

By following Guidelines 6.1 through 6.5, you will have information that will help you judge the overall quality of a journal. Also, consider whether the journal seems to be professionally edited (e.g., free from mechanical flaws such as spelling and grammatical errors) and that there is overall consistency in quality from article to article. Journals that

---

[2] Instructions to authors are usually published near the beginning of journals or at the end. Some journals publish their instructions in only one issue per year. Major publishers of journals maintain Web sites where these instructions can often be obtained.

receive only a small number of very good submissions and, thus, must choose among poor ones to fill their journals, tend to be second-tier journals.

Part of the "publish or perish syndrome" in academe is not only the question of whether a professor's research has been published but also whether he or she has been published in journals of high quality.[3] While this is a somewhat subjective matter, professors are aware that there are degrees of quality across journals and consider this when choosing journals to which they submit their manuscripts. Thus, journals that are known for publishing high-quality research tend to attract high-quality submissions. These journals are known for their overall high quality.

⚓ Guideline 6.7
Consider the typical length of articles published in a journal.

As you know, longer pieces of writing are not necessarily better than shorter ones. However, in many fields, there are journals that specialize in publishing large numbers of short articles, often no more than a couple of pages in length (on small-sized pages). While research articles in such journals may contain some useful facts that you might want to use in a literature review, the shortness of the articles precludes a thorough discussion of the rationale, methodology, findings, and theoretical underpinnings of the individual reports of research—issues that are typically found in longer research articles.

Exercise for Chapter 6

1. Very briefly name the three major reasons why methodologically weak articles are sometimes published (even in highly respected journals).

2. Name the major sponsors of journals (i.e., types of publishers).

3. What indicates the "independence" of an editorial review board?

4. Many journals use a "blind peer-review process" to assist in the selection of manuscripts for publication. What is the meaning of the word "blind" in this context?

---

[3] Typically, recommendations regarding promotions and tenure for professors are made by committees of full professors who teach in the same or related fields. Because of their long participation in a field, they often know the reputations of various journals. Also, they often will consider whether a professor has published in peer-reviewed journals (see Guideline 6.4) as well as whether authors of other articles have cited the articles published by the professor being considered. The reference sections of libraries usually have citation indices that keep track of who is citing whom and in what publications.

5. In this chapter, a rationale is given for the statement that journals that specialize in publishing very short articles might be less useful than those that typically publish long articles. What is the rationale?

6. In your opinion, does this chapter imply that you should cite in your review only articles published in prestigious journals? Explain.

7. Name several journals in your field of study. Who publishes them? In your opinion, are they prestigious? Explain.

Chapter 7

Evaluating and Interpreting
Research Literature

Although the guidelines in this chapter emphasize the evaluation of research reports published in academic journals, they also apply to other sources of original research, such as books, conference papers, reports on preliminary research presented at conferences, and so on. All the guidelines apply to both qualitatively oriented and quantitatively oriented research reports. However, there are differences in exactly how some of the guidelines are applied to the two types of research. These differences are noted at appropriate points throughout this chapter.

✎ Guideline 7.1
Be wary of sources offering "proof," "facts," and "truth" based on research evidence.

There are certain "proofs" in mathematics and other fields that rely on deduction. Stated simply, scholars start with certain assumptions and derive a solution that must be true *if* the assumptions are correct. Also, there are certain everyday "facts" that we can probably all agree on as being true. For instance, all people who even briefly look into the matter would probably agree with the "fact" that more voters in California are registered as Democrats than are registered as Republicans. However, when we study complex human behavior, we almost always have at least some degree of uncertainty regarding important principles and theories. Often, we usually have more uncertainty than certainty about most "facts" regarding complex issues.

Note that decisions on how to gather information on a particular topic vary from researcher to researcher. The first decision is whether to use a qualitatively oriented or quantitatively oriented approach (or a combination of both). Quantitatively oriented researchers usually start with well-defined plans for obtaining new information, which is reduced to statistics. Qualitatively oriented researchers start with less well-defined plans. They are more likely to make changes in their methodology (e.g., changes in the wording of questions for an interview as they gain insights from participants). Given that there are two fundamentally different approaches to conducting research on a topic (both of which are generally recognized as valuable), you can see that it will be difficult to arrive at a single "truth" about a topic examined with the two approaches.

Even among quantitatively oriented researchers, there are often differences of opinion on how to interpret even basic statistical results. For example, one researcher might interpret a particular correlation coefficient as representing a "strong" relationship while another might interpret it as representing a "very strong" one.

Many of the reasons for uncertainty in our knowledge will be covered in the next five guidelines, which discuss issues regarding sampling (identifying a sample of participants from a population) and measurement (measuring participants' traits).

In the face of this inherent uncertainty associated with research, consumers of research should make decisions based on principles and theories that seem most likely to be true. In fact, this is the primary purpose of a literature review: to synthesize the often contradictory literature on a topic to arrive at defensible conclusions regarding what seems most likely to be true based on the whole body of research on a topic. Note that the validity of theories, which should be carefully considered when writing literature reviews, should be assessed on the basis of the extent to which research seems to confirm them.

A secondary purpose for conducting a literature review is to establish through the synthesis which areas need more research attention in order to reduce the amount of uncertainty about the tentative conclusions drawn in the literature review. Box 7A summarizes the primary and secondary purposes for preparing a literature review.

Box 7A *The primary and secondary purposes for preparing a literature review.*

> The primary purpose for preparing a literature review is to synthesize literature on a topic in order to arrive at defensible conclusions regarding what is *most likely to be true* in the face of the inherent uncertainty of the results reported in both qualitatively oriented and quantitatively oriented research reports.
>
> The secondary purpose is to establish which areas need more research attention in order to reduce the amount of uncertainty about the tentative conclusions drawn in a literature review.

Instead of using the words "prove" or "proof," most researchers hedge by using wording that indicates uncertainty. In fact, most will hedge even when there is seemingly overwhelming evidence that something is true because researchers know the largest advances in science have been made when a concept or principle that was almost universally regarded as being true (e.g., the world is flat) has been shown to be untrue. Box 7B shows examples of how carefully worded statements are made in the face of varying degrees of uncertainty.

As a general rule, give higher evaluations to the conclusions stated in literature in which the statements indicating the degree of certainty are consistent with the amount and quality of the evidence analyzed and presented. Beware of researchers who claim to offer "proof," establish universal "facts," and offer "truth."

When you write your review, you may want to refer to Box 7B and consider how to phrase the conclusions you reach in your synthesis of the literature. In other words, you should express your conclusions carefully to indicate the extent to which you are certain of them based on your evaluations of the research on your topic.

Box 7B *Expressions indicating degrees of certainty in the absence of proof.*

Degree of Certainty	Sample Expressions	Sample Topic
Almost absolutely certain	Almost without exception, the medical community believes… The evidence from all major studies overwhelmingly supports the finding that…	The effects of cigarette smoking on health (i.e., it is harmful to health).
Close to certain	Few who have reviewed the body of literature on XYZ would disagree with the contention that…	Topics will vary.
Fair degree of certainty	Recent studies seem to confirm the major premises of the ABC theory. Specifically, …	Topics will vary.
Rather uncertain	Although the single study that supports this finding is strong methodologically, additional studies and replications are needed before reaching firm conclusions regarding…	Topics will vary.
Very uncertain	The results of an initial pilot study suggest that… Some very preliminary evidence leads us to believe…	The effects of a new educational virtual reality computer program tested with sixteen students without a control group.

✤ Guideline 7.2

Research is almost always flawed by inadequate samples.

Quantitatively oriented researchers emphasize the desirability of identifying all members of a population of interest (such as all students majoring in economics in the United States) and drawing a random sample (such as drawing names out of a hat). Often, there are problems in identifying all members of a population (e.g., contacting all universities and colleges in the United States to get the names and contact information for all economics majors would be a daunting task). When this is true, quantitatively oriented researchers tend to use a population (such as the students majoring in economics in *one* university) that is more limited than the one they want to study. In a more limited setting, it is often possible to draw names at random. However, participation in studies is almost always voluntary, and in most samples, at least some (and sometimes many) of those selected at random refuse to participate. This leads to what is known as a "biased sample," which might easily lead to biased results.

Qualitatively oriented researchers prefer "purposive sampling" over random sampling. They establish a general purpose for their research (such as identifying the factors that lead minority women to be successful in engineering) and then seek out and select participants who are likely to provide useful information for achieving their purpose (such as contacting some local employers of engineers to determine if they have successful engineers who belong to minority groups who might be willing to be interviewed). Qualitatively oriented researchers stress gaining a thorough understanding of their particular participants by using intensive measurement methods such as extensive interviews or observing them extensively in natural settings. In general, qualitatively oriented researchers are less concerned with generalizing to populations than are quantitatively oriented researchers. Still, a reviewer of research should be concerned with whether the search for a purposive sample in qualitatively oriented research was conducted with care and whether the results were tilted in one direction or another by the refusal of some to participate in qualitatively oriented studies.

Give lower evaluations to quantitatively oriented and qualitatively oriented research reports in which the researchers used individuals who just happened to be available as their research participants. This is called an "accidental" or "convenience" sample. Such a sample does not allow a quantitatively oriented researcher to generalize to a population. It also is counterproductive for qualitatively oriented researchers who need particular types of participants (who may not be the ones who are readily available) to achieve their research purposes.

✎ Guideline 7.3
Be cautious when a body of literature has a common sampling flaw.

It is not unusual to find an entire body of research literature on a topic that has a common sampling flaw. For instance, most research in the social and behavioral sciences is conducted by professors who often have limited resources. As a result, a large proportion of studies are conducted with college/university students who volunteer to participate. This provides us with no knowledge of how nonvolunteers would respond or how individuals who are not college students would respond.

When there is a common sampling flaw in all (or most) of the studies being reviewed on a particular topic, this should be pointed out in the literature review as a weakness in the body of the research as a whole.

✎ Guideline 7.4
Research is almost always flawed by inadequate measures.

Measures in research (often called "instrumentation") vary greatly from highly structured (such as multiple-choice achievement tests or personality scales) to highly unstructured (such as loosely structured, free-flowing interviews). In addition, some traits are inherently easier to measure (such as first-grade math achievement) than others (such as proneness to engage in violent behavior). However, even the most objectively measured and easy-to-measure traits are measured with imperfect instruments, often under imperfect circumstances. For instance: (a) some first graders taking a math test might be ill on the day the test is administered, (b) some might be distracted, (c) others might not understand the test directions or understand the nature of the time limits for testing, and so on. In addition, because of questionable judgment on the part of the test maker, a given test might not include one or more important math concepts or might have poorly phrased math word problems.

Consider this example: A researcher is planning a study on the incidence of driving under the influence (DUI) of alcohol. Box 7C lists some measurement approaches that might be used. Note that each has drawbacks that might potentially flaw the results of the study.

Ideally, a study on DUI should consider a number of potentially related variables (e.g., risk-taking propensities, self-esteem, self-control, addiction to alcohol) that potentially might tie the DUI behavior to one or more theories. Note that there also would be no perfect way to measure any of these other variables.

Box 7C *Approaches to measurement in a study on DUI.*

Approach	Potential Drawback
Questionnaire with objective-type items asking about DUI behavior in the past	Respondents might not be willing to admit to the behavior and may give socially desirable responses even if responses are anonymous.
	Respondents might interpret "under the influence" in various ways. The questionnaire might provide a definition, which would help reduce the problem.
Brief structured interviews	Same drawbacks as the first approach except that responses will not be anonymous, increasing the possibility of failing to admit to DUI behavior.
In-depth interviews	If rapport is established, respondents might be more likely to admit to DUI behavior.
	Subjectivity required to interpret and summarize results across a group of respondents may lead to errors in analysis.
Direct observation	Participants might behave differently if they know they are being observed (such as when leaving a bar).
	The sample of observations will probably be limited (e.g., cannot follow subjects everywhere; subjects might drink in private).
Questioning significant others	They might be unwilling to "squeal" on their significant others.
	They might not be with the subjects at appropriate times (e.g., parents not going out with the adolescents on their dates).
Examining criminal records available to the public	Would yield information on *only* those who were driving under the influence *and* were stopped by police *and* were charged *and* convicted.

✢ Guideline 7.5

Consider the reliability of measures used in research.

Reliability refers to the consistency of results. Researchers often address this issue in their research reports, which you should consider when evaluating the overall dependability of the results.

Qualitatively oriented researchers often report the extent to which two or more independent individuals identified the same themes when analyzing participants' responses to loosely structured interviews. Their level of agreement is often expressed as a percentage.

Quantitatively oriented researchers (who tend to use objectively scored measures) often report on reliability using correlation coefficients (ranging from 0.00 for no reliability to 1.00 for perfect reliability).[1] Often, you will find reliabilities ranging from about 0.65 to 0.85 reported for measures used in quantitative research, indicating moderate to high reliability.

Other things being equal, give higher evaluations to studies in which the reliability of the measures have been established and reported at acceptable levels such as 80% or higher agreement in qualitatively oriented studies or correlation coefficients of 0.65 or higher in quantitatively oriented studies.

✢ Guideline 7.6

Consider the validity of measures used in research.

Validity refers to the extent to which an instrument measures what it is supposed to measure. Note that a measure can be highly reliable without being valid. For instance, consider an extreme example that makes this point clear. If a researcher tried to measure the cognitive skills of legal immigrants passing through the U.S.–Mexican border with a series of questions asked in English, those with limited English-language skills would understandably perform poorly. Asking these immigrants the same questions repeatedly would likely yield consistent (i.e., reliable) results. Yet, the results would be of extremely dubious validity because the questions were posed in a language with which the immigrants were not fluent. Hence, when evaluating a measure, it is not sufficient to consider only its reliability. Its validity should also be assessed.

Most professionals in measurement would agree that most widely used measures have higher reliability than validity. It is beyond the scope of this book to explore the many approaches and controversies concerning how to estimate the validity of a measure. However, even if you have not taken a course in tests and measurements, you can look for obvious flaws (e.g., asking questions about sensitive measures without anonymity and/or without establishing rapport with the participants) when you evaluate a research article.

---

[1] Quantitative researchers often report coefficient alpha (α), which is a type of correlation coefficient, to indicate "reliability." It indicates the extent to which the individual items in a measure yield similar results, that is, yield results that agree with each other. (This is somewhat analogous to reporting the extent to which researchers in qualitative studies agree with each other.)

Note that in good scientific reporting, researchers address the issue of the validity of their measures. Often, they use published measures for which you can obtain validity information from the test publisher. Probably as often as not, researchers use measures they have constructed especially for use in their research. You should give lower evaluations to studies in which the researchers fail to discuss the validity of their measures because in the absence of such a discussion, you will often have no basis for judging whether the measures are valid.

Sometimes researchers report the actual wording of questions posed on questionnaires or in interviews. When this is the case, consider the questions carefully. Ask questions such as: Are they clearly stated? Could they be misinterpreted? Do they cover the topic thoroughly? Are they worded in such a way that they might influence the respondents to answer in one way rather than another? Box 7D shows examples of defective interview/questionnaire items. Such items lower the validity of the measures.

Box 7D *A sample of defective interview/questionnaire items.*

Item	Defect
As you may know, the President of the United States believes that X is greater than Y. Do you think that X is greater than Y?	Citing the opinion of an authority might sway the opinions of the respondents to the question.
Are you confident that the economy of the United States is improving? __ Yes __ No	The item fails to allow for degrees of opinion. For instance, it does not provide a choice for someone who is "fairly confident" but not sure enough to respond simply "yes" or "no."
When is the last time you hit your child with your hand?	The question assumes that a parent engaged in this behavior. The question is suitable only if the parents have been prescreened, and the researcher already knows that all have hit their children with their hands.
During your career, how many times have you been ill enough to miss two or more consecutive days of work?	For adults, the timeframe is too long. For instance, an older worker might not be able to remember how many times this happened. Note that it is better to use a shorter timeframe such as "in the last year."
Have you used any tobacco products during the last seven days? __ Yes __ No	As an anonymous question, it is satisfactory. However, it is unsatisfactory if it is administered to students who will be handing their completed questionnaires to their teachers because students might not be willing to admit to the behavior to their teachers.

✥ Guideline 7.7
Consider researchers' self-critiques of their own research methods.

In good scientific writing, researchers point out the major flaws in the research methodology. Typically, these are flaws that the researchers could not overcome because of limited resources such as time, access to participants, and so on. Very often, these are referred to as "limitations" and are usually discussed briefly near the end of research reports in the Discussion section. Example 7.7.1 shows a discussion of limitations, which appeared in the Discussion section of a research article in an academic journal. It illustrates the usefulness of following this guideline in order to identify methodological weaknesses that might otherwise be overlooked by those writing literature reviews who may not be expert in research methods.

Example 7.7.1[2]

Sample statement by the researcher regarding limitations:

There were some limitations to this study. First, we provided adolescent participants with specific smoking categories (i.e., casual or addicted smoker) rather than allowing them to provide their own categories, which may have caused some confusion among adolescents not familiar with such terms. Another possible limitation is the fact that we only evaluated adolescents who had never smoked even a puff of a cigarette and thus were unable to explore how experiences with cigarette smoking affect discrimination of types of smokers.... Finally, the racial distribution is not necessarily representative of the United States as a whole. African Americans are relatively underrepresented in this sample, while Asians are overrepresented.

Also, researchers often will point out major methodological strengths of their studies, especially if they were the first to have these strengths (e.g., the first study on a topic that used a random sample from a population).

By paying close attention to self-critiques of research methodology, you will be in a better position to evaluate the research reports you will refer to in your literature review. For instance, if a researcher states that his or her study has a major strength, you might check the other studies you have collected to see if they have the same strength. If not, these studies might be weaker than the one claiming a major strength.

✳ Guideline 7.8

Be cautious when researchers refer to causality.

It is easy to fall into the logical trap of assuming that because X precedes Y, then X must be the cause of Y. By definition, it is true that a cause must occur before its effect appears. However, not every variable that occurs first is necessarily a cause. Here is a simple illustration: Someone notices that students in a particular first-grade classroom, on average, are high achievers in reading. The person also notices that the classroom has a large number of books that were available to the students from the beginning of first grade. Did the large number of books *cause* the high reading achievement? It is not possible to know because many other variables also preceded their achievement. Some examples are: having a well-

_____

[2] Rubinstein, Halpern-Felsher, Thompson, & Millstein (2003, p. 661).

qualified teacher assigned to the class, having self-selection (by their parents) of high-potential students to the class, having an effective computer-assisted reading instruction program available in the classroom, and so on.

The study of causality is the source of a major divide between quantitatively oriented and qualitatively oriented researchers. To study causality, quantitatively oriented researchers prefer random assignment to treatment and control groups in an attempt to control extraneous variables. Thus, in the example we have been considering, half of the students would be selected at random to learn reading in a classroom with many books while the remaining ones would be taught reading in a classroom with few books. The researcher would try to establish equality between the two settings on other variables such as the qualifications of the teachers and the availability of other resources such as computer-assisted reading instruction programs that might also affect achievement in reading.

Qualitatively oriented researchers, on the other hand, eschew random assignment. Instead, they take an in-depth look at their participants through intensive interviews, open-ended questionnaires, observations, and so on. Note that self-reports can be difficult to interpret when attempting to identify causal variables not only because participants might not tell the truth about certain aspects of their lives, but they might not have the self-insights to understand why they do what they do (i.e., the cause of their behavior). Thus, a group of juvenile inmates in jail might be interviewed by a qualitatively oriented researcher to study the causes of their delinquent behavior. It is the qualitatively oriented researcher's job to question the participants in such a way that the researcher ferrets out information on causation even if the participants are not aware of it or are unable to verbalize it directly. This can be a daunting task.

If you will be writing a literature review on a topic relating to causation, you should carefully evaluate the evidence presented in research reports to determine the credibility of various purported causal explanations that are offered by researchers.[3] In well-crafted research reports dealing with causality, researchers will discuss various causal explanations and the degree of success they had in ruling out some in favor of one or more other explanations. It is especially important to read such discussions when preparing literature reviews.

✥ Guideline 7.9

Assess the strengths of trends across studies when evaluating literature.

Because it is safe to assume that all research is flawed, it is important to consider the trends across the body of research on a topic and give greater emphasis to the methodologically stronger studies than to weaker ones when writing your review. If the vast

---

[3] Like many other issues in this chapter, only the basics of this topic are covered. If you will be writing a literature review for an advanced purpose such as a master's thesis, you should take courses in research methods, statistics, and tests and measurements before undertaking the task of writing a review. On the other hand, for undergraduates who have not taken such coursework, this chapter provides general guidance on many of the basics that should be considered.

majority of studies on a topic has a particular kind of result, while only a slim minority has a different kind of result, give more emphasis to the majority while noting the minority in your literature review. The exception to this principle is if the slim minority clearly has used superior research techniques and presents arguments that are more consistently logical and related to appropriate theories. In this case, you might emphasize the minority while pointing out the flaws of the majority.

✤ Guideline 7.10

Recognize the limitations of significance testing.

Quantitatively oriented researchers typically conduct significance tests. As a result, you will read statements such as "the mean (average) for Group A is significantly higher than the mean for Group B ($p < .05$)."[4] Saying that it is *significantly higher* is equivalent to saying it is *reliably higher*. It is *not* equivalent to saying that the difference is large. In other words, a researcher is saying that a reliable difference has been detected, *not* that the difference is large or important.

Because this concept may be difficult to understand at first, consider this example: Suppose that a disgruntled employee decides that he will clock in to work exactly 30 seconds late each day. Because management is strict about punctuality and the other workers value and enjoy their jobs, the other workers clock in before or just on time. This happens day after day for months on end. At some point, a large enough sample of days would be observed that a significance test would declare the difference in clock-in times between the disgruntled employee and the other employees to be statistically significant *just because it is a reliable phenomenon*, not because the difference (30 seconds) is large enough to be of any practical consequence.

This is an important guideline because many researchers who did not major in statistics but conduct research in their content areas are unaware of it. Thus, it is not uncommon to find researchers discussing their "statistically significant" results as though they were large enough to be of practical significance. One way you can avoid falling into the trap they are unwittingly setting is to consider the raw statistics that underlie the significance tests. For instance, if two means are significantly different, examine the values of the means and consider by how many points they differ and whether that amount of difference is of any practical concern or has practical implications.

Concluding Comments

This chapter presents only a brief overview of some of the basics for evaluating qualitatively oriented and quantitatively oriented research. Admittedly, you will be at a handicap if you have not previously mastered the material in courses in research methods,

---

[4] As you may know, "$p < .05$" indicates that there are only 5 chances in 100 that the researcher is in error in making the statement that the difference is statistically significant.

statistics, and tests and measurements. However, you will find that many research reports published in academic journals are clearly written and provide enough context and self-criticism to keep you from getting too far astray in your evaluation and interpretation of them.

Exercise for Chapter 7

1. Have any of your peers, colleagues, or instructors ever stated that a study "proves" something? If so, briefly describe what he or she said. In light of this chapter, would you be cautious about believing such a statement? Explain.

2. According to this chapter, what is the primary purpose for preparing a literature review?

3. What do quantitatively oriented researchers emphasize when sampling that qualitatively oriented researchers do *not* emphasize?

4. Name an example of a common sampling flaw.

5. Under Guideline 7.4, this statement is made: "…some traits are inherently easier to measure…than others…." Name a trait other than the ones mentioned in this chapter that you think is inherently *difficult* to measure.

6. Briefly explain why a highly reliable measuring instrument can be invalid.

7. According to this chapter, should you be surprised to find that the author of a research report points out weaknesses in his or her own research methodology?

8. To study causality, what do quantitatively oriented researchers prefer to do?

9. What is the reason given in this chapter for assessing the strengths of trends across studies when evaluating literature?

10. If a difference is statistically significant, is it necessarily large? If not, what does the fact that a difference is statistically significant tell you?

Notes:

Chapter 8

Planning and Writing
the First Draft

At this point, you should have collected the literature relevant to your topic, read it and made notes, and evaluated the literature that reports the results of research. Now you should begin planning and writing your first draft.

♆ Guideline 8.1
Before preparing an outline, review your notes and group them according to content.

Grouping by content is often superior to putting sources in chronological order unless the primary intent of your review is to synthesize information on the history of some topic.[1] Thus, for a literature review of variables associated with investment strategies, you might group together those that deal with gender differences. In another group, you might have those that deal with age differences in investment strategies. In yet another, you might group those that name and define various strategies. Looking at your groupings should help you prepare an outline for your literature review.

♆ Guideline 8.2
When beginning to build a topic outline, consider the order in which other writers have presented material on your topic.

For instance, if your topic is regional differences in voting patterns in national elections, consider the various ways and the order in which material was presented by previous authors. Did they begin by defining what they mean by voting patterns? Did they define the regions of interest to them? Did they provide a historical overview and, if so, where did they do so? Near the beginning? Near the end? Noticing patterns such as these should give you some ideas on how to organize your outline.[2]

---

[1] Even for a historical review, you should group according to content within each historical time period.
[2] Note that even a brief literature review that precedes a report of original research will have some type of organization even if it does not have subheadings for major content groupings.

☙ Guideline 8.3
Consider your first topic outline as a tentative one that is subject to change.

This guideline is suggested for two reasons. First, if you are considering a substantial amount of material on a topic, you might feel overwhelmed as to how to organize it. Considering the outline for it as only tentative and subject to change may make you feel more comfortable and help you overcome initial writer's block. After all, it is only a tentative first stab, not the final product. Second, you will be more willing to change it after showing it to others (such as your instructor) for feedback.

Unless your instructor requires that you strictly follow an approved outline, feel free to change it (by adding, subtracting, or rearranging topics) during the writing process. Good writers often change directions several times during the process of writing an important work.

It is important to put your outline in writing. While highly skilled writers sometimes can work effectively without a written outline, it is unwise for most writers to use only a mental outline.

Example 8.3.1 shows a topic outline. Note that it starts with a general introduction. In a thesis or dissertation, the introduction might be a separate chapter (usually Chapter 1) from the literature review (usually Chapter 2). In journal articles, the introduction is typically integrated with the literature review, with references to literature being referred to as early as the first sentence. Check with your instructor as to which arrangement he or she prefers.

Example 8.3.1

A topic outline for a literature review: [3]

Title: The Effects of Praise on Children's Intrinsic Motivation

General Introduction to the Topic
Defining Praise and Motivation
Two Contrasting Views
Praise Enhances Intrinsic Motivation
    –Beneficial mechanisms
Praise Undermines Intrinsic Motivation
    –Detrimental mechanisms
Conceptual Variables Influencing the Effects of Praise on Intrinsic Motivation
Sincerity
Performance Attributions
    –Attributions as mediators
    –Ability versus effort praise
    –Person versus process praise
    –Overview of attributions

Continued on next page.

---

[3] This outline is loosely based on the work of Henderlong & Lepper (2002).

Example 8.3.1 (continued)

Perceived Autonomy

  –Praise as extrinsic reward

  –Informational versus controlling aspects of praise

  –Gender differences in perceived autonomy

  –Overview of autonomy

Standards and Expectations

  –The moderating function of standards and expectations

  –Gender differences in familiarity of standards and expectations

  –Overview of standards and expectations

Summary of Conceptual Variables

A Cultural Caveat

Directions for Future Research

Appropriate Control Conditions

Appropriate Dependent Measures

Appropriate Manipulations

Summary and Conclusions

Note that in the outline in Example 8.3.1, the main headings are in bold, the second-level headings are in italics, and the third-level headings are indented with dashes in front of them. Any arrangement of this sort is acceptable if it is only a working topic outline for your use while writing. If you must submit an outline to an instructor, you might want to use the method commonly taught in English composition courses: Roman numerals for first-level headings, capital letters of the alphabet for second-level headings, and so on.

When writing your literature review, consult with the recommended style manual for your university or for your field of study for guidance on how to format the levels of headings. For example, the *Publication Manual of the American Psychological Association* has specific guidelines for various levels of headings, some of which are shown in Example 8.3.2.

Example 8.3.2

Some levels of headings from the Publication Manual of the American Psychological Association:

Level one:

Centered Uppercase and Lowercase Heading

Level two:

Centered, Italicized, Uppercase and Lowercase Heading

Level three:

Flush Left, Italicized, Uppercase and Lowercase Side Heading[4]

---

[4] American Psychological Association (2001, p. 113).

✍ Guideline 8.4

Consider filling in your outline with brief notes (including unique identifiers) before beginning to write your review.

Guideline 5.5 in Chapter 5 suggests that you give each piece of literature a unique identifier, such as the surname of the first author. You can start filling in your outline by writing notes within the outline that indicate which material will be presented under each heading (and subheading) and which sources will be used. This is done in Example 8.4.1 below, where the notes are shown in smaller type in brackets below some of the early topics in the outline in Example 8.3.1.

Example 8.4.1

A topic outline for a literature review, with notes and identifiers on what to cover and the sources to be used. Notes and identifiers are shown in brackets: [5]

Title: The Effects of Praise on Children's Intrinsic Motivation

General Introduction to the Topic

[Topic is important because praise is so widely used: Smith & Small; Doe.

Teachers' and parents' beliefs on the importance of praise: Doe; Brown.

Failure of parents and teachers to recognize that different schedules of praise may have different effects: Blackwell & Wright; Logan; Manchester & Lake.]

Defining Praise and Motivation

[Use Black's definition of "praise."

Define "intrinsic motivation" and "extrinsic motivation" separately by paraphrasing definitions in Doe & Barnes.

Stress that this review is on *intrinsic* motivation only. Justify this restriction using Noble & Smith's rationale. Mention Jackson's theory, which supports Noble & Smith.]

Two Contrasting Views

Praise Enhances Intrinsic Motivation

[Describe circumstances and studies that support enhancement: Franklin & James; Smith & Smith; Jackson, Washington, & Adams.

Outline theory that explains this phenomenon: Blackwell, Wright, & Logan; Honeywell; Langly & Sears.

Provide details on Doe's classic study with attention to circumstances when enhancement was found in her study. Mention replications: Bruce, Harris, & Corwin; Moeller; Brahm & Lake; Doe.]

---

[5] This outline is loosely based on the work of Henderlong & Lepper (2002).

Notice in Example 8.4.1, the reviewer is making the topic outline more concrete by adding cryptic notes. Also notice that several of the notes have more than one source. For instance, the works of Smith & Small *and* Doe will be cited for the first note made in the outline. In addition, it is important to notice that a given source may appear in several places within the outline. For example, Doe is cited for the first note as well as in the last one in the example.[6] This repetition of sources in various places in the outline occurs because it is an outline built around *topics*, not around individual pieces of literature. Thus, a work such as Doe's may have information that is relevant to more than one topic within the outline.

If they are readily available when you make your cryptic notes within your topic outline, relevant page numbers should be included.

✎ Guideline 8.5
Establish the importance of the topic that you are reviewing in the introductory paragraphs of your review.

When following this guideline, the word "importance" may be used as illustrated in Example 8.5.1, in which literature is cited to justify the assertion that a topic is important.

Example 8.5.1

A statement of importance from the introduction to a literature review:

The importance of values in social work is indisputable, for values represent a fundamental working element in social work practice and ethics (Bartlett, 1958;...Loewenberg & Dolgoff, 1992). Social work values embody social workers' preferred views of people, what they prefer for people, and how they work with people (Levy, 1973). Values guide social work practice, and, ultimately, express social workers' commitments to action.[7]

The importance of a topic can also be established by citing the statistics on the numbers of people (or percentages of people) affected by the topic.[8] This is illustrated in Example 8.5.2. Even though it involves reporting statistics, this approach can be used by both those writing qualitatively oriented and those writing quantitatively oriented literature reviews.

Example 8.5.2

Importance of a topic (ADHD) established by citing statistics:

In the last decade, there has been a rapid rise in the reported prevalence rates of ADHD. Robinson, Sclar, Skaer, and Galin (1999) examined the National Ambulatory Medical Care Survey data for the years 1990 through 1995. They found

---

[6] Of course, if two different authors have the same surname, add first names (such as Doe, Monica and Doe, John) or years of publication (such as Doe [2000] and Doe [2002]). Using years of publication is desirable if the author has written more than one source that will be cited in the review.

[7] Pinto (2002, p. 85).

[8] A topic might be justified in terms of the seriousness of the consequences for a *small* percentage of people. For instance, a life-threatening disease that affects only a fraction of one percent of the population is an important topic because of its potentially devastating effects.

that the number of office-based visits documenting a diagnosis of ADHD increased from 947,208 in 1990 to 2,357,833 in 1995. This increase in diagnosis was matched with a 2.9-fold increase in the number of ADHD individuals prescribed stimulant medication.[9]

The U.S. Census Bureau, which can be accessed via the Internet at www.census.gov/, is a good source of statistics on many matters. One of the statistics from this Web site is used in Example 8.5.3 to help establish the importance of the topic.

Example 8.5.3

Example of establishing the importance of a topic using Census Bureau statistics:

Almost 30% of all children are currently being raised in single-parent homes and have a nonresident parent (U.S. Census Bureau, 1999).[10]

✍ Guideline 8.6

Avoid vague references to statistics—especially in the first paragraph of your review.

Many literature reviews *inappropriately* begin with sentences such as the two shown in Example 8.6.1. They are inappropriate unless they are followed shortly afterwards with specific statistics that support them. Without statistical support (even in qualitatively oriented reviews), nonstatistical statements about statistical matters cause insightful readers to wince at the thought that you are giving your personal impressions of what statistics *might* reveal instead of being a careful researcher who has collected relevant statistics from the literature. (If you insist on *not* following this guideline, you should at least make a statement to this effect: "It is *my general impression* that economists are increasingly interested in....)

Example 8.6.1

Two statements with vague references to statistics (inappropriate unless they are followed by specific supporting statistics with sources):

First statement (inappropriate):

In recent years, economists increasingly have become interested in the XYZ theory of economic trends and have.... [*Note*: In which recent years? How does the author know there is an increase? What is the size of the increase?]

Second statement (inappropriate):

More and more teachers are facing the dilemma of integrating special-needs children into their classrooms without adequate training on techniques and.... [*Note*: How many are "more and more"? What is the source of this vague quantity?]

---

[9] Purdie, Hattie, & Carroll (2002, p. 63).
[10] Bloomer, Sipe, & Ruedt (2002, p. 77).

☙ Guideline 8.7

Provide specific definitions of major variables early in the literature review.

Definitions of major variables are essential to avoid miscommunication between you and your readers. Also, differences in how various researchers define variables may help to explain discrepancies in results across studies, which is an issue that should be addressed in your review. Specifically, those researchers using one type of definition may be consistently finding results different from those using another type, a possibility that you should consider while writing your review. For instance, if one researcher defines "physical child abuse" as "any form of physical punishment" while another researcher defines it to exclude mild forms of spanking with an open hand, you would expect differences between the results of the two studies.

It is acceptable (and sometimes desirable) to use a previously published definition as long as you cite its source, as is done in Example 8.7.1. The first sentence in the example provides the definition while the two sentences that follow help clarify the definition by citing some characteristics of those who fit it. If there is a previously published definition that prevails in the literature you are reviewing, it is a good idea to use it as your definition also for the sake of consistency in communications, unless you think it is a flawed definition, in which case you should point out its flaws and offer your own definition.

Example 8.7.1

A definition attributed to another source (an acceptable practice):

Job burnout has been defined as a syndrome characterized by physical and emotional exhaustion resulting from excessive demands on the energy, strength, and resources of the worker (Spicuzza & De Voe, 1982). Workers who suffer from job burnout are less effective on the job. They are more likely to be emotionally exhausted, depersonalize their clients, feel less personal accomplishment, and feel less commitment to their occupation (Miller et al., 1995).[11]

☙ Guideline 8.8

Write an essay that moves logically from one point to another. Do not write a string of annotations.

An annotation is a summary of a piece of literature. Most academic literature (especially journal articles) has already been annotated, and the annotations have been published both in print and on the Web. As a reviewer of literature, it is your task to make an original contribution—not just annotate literature again—and write an essay that moves logically from topic to topic. References should be cited as needed, and a given reference may be cited repeatedly in different parts of your essay in order to support various points you are making.

---

[11] Franze, Foster, Abbott-Shim, McCarty, & Lambert (2002, p. 259).

An essay will result if you build and follow a *topic* outline (see Guidelines 8.1 through 8.4). In short, your narrative should move from topic to topic as indicated on your outline, not from the work of one author to the work of another author.

✺ Guideline 8.9

When they are available, use more than one reference to support each point you make while avoiding very long strings of references for a single point.

Example 8.9.1, in which two sources are cited for a single point, illustrates this guideline.

Example 8.9.1

An example of citing two sources for a given point:

Interest groups purchase advertising space in mass media to explain their views because it is an economical means of communicating their message to the general public, and they believe that their ads have had an effect on the general public (Kollman, 1998; Loomis & Sexton, 1995).[12]

On the other hand, do *not* cite very long strings of references for a single point. Instead, cite a limited number of the more important ones, starting with "e.g.," as illustrated in Example 8.9.2.

Example 8.9.2

An example of using "e.g.," when there are many sources for a single point:

The XYZ theory has wide support (e.g., Smith, 2001; Jones, 2002).

If you want to stress that there are a very large number of supporting studies (and/or theoretical literature), you can also make a statement such as the one in Example 8.9.3, in which the number of studies is mentioned but only a few are cited.

Example 8.9.3

An example of using "see especially" when there are many sources for a single point and mention is made of the number of studies that have such support:

The XYZ theory has wide support, with 14 studies published within the last decade that provide supporting data (see especially: Smith, 2001; Jones, 2002).

A major exception to this guideline sometimes occurs when students are writing literature reviews for theses and dissertations, which are, in essence, long-term take-home tests (i.e., performance tasks). Students writing these documents may be asked to cite *all* relevant literature as a test of their ability to locate it and appropriately cite it. Occasionally, this may also be required for a class paper or senior project for the same reason. Consult with your instructor for further clarification on this issue.

---

[12] Hunter (2002, p. 390).

✋ Guideline 8.10

Write the literature review using your own words; use quotations very sparingly.

Strings of quotations will result in a paper that is uneven in style. Even more important, as a reviewer of literature, you are expected to make an original contribution by recasting the literature you have read in your own words so that your entire narrative makes sense logically, flows smoothly, and is cohesive.

The main exception to this guideline is when an idea is expressed so aptly that its impact or intensity achieved through the use of rhetorical devices would be lost in paraphrase. Arguably, the impact of the quotation in Example 8.10.1 would be lost if it were merely paraphrased.

Example 8.10.1

A quotation whose impact might be lost in paraphrase:

Willis (1994), for example, writes that "to succeed as an athlete can be to fail as a woman, because she has, in certain symbolic ways, become a man" (p. 36).[13]

Be especially cautious about beginning your literature review with a direct quotation from the literature. Remember, it is *your* literature review, and it makes sense for you to begin it in your own words. An exception is when a quotation is exceedingly apt and very clearly sets the stage for what you are about to write. In scientific writing, there seldom is a quotation that meets the standards for this exception.

✋ Guideline 8.11

Explicitly state what you think are reasonable conclusions based on the literature for each major subtopic that you cover.

It is not sufficient merely to present the evidence from the literature without discussing at least the major conclusions that you think are supported by it, as illustrated in Example 8.11.1.

Example 8.11.1

A tentative conclusion based on a review of the literature:

In sum, despite discrepant results in a minority of studies, this review of the literature on XYZ clearly suggests that the ABC model is more predictive of future alcohol behavior than the DEF model when the entire body of literature on this topic is considered.

Remember to avoid using the words "prove" and "proof" when following this guideline. See Guideline 7.1 in Chapter 7.

---

[13] Christopherson, Janning, & McConnell (2002, p. 172).

Note that Guideline 8.11 should be followed in conjunction with the next three guidelines.

ꙮ Guideline 8.12
Consider theories and/or models when reaching conclusions.

This guideline is suggested because conclusions regarding theories and models are likely to be more important than conclusions about simple factual matters because they have more implications. Example 8.11.1 above illustrates a statement that refers to models.

If you reach a conclusion that a widely accepted theory may be flawed or invalid, reread your literature review to be certain that you have sufficient supporting material to reach such a conclusion (one that runs contrary to prevailing opinion). Also, check to see that you have included all the relevant literature. If so, then feel free to make statements that run counter to the mainstream.

ꙮ Guideline 8.13
Critique the research you cite, which will help you show your readers why you have reached particular conclusions.

Close examination of the literature on almost any complex topic will reveal at least minor contradictions (and sometimes major ones) in the results of the research on the topic. In general, consider basing conclusions on the studies with superior research methodologies. (Chapter 7 provides a number of guidelines for evaluating research.)

Note that if you fail to point out that one research study is superior to another, your readers are likely to assume that both are about equal in their research methodology. If they are not equal in your opinion but you do not say so, you may be misleading your readers. Example 8.13.1 shows a potentially misleading statement about two groups of contradictory studies followed by one that differentiates between the two groups in terms of methodology.

Example 8.13.1
A statement that misleads because no differentiation is made between studies:

Several studies (Doe, 2002; Smith, 2001) provide support for the contention that XYZ is correct. In contrast, other studies (Jones, 2001; Long, 2002) fail to support this contention.

A statement that makes distinctions based on research methodology:

While several studies (Doe, 2002; Smith, 2001) provide support for the contention that XYZ is correct, others (Jones, 2001; Long, 2002) fail to support this contention. It is important to note that the latter studies used more representative samples than the former, lending credence to the conclusion that XYZ is possibly incorrect.

Example 8.13.2 shows a brief part of the conclusion from a literature review in which the writers conclude that goal-setting theory is supported by the research literature. Notice that they point out flaws in studies that fail to support the theory.

Example 8.13.2

A conclusion about goal-setting theory that is based on a critique of research methods:

The effects of goal setting are very reliable. Failures to replicate them are usually due to errors, such as not matching the goal to the performance measure, not providing feedback, not getting goal commitment....[14]

ᗑ Guideline 8.14

Point out gaps in the literature, explain why they are important, and mention them in your conclusions.

The conclusions that you reach near the end of your literature review may need to be stated as being tentative if there are no (or only a few) studies on some important aspects of issues that are highly relevant to your topic. When this is the case, point out why the gap hinders our understanding of the phenomenon. This is illustrated in Example 8.14.1.[15]

Example 8.14.1

A statement about a gap in the literature and its importance:

With the exception of research into the influence of sibling smoking status on youth imitation, few studies have examined the role of nonparental family members in smoking onset. This may be a fruitful area for investigation because the extended family plays a more salient role in the lives of children in some nonwhite cultures.[23,24] [This is important because] extended family members...may engage in meaningful anti-smoking socialization or may contribute to teen smoking through the same mechanisms as parents and siblings.[16]

ᗑ Guideline 8.15

Consider concluding your review with suggestions for future research.

Having carefully considered and synthesized the research on your topic, you are in an especially good position to make suggestions for possible fruitful areas for future research. Often, these suggestions will be for research that will help to fill out the gaps you identified (see Guideline 8.14). They may also refer to conducting research that is less methodologically flawed than the research conducted to date.

---

[14] Locke & Latham (2002, p. 714).

[15] Note that superscripts 23 and 24 in example 8.14.1 refer to references in the original review that support the statement about the gap. Superscript 16 identifies the reference for the quotation shown in the example.

[16] Kegler et al. (2002, p. 475).

Concluding Comments

By reading a large number of well-crafted literature reviews (such as those that typically appear in journals), you will see a variety of structures and techniques used to introduce a topic, critically summarize what is known about it, write a cohesive essay that synthesizes literature, reach defensible conclusions, and make sound suggestions for future research.

If you have carefully built a topic outline as described at the beginning of this chapter and followed the remaining guidelines, you should have a suitable *first draft* of your literature review. In the next two chapters, we will consider some additional refinements you might use to improve your first draft when you rewrite it to produce a second draft. The old truism deserves mention here: The key to effective writing is rewriting.

Exercise for Chapter 8

1. If you have already gathered literature, name several of the groupings you will use. If you have not gathered literature yet, name some groupings you anticipate that you will use. See Guideline 8.1.

2. Notice that "Defining Praise and Motivation" is the second major heading in Example 8.3.1. What major terms do you anticipate defining in your literature review? Will you define them in a separate section with its own major heading such as in the example, *or* will you integrate the definitions into your narrative (defining each when it is first introduced)?

3. Examine Example 8.3.1. Excluding the title, how many levels of headings are shown? How can you distinguish among the levels in the example?

4. Have you been assigned a style manual that covers formatting matters such as levels of headings and other matters regarding presentation of material? If so, name it. If not, will you use a style manual? If yes, which one?

5. Examine Model Literature Review 6 on religion-accommodative counseling. Read the title and then read the first- and second-level headings (without reading the text). To what extent do the headings help you get a sense of what is covered in the review? In your opinion, is the review long enough to justify the number of headings and subheadings the authors used?

6. What is your opinion on Guideline 8.4? Do you plan to follow it? Why? Why not?

7. Notice that some authors' names appear in more than one place in the outline in Example 8.4.1. According to the material in this chapter, why does this occur?

8. If you have access to the Internet, go to www.census.gov/ and explore the Web site, looking for statistics that are relevant to your topic. Very briefly describe your findings here.

9. According to this chapter, what is wrong with starting a review with a statement such as "Each year, more and more adolescents drop out of high school, which increases their odds of never finding a well-paying job."?

10. According to this chapter, is it acceptable to cite and use a previously published definition of a variable you are discussing in your review? Explain.

11. Select one of the variables you will be covering in your literature review. Define it here. Indicate whether it is a draft of the definition *or* a finalized definition.

12. According to this chapter, what are some alternatives to citing a long string of references for a single point?

13. According to this chapter, why should direct quotations be used sparingly in literature reviews?

14. According to this chapter, should writers of literature reviews state their own conclusions drawn from the literature, *or* should they describe the literature in a cohesive essay but "let the facts speak for themselves" instead of stating their own conclusions?

15. According to this chapter, if several research studies are cited but not critiqued, what are readers likely to assume?

16. If you have already searched the literature, are you aware of any important gaps in the research on your topic? If so, very briefly describe them here.

Notes:

Chapter 9

Revising and Refining
the First Draft

Having written your first draft, review it while considering the following guidelines. Usually, it is best to allow at least a couple of days to intervene between finishing the first draft and reviewing it for revision in order to be fresh during the revision process.

✛ Guideline 9.1
Recheck headings and subheadings, and modify them, as necessary.

In the last chapter, you were urged to build a topic outline and make cryptic notes for each of the major headings and subheadings in the outline. By flushing out your notes, you were able to create a first draft in which you used the topic headings/subheadings in your outline as the headings/subheadings in the first draft of your literature review.

While you revise your first draft, consider whether any of the headings/subheadings should be reworded in light of the narrative you wrote. Also, consider whether additional headings/subheadings are needed. For example, you may have quite a bit of material on how participants at various educational levels responded to variables related to your topic. In such a case, consider whether this set of literature might be broken into two or more categories. For instance, instead of using "education" as a single subheading, you might use "high school dropouts" and "high school graduates."

If you find that you have only one piece of literature for each of a number of headings, you might want to combine them so that you can discuss several pieces of literature under one heading.

As a general rule, be generous in the use of headings and subheadings. They help readers understand the organization of your review and help them follow your transitions from one topic or subtopic to another. Although it is difficult to quantify this matter in the abstract without referring to specific content, a useful guideline might be that you should aim to have at least one heading or subheading for every two double-spaced typewritten pages of your review—while allowing for somewhat more or less as needed to cover the material.

✛ Guideline 9.2
Check to see that all your paragraphs are straightforward and reasonably short.

Good scientific writing is clear writing. Unlike creative writing, in which one might strive for variety, the purpose of scientific writing is to communicate information clearly and unambiguously. It is perfectly acceptable in scientific writing to write paragraphs that follow the simplest model for paragraph writing: Write a topic sentence first (e.g., "Studies of the use of polygraphs in employment selection in major corporations have had mixed results") and then write sentences that provide details on the topic (e.g., "One of the earliest studies of its use for this purpose [Doe, 1981] showed promising....").

Check any overly long paragraphs to see if they have two or more main topics. If so, revise them to make one paragraph per main topic.

Remember that readers of literature reviews are reading to learn content—not to be entertained. Writing that might be considered pedestrian in a creative writing class may be desirable when writing a literature review. Readers who are interested in the content you are covering will appreciate simple, unpretentious writing that employs straightforward paragraphs that are no longer than needed to support the topic sentences of each one.

✬ Guideline 9.3
Check to see that you have used rhetorical questions very sparingly.

A rhetorical question is one that the writer answers immediately. Such a question can be used as the topic sentence of a paragraph. Occasional use can provide variety in paragraph beginnings. Too many rhetorical questions, on the other hand, can be distracting. Example 9.3.1 shows the use of a rhetorical question at the beginning of a paragraph. The answer to the question is discussed in the six paragraphs that follow it; only a portion of the first of the six is shown in the example.

Example 9.3.1

A paragraph that begins with a rhetorical question:

Why do people die in famines? This question seems to invite a simple answer, but in fact the answer is the subject of much contention. This is a problem because views on the issue have major implications for policies toward malnourished populations....[1]

✬ Guideline 9.4
Consider using transitional terms to make one paragraph flow from the previous one.

Example 9.4.1 shows the beginnings of the five sequential paragraphs in a literature review. Notice how the transitional terms, which are italicized in bold, help smooth out the transitions from one paragraph to the next. Check the paragraphs under each of your headings/subheadings to make sure they flow, using transitional terms when possible.

---

[1] Loosely based on Hionidou (2002, p. 65).

Example 9.4.1

*The beginnings of five paragraphs. Paragraphs 2 through 5 contain transitional terms (**italicized in bold**)*:

A considerable body of theory suggests that elected public officials in a democracy have reason to pay attention to public opinion. Rational choice theorists, for example, have long argued....

Empirically, ***too***, there is substantial scholarly evidence of rather close connections between citizens' preferences....

Moreover, there has been an enormous increase in policy-related polls and surveys of public opinion....

Given this abundance of information about public opinion, most of us would probably ***also*** expect that politicians would take note of....

Thus, our hypotheses...are the following....[2]

In his book on rhetoric and style in writing, Harris (2003) illustrates the use of transitional terms. Portions of his statements about them are shown in Box 9A. Note that he advises against the use of too many strong transitions. Box 9B provides many examples of transitional terms. Harris has classified them according to function (e.g., "addition" and "comparison") as well as according to strength (i.e., "milder" and "stronger"). As you revise your first draft, refer to these terms for ideas on how to improve the transitions among the paragraphs on each topic and subtopic within your review. Also, consider whether you have used appropriate ones *within* individual paragraphs.

Box 9A *The use of transitional terms.*[3]

1. Use transitions between paragraphs to signal connections (addition, contrast, and so forth) between idea segments. Use transitions within paragraphs to signal a change from one sentence to another or from one section of the paragraph to another.

2. Use sufficient transitions to provide coherence (holding together, like glue) and continuity (making the thought process easy to follow). Less experienced writers tend to supply too few transitions.

3. Avoid using too many strong transitions. Be careful to avoid littering your writing with *however* and *nevertheless*. Strong transitions should be used sparingly.

4. Transitions become stronger when they are placed at the beginning (or end) of a sentence, milder (or less strong) when they are moved into the sentence. Generally, moving transitions into the sentence is the better choice.

---

[2] Cook, Barabas, & Page (2002, pp. 237–238).
[3] Harris (2003, p. 35).

Box 9B *Transitional terms that can be used to provide coherence.*[4]

	Milder		Stronger	
Addition	a further x also and and then another	next nor other then too	additionally again besides equally important finally, last	first, second further furthermore in addition moreover
Comparison	a similar x another x like	just as…so too	comparable in the same way	likewise similarly

Contrast	and yet
	but
	but another
	or
	otherwise
		rather
		still
		though
		yet
			alternatively
			at the same time
			conversely
			even so
			for all that
			however
			in contrast
			instead
			nevertheless
				nonetheless
				notwithstanding
				on the contrary
				on the other
				   hand
				otherwise
				still
				though this may
				   be

Time	after afterward before earlier first, second, third later next	now recently shortly soon then today tomorrow	at last at length at that time currently eventually finally	immediately meanwhile presently subsequently thereafter
Purpose	because of this x	to do this	for that reason for this purpose	to this end with this object
Place	beyond here	nearby there	adjacent to at that point in the back	in the front on the other side opposite to
Result	and so so	then	accordingly as a result consequently hence	in consequence therefore thereupon thus

---

[4] Harris (2003, p. 36).

✏ Guideline 9.5

If more than one paragraph is based on the same reference, use wording that makes it clear.[5]

You may find yourself writing more than one paragraph based on a single reference. When you do this, provide the reference in the first paragraph, and provide transitions in subsequent paragraphs to make the continuity of the citation clear. Otherwise, readers might think that the ideas in subsequent paragraphs are yours. Example 9.5.1 shows how the identification of the source of the second two paragraphs is made clear. Note the terms in bold italics.

Example 9.5.1

Three paragraphs based on the same reference:

In one of the most comprehensive studies of consumer behavior during national recessions, Smith (2004) surveyed more than 1,000 consumers who....

In addition, the results *of the same survey* shed light on three related issues important to understanding....

Perhaps the most important result *of Smith's survey* was the segmentation of consumers into groups according to....

✏ Guideline 9.6

Avoid beginning your literature review with truisms.

Starting your literature review with a general "truism" (something all educated people probably know and believe) is usually a mistake. Instead, start with a paragraph that is specific to your review and contains specific, new information.

Example 9.6.1 is a poor start for the first paragraph of a literature review because it starts with a truism. The improved paragraph is superior because it more specifically names the law and its effects, which will be covered in the literature review.

Example 9.6.1

Poor first paragraph that states only truisms:

The importance of good nutrition is very widely recognized. One of the underlying requirements for making good nutritional decisions is having available reliable information on the nutritional contents of various foods and food products. Without such information, consumers will have a difficult time making decisions that are beneficial to their health.

Improved first paragraph, which refers directly to the topic of the review:

The 1990 Nutrition Labeling and Education Act (NLEA) dramatically changed nutrition labels on packaged foods in supermarkets, thereby increasing the amount

---

[5] This guideline is implied in Guideline 5.3. It also should be considered during the revision process.

of nutrition information available at the point of purchase. This law requires packaged foods to display nutrition information prominently in a new label format, namely, the Nutrition Facts panel. It also regulates serving size....[6]

✍ Guideline 9.7
Consider using a first paragraph that provides historical context *if* the context is clearly on target and interesting.

Interesting historical notes can be an effective way to begin a literature review. However, be careful that they relate directly to the topic of your review.

Example 9.7.1 is the first paragraph in a literature review on an international comparison of students' attitudes toward cheating. The historical anecdote is both interesting and relevant to the review.

Example 9.7.1
First paragraph that begins with an interesting historical anecdote:

The Chinese have been concerned about cheating for longer than most civilizations have been in existence. Over 2,000 years ago, prospective Chinese civil servants were given entrance exams in individual cubicles to prevent cheating and were searched as they entered the cubicles for crib notes. The penalty for being caught at cheating in ancient China was not a failing grade or expulsion, but death, which was applicable to both the examinees and the examiners (Brickman, 1961). Today, while we do not execute students and their professors when cheating is discovered, it appears that we....[7]

✍ Guideline 9.8
Remove any material that is meant to be clever, amusing, or flippant.

Scientific writing is serious writing, and your readers will be interested in your analysis of the material on your topic—not in your ability to be clever or to amuse. Likewise, flippant remarks distract from your message. Note that in oral presentations, a skilled speaker can sometimes use a bit of humor to engage an audience, which is sometimes done in academic presentations. It should be avoided, however, in written literature reviews.

✍ Guideline 9.9
Revise to reduce the amount of anecdotal material.

An anecdote is a brief description of an interesting (or amusing) incident. Anecdotal evidence, which is based on isolated and perhaps nonrepresentative incidents, is one of the weakest forms of scientific evidence. Hence, it should be used very sparingly. Another

---

[6] Balasubramanian & Cole (2002, p. 112).
[7] Lupton & Chapman (2002, pp. 17–18).

drawback is that an incident that you find interesting or amusing may not be perceived as such by your readers.

↳ Guideline 9.10

When using the Harvard method for citation, it is often better to emphasize content over authorship.

In the Harvard method, citations to literature are provided by citing the surname(s) of the author(s) followed by the year of publication. The reference list at the end of the literature review is arranged alphabetically by surnames when this method is used.[8]

Surnames of authors can be integrated into the sentences or placed in parentheses at the end of the sentences or paragraphs. Notice in Example 9.10.1 that the first version emphasizes authorship by mentioning the authors' names first; the second one emphasizes content of the statement by putting the surnames of authors in parentheses at the end of the first sentence.

Example 9.10.1

Paragraph emphasizing authorship (usually not appropriate):

Mead (1955); Portes & Rumbaut (2001); and Sapocznik, Scopetta, Kurtines, & Arandale (1978) noted that when a family immigrates to a new country, the acculturation process typically is not uniform across generations of the family. When children learn the new culture more quickly than their parents, parental authority can be undermined....

Improved paragraph, which emphasizes content:

When a family immigrates to a new country, the acculturation process typically is not uniform across generations of the family (Mead, 1955; Portes & Rumbaut, 2001; Sapocznik, Scopetta, Kurtines, & Arandale, 1978). When children learn the new culture more quickly than their parents, parental authority can be undermined....[9]

The main exception to this guideline is when the authorship is important, such as when you refer to an important theorist or a landmark research report that is widely identified with its author. Under these circumstances, authorship is important. Example 9.10.2 illustrates this.

Example 9.10.2

Paragraph emphasizing authorship by making the author's surname part of the sentence (appropriate if the author is someone who is widely known):

---

[8] The Harvard method is also known as the APA method because it is recommended in the *Publication Manual of the American Psychological Association*.
[9] Unger et al. (2002, p. 226).

Research on note taking and note review often references Wittrock's (1990) theory of generative processing. The supposition is that students who make associations between materials presented…and their own previous knowledge learn new material better than those students who do not generate links in the material….[10]

Another exception to this guideline occurs when you want to discuss differences of opinion between two or more researchers or theorists. Sometimes the text flows more smoothly if you use their names nonparenthetically, as was done in Example 9.10.3.

Example 9.10.3

Paragraph emphasizing authorship (may be appropriate when discussing differences of opinion among authors):

However, to date there is little empirical support for Langly's (2002) theory. What support exists is based on a logical analysis of….

In contrast, Doe (2002) has criticized Langly's theory and has presented data that suggest the theory is flawed. The data consist of….

✤ Guideline 9.11

Cross-check the references cited in the body of your review against those in your reference list at the end.

Make sure that the reference list at the end is complete and accurate. Attention to this matter can save you the embarrassment of having your readers call to your attention any missing or incorrect references in your paper. Note that the reference list serves the important purpose of helping your readers locate the literature that you have cited.

The following types of errors are sometimes found in published journal articles: (a) the spelling of a surname in the citation is different from the spelling in the reference list, (b) the year given in the citation is different from the one in the reference list, and (c) a name in a citation does not appear in the reference list.

✤ Guideline 9.12

Have your first draft critiqued by others, and assume they are correct if anything is unclear to them.

A truism in publishing is that "you can never have too many eyes look over a manuscript prior to publication." Your first concern should be to identify unclear material. Ask your reviewers to mark anything that is unclear to them with red ink and then discuss with them the marked sections. Avoid the pitfall of blaming your reviewers for not understanding your writing. If an educated person is confused by some sections of your first draft, be open to revising those sections. Otherwise, you might fall prey to the "clear if

---

[10] Elliot, Foster, & Stinson (2002, p. 26).

already known fallacy." Box 9C shows an analogy often used by one of the leading early researchers on the comprehensibility of written text. The analogy is designed to illustrate clearly that if you already know the material you are writing about, your expression of it may be clear to you but not to others.

Box 9C *An analogy that illustrates the "clear if already known fallacy."*[11]

> A tourist drove into town and was having trouble locating a motel at which he had a reservation. He stopped at a gas station to ask for directions. Trying to be helpful, the attendant said, "Go down this road and turn right where the old oak tree used to be before it died and was cut down. Then, turn left at the house that used to be painted red but now is some other color. Proceed for about a mile and the motel will be on your left."

Concluding Comments

The guidelines in this chapter and the previous one apply to both qualitatively oriented and quantitatively oriented literature reviews. Both types need strong, clearly written narratives to introduce the topics, establish their importance, and provide readers with an overview of the literature.

Exercise for Chapter 9

1. According to this chapter, why should you be generous in your use of headings and subheadings in your literature review?

2. If you have written your first draft, how many major headings and how many subheadings do you have? If you have not written it yet, list some of the headings and subheadings you might use.

3. According to this chapter, the "simplest model" for writing a paragraph is acceptable for use in literature reviews. Very briefly describe this model.

4. How is the term "rhetorical question" defined in this chapter? Is the use of rhetorical questions in literature reviews recommended in this chapter?

5. This statement appears in Box 9A: "Less experienced writers tend to supply too few transitions." Reflect on your first draft. Do you think you have used a sufficient number

---

[11] Loosely based on a personal communication with Edgar Dale, March 8, 1977.

of transitional terms? Has the material in Box 9B helped you in the selection of transitional terms? Explain.

6. What should you make clear if more than one paragraph is based on a single reference?

7. Examine the first paragraph of your first draft of your literature review. Does it begin with a truism? If so, do you plan to change it? If not, does your first paragraph provide information that is highly specific to your topic? Explain.

8. What is characterized in this chapter as "one of the weakest forms of scientific evidence"?

9. When using the Harvard method for citing references, what should you do if you want to emphasize content over authorship?

10. Have you obtained feedback on your first draft from others? If so, who critiqued it? Describe the types of changes, if any, that you made on the basis of their criticism. If you have not yet obtained feedback, whom do you plan to ask to review your first draft?

11. Consider the following material, which appeared at the beginning of the literature review for a research report.[12] In your opinion, does the first sentence provide a strong beginning for the review? Does the second sentence emphasize authorship *or* content?

> The beneficial effects of social support have been conclusively established over decades of scientific research. The availability of social support significantly enhances people's general well-being and happiness as well as their ability to withstand a variety of major stressors such as serious illness (Coyne & Smith, 1994). On the other hand, people who lack social support appear to be at risk for developing a range of physical and mental health problems. For instance, those who do not have satisfying....

12. Are there any transitional terms within the sample material in Question 11? If yes, what are they?

---

[12] Segrin (2003, p. 317).

Chapter 10

Blending Qualitative and Quantitative Approaches

The purpose of this chapter is to provide guidelines on how to make a *qualitatively oriented* review more *quantitatively oriented* through the judicious reporting of statistical material in the review from the literature being covered, thus arriving at a blend of approaches for writing literature reviews. The more statistical material you include in your qualitatively oriented review, the more quantitatively oriented it becomes. Hence, you should think of the two types as existing on a continuum from highly qualitatively oriented to highly quantitatively oriented. Four of the many points along this continuum are shown in Box 10A. Note the term "meta-analysis" in the heading of the last column of the table. Procedures for conducting a meta-analysis are covered in the next chapter.

Box 10A   *Four points on the continuum from highly qualitatively oriented to highly quantitatively oriented literature reviews.*

Almost exclusively qualitative	A blend leaning toward the qualitative	A blend leaning toward the quantitative	Very highly quantitative (i.e., a meta-analysis)
Absence of statistics. However, when reviewing statistical literature, statements that imply the use of statistics are made. Example: "Overall, the literature indicates that men generally have more XYZ than women."	Occasional mention of statistics by making statements such as: "Twelve of the 17 studies showed men had significantly more XYZ than women."	Frequent reporting of selected statistics such as: "Table 1 shows the percentages of men and women separately for each of the 17 studies on gender differences in XYZ."	Large numbers of statistics reported (often in extensive tables). Statistics are combined across studies. Example: "The average man in the 17 studies combined is 0.52 standard deviations above the average woman, which is a large effect size...."

✍ Guideline 10.1

Consider your audience's needs for reporting specific statistics in your literature review.

If your instructor is your primary audience, he or she may provide you with some guidance on following this guideline. For some audiences, such as those who have not studied statistics, you might want to write a highly qualitatively oriented literature review. For a committee of professors overseeing your work (e.g., a doctoral dissertation), you might include much more quantification.

If your goal is publication in a journal, examine reviews in journals to which you might wish to submit your literature review to determine how quantitatively oriented the typical reviews are.

✥ Guideline 10.2
If you fail to state that a difference or relationship is statistically significant, your readers will assume that it is, which is acceptable if this is true.

Literature reviews typically contain many statements about differences and relationships reported in the literature. If reviewers were required to use the term "statistically significant" each time they mentioned a difference, many literature reviews would be cluttered with this term, which might appear dozens of times in a review.

Statements such as the one in Example 10.2.1 are extremely common in literature reviews. Notice that the statement does *not* indicate that the benefits for those who exercise regularly are significantly greater than for those who do not. However, it is safe to assume that they are. Otherwise, the reviewer would probably warn us with some type of caution such as "preliminary research has revealed an *in*significant increase in physical benefits from regular exercise."

Example 10.2.1

A statement about differences without mentioning statistical significance (acceptable if the differences are significant):

Regular physical activity has physical (e.g., improving cardiovascular endurance) and psychological (e.g., increasing self-esteem) benefits for children and adolescents (United States Department of Health and Human Services [USDHHS], 1996, 2000)....[1]

Of course, there will be times when you will want to report on *insignificant* differences. This is especially true when comparing a difference between groups. Consider Example 10.2.2. Readers will assume that the first difference is statistically significant and assume that the second one is not because it is referred to as "no difference." Note that quantitatively oriented reviewers equate an "insignificant difference" with "no difference."[2]

Example 10.2.2

A statement about differences with the first part implying statistical significance and the second part implying insignificance:

While young adult Republicans differed from young adult Democrats on the XYZ issue, there was no difference between middle-aged Republicans and middle-aged Democrats on this issue.

---

[1] Hausenblas, Nigg, Downs, Fleming, & Connaughton (2002, p. 436).
[2] Note that a statistically insignificant difference is a difference that is no greater than would be expected on the basis of chance alone (such as getting 51 heads and 49 tails when tossing a coin 100 times).

Note that the term "no difference" as used in Example 10.2.2 almost always means "no statistically significant difference." When we compare two large samples (such as large samples of middle-aged Republicans and Democrats), it is almost certain that some difference will be observed even if it is as small as 62.5% for Republicans and 62.3% for Democrats. If this difference is not statistically significant, reviewers often use "no difference" as shorthand for "no statistically significant difference." While this is an accepted practice when writing literature reviews, it is more precise to state that there was no statistically significant difference.

✣ Guideline 10.3
Consider pointing out especially large (or strong) and especially small (or weak) differences or relationships.

As you know from Guideline 7.10, just because a difference (or relationship) is statistically significant does *not* necessarily mean that it is large (or strong). It means only that it is *reliable*. Even very small differences can be quite reliable (i.e., statistically significant). An example that illustrates this is given in the discussion of Guideline 7.10. Because this is such an important point, consider the following additional example: A third-grade teacher very precisely measures the heights of the students in his class on the first Monday of September and on the first Monday of October each year and records the data. After 35 years, he carefully examines the data and sees that year after year, there is a minuscule increase in height from September to October. Thus, he has detected a *reliable but small difference*. A statistical significance test tells us *only* whether a difference (or relationship) is *reliable*, which it is in this example. It does *not* address the issue of whether the difference is large, which it is *not* in this example.

One of the most common flaws in writing literature reviews is to treat all statistically significant differences or relationships as being large and equal in magnitude. Thus, it is common to see discussions of literature as shown in Example 10.3.1. This problem has been fixed in the improved version shown in Example 10.3.2. Notice that the improvement does not require reference to any specific statistics, although it would be acceptable to mention them.

Example 10.3.1
A discussion of relationships in which all are treated as equal due to the lack of differentiation in terms of magnitude (not recommended):

One of the most consistent findings in research on achievement testing is that there is a positive relationship between scores on vocabulary knowledge tests and scores on reading comprehension tests (e.g., Doe, 2004; Jones, 2003). Positive relationships have also consistently been found between scores on reading comprehension tests and scores on mathematics word problem tests (e.g., Black & Smith, 2003).

Example 10.3.2

An improved version of Example 10.3.1 (differences from Example 10.3.1 are shown in italics):

One of the most consistent findings in research on achievement testing is that there is a *strong* positive relationship between scores on vocabulary knowledge tests and scores on reading comprehension tests (e.g., Doe, 2004; Jones, 2003). *Although* positive relationships have also consistently been found between scores on reading comprehension tests and scores on mathematics word problem tests (e.g., Black & Smith, 2003), *these relationships are almost always much weaker than the relationships between vocabulary and reading comprehension.*

Box 10B *One of the most common flaws (see Guidelines 7.10 and 10.3).*

> One of the most common flaws in writing literature reviews is to treat all statistically significant differences or relationships as being large and equal in magnitude.

✦ Guideline 10.4

Examine your literature review to identify vague terms that refer to quantities, and consider replacing them with specific statistics.

Terms such as "more," "less," "stronger," "weaker," "higher," "lower," "majority," and "minority" refer to quantities. If the quantities you have referred to with these terms are simple and easy to understand, consider supplementing them with the specific statistics. The specificity of the second sentence in Example 10.4.1 makes it superior to the first.

Example 10.4.1

Two statements based on the same piece of literature. The second one names specific statistics (as they appeared in the original source):

First statement: Although a minority of AFDC [Aid to Families with Dependent Children] recipients are married women (Moffitt, Reville, & Walker, 1998)....

Improved statement: Although 19 percent to 30 percent of AFDC recipients are married women (Moffitt, Reville, & Walker, 1998)....[3]

Example 10.4.2 also contains a statement that vaguely refers to a quantity (i.e., "many"). Because there is a statistical estimate of this, the improved version quantifies it with a specific statistic (i.e., "almost four in every 10"). Note that such quantification is appropriate even in a qualitatively oriented review because the statistic provides more information and is easy to understand.

---

[3] Cheng (2002, p. 161).

Example 10.4.2

Two statements based on the same piece of literature. The second one names specific statistics (as they appeared in the original source):

First statement: Many children in the United Kingdom experience the breakup of their parents' relationship by the time they reach the age of 16 (Office for National Statistics, 2002).

Improved statement: Almost four in every 10 children in the United Kingdom experience the breakup of their parents' relationship by the time they reach the age of 16 (Office for National Statistics, 2002).[4]

✤ Guideline 10.5

Consider summarizing key statistics in a table.

Readers may find it easier to peruse and get an overview of the statistics on a topic if they are tabled. If you table statistical values, you can point out the highlights of the table without necessarily repeating all the exact statistics in your narrative. Example 10.5.1 shows a portion of a table containing specific statistics that were included in a literature review.

Note that when statistics on an issue are scattered throughout the narrative of a literature review, it can be difficult for readers to make comparisons across studies. Notice that the table in Example 10.5.1 makes it easy to compare specific findings from study to study.

Example 10.5.1

Table containing statistics that appeared in a literature review of research on needlestick injuries among healthcare workers (for instructional purposes, only two of the seven columns and only 5 of the 16 study findings are shown here):[5]

Study	Study Findings
Ribner (1990)	Decreased injury due to recapping from 61% to 16% of total needlesticks.
Haiduven (1992)	Decreased injuries by 45%; decreased injury due to recapping by 53%.
Orenstein (1995)	Decrease in injuries from 33 to 14; cost of each prevented needlestick estimated at $789.
CDC (1997b)	46% of injuries unreported; 20% of safety units not activated.
Lawrence (1997)	Decreased IV injury rate; 94% user satisfaction reported.

---

[4] Walker (2003, p. 406).
[5] Porta, Handelman, & McGovern (1999, p. 240).

A narrative describing the number of families that graduated from a program designed to help them become more adaptable and cohesive is described in Example 10.5.2. Example 10.5.3 shows the same statistics in a table, which is much easier to read.

Example 10.5.2

Statistics presented in a narrative (more difficult to follow than the same statistics tabled in Example 10.5.3):

During the four years of the program, a total of 427 families graduated from the program. In the first three school years (i.e., 1996–1997, 1997–1998, and 1998–1999), families from seven schools participated, while nine schools were represented during the last year (i.e., 1999–2000). During the first three years, the number of families graduating were 94, 110, and 111, respectively. During the last year, 112 families graduated.

Example 10.5.3

Same statistics as in Example 10.5.2 (tabular form in this example is superior to the narrative form in Example 10.5.2):[6]

School Year	Number of Schools	Number of Graduating Families
1996–1997	7	94
1997–1998	7	110
1998–1999	7	111
1999–2000	9	112
Total		**427**

✵ Guideline 10.6

Avoid overburdening readers with statistics.

Under the previous guideline, you learned that if you are going to present a number of related statistics, it is often better to present them in a table. In contrast, this guideline suggests that you avoid presenting too many statistics whether in the narrative or in numerous tables. Because the goal of a review is to provide an overview and a synthesis, too many statistics can interfere with your readers' ability to obtain an overview. Also, note that because almost all the studies you will refer in your review are already published, readers can consult them for additional statistics after reading your review if they need the statistics that you choose not to report.

This guideline can be implemented in four ways. First, it can be done through the judicious selection of statistics to state in your review. For instance, a report that you are citing may have many means[7] and standard deviations. Depending on the point(s) you are

---

[6] Fischer (2003, p. 341).
[7] The arithmetic mean is the most widely used average in research.

making, you might mention, for example, only the highest and lowest means in the entire set of studies (and possibly omit all the standard deviations), as illustrated in Example 10.6.1.

Example 10.6.1

A statement citing only two means, which show the range of results across a large number of means found in a large number of studies:

Means on the Avis Risk-Taking Scale in the 23 studies in which it has been used in published research range from 39.36 in a study of juvenile delinquents (Doe, 2004) to 18.97 in a study of high school honor students (Smith, 2003). A score of 39.36 is far above the clinical cutting point for abnormally high risk-taking propensities while a score of 18.97 is near the national average of 21.95.

Note that when reporting a range of values that vary greatly, such as we see in Example 10.6.1, it is desirable to point out any distinctive characteristics of the group with the highest value (in this case, being juvenile delinquents is distinctive) as well as distinctive characteristics of the group with the lowest value (in this case, high school honor students). Also, if you know how the "average" person performs, such as the national average on a published test or scale, it is helpful to include it as a reference point for readers of your review.

A second way to implement Guideline 10.6 is to cite specific statistics for only a limited number of studies that are especially important in helping you create your synthesis. For the other studies you cite, you might report on differences and relationships in words without statistics (while mentioning which ones are large or strong and which ones are small or weak).

Third, you can use tables, as suggested in Guideline 10.5, to which your readers can refer for specific statistics when they want to do so while you point out only the statistical highlights in your narrative. However, note that this guideline implies that you should avoid the overuse of tables in order to avoid overburdening your readers with statistics. The number of tables to include is a subjective matter. Note, however, that if your narrative is clear, most readers will be able to skip over some of the tables (if you have a number of them) while other readers might be glad they are included due to their interest in specific statistics.

Fourth, you can include a brief meta-analysis, which can concisely summarize a number of statistics, within a qualitatively oriented review, a possibility that is discussed in the next chapter.

✎ Guideline 10.7

If a particular statistic is especially important, consider commenting on the quality of the study that produced it.

As you know from Guideline 8.13, you should consider commenting on the quality of the research you cite in your literature review. Often, this can be done with phrases that indicate the quality of the research. Box 10C shows some phrases that can be used to indicate whether a study is weak or strong. If you do not use any phrases of these types when citing studies, readers will probably assume that you believe that they are reasonable in quality.

Relying on and citing statistics from methodologically weak studies to support the main points in your review is potentially misleading unless you point out those weaknesses. You can point them out by discussing the methodology of such key studies in some detail or by using one or more of the phrases of the type shown in the first column of Box 10C. It is usually undesirable to provide detailed evaluations of all studies that you cite. The more important a study (and its resulting statistics) is to your conclusions, the more detailed your evaluation and discussion of its strengths and weaknesses should be.

Box 10C   *Phrases that indicate strengths and weaknesses (consider using them when discussing statistical results).*

Phrases that indicate weaknesses:	Phrases that indicate strengths:
In a preliminary study, Doe (2002) reported data that indicates….	A definitive study by Doe (2002) indicates….
The results of a local survey by Doe (2002) suggest….	A major nationwide poll conducted by Doe (2002) supports….
While the results of Doe's (2002) pilot study are interesting, additional research should be conducted in order to confirm the major findings that….	While the earlier studies on the topic had mixed results, Doe's (2002) study is probably the most reliable because she used random….
All five studies on the effects of XYZ have two major flaws: use of volunteer samples and lack of random assignment to….	The use of random assignment in the five studies on the effects of XYZ give us confidence in the finding that XYZ has an important effect on….

It is important to note that it is acceptable to rely heavily on methodologically weak studies in creating a synthesis and reaching conclusions in a literature review if the studies provide the best available evidence. Of course, you will want to point out the weaknesses of the studies in your narrative and warn your readers that your synthesis and conclusions are tentative because they are based on weak studies. In addition, you might consider suggesting future research that will overcome the weaknesses you have identified. Sometimes this is done near the end of a review in a separate section with its own heading such as "Suggestions for Future Research," which might also suggest areas that have not yet been explored even with weak studies.

✎ Guideline 10.8
Use wording that indicates which statements are supported by data.

Sometimes literature reviews are flawed because readers cannot determine from the wording which statements are based on data (i.e., based on statistical findings). Example 10.8.1 shows two statements from a single literature review, both of which are clearly data-based. The data-based nature of the first one is clear from the mention of a specific statistic (20.5%). The second one is clearly data-based because of the use of the terms "studies" and "study." Other phrases and terms that provide readers with cues that the statements are data-based are: "In an experiment....," "This survey shows....," "Smith (2003) investigated the relationship between....," "Researchers have found that....," and "In the first study on this topic...."

Example 10.8.1

Two statements from a literature review that are clearly data-based:

First statement: Child poverty is currently 20.5% (CDF, 1998)....

Second statement: Studies have shown mixed results in understanding the impact of homelessness beyond poverty. A study by Bassuk and Rosenberg (1988) suggests....[8]

Reviewers also should use terms and phrases to indicate that a statement is *not* data-based. Two samples are shown in Example 10.8.2. The term "speculated" in the first statement, the term "mentioned the possibility" in the second one, and the term "pointed out" in the third suggest that the assertions are not based on data. Other terms and phrases that indicate the lack of underlying data are: "Doe (2003) argued that....," "It is reasonable to infer from everyday observations that....," "On the basis of anecdotal evidence, it seems reasonable to conclude that....," and "Jackson (2004) suggested that...."

Example 10.8.2

Three statements that are clearly not data-based:

First statement: Doe (2003) has speculated that consumer confidence in the economy will rise....

Second statement: Several authors have mentioned the possibility that consumer confidence in the economy rises when....

Third statement: Following the theory to its logical conclusion, Jones (2004) pointed out that....

It is important to note that it is perfectly acceptable to report experts' opinions and speculations in literature reviews. However, failure to indicate whether statistics underlie them in a literature review is a flaw because the distinction between an "opinion" and a "statistical finding" is important to many readers. Example 10.8.3 shows statements that are

---

[8] Schmitz, Wagner, & Menke (2001, p. 69).

not clear in terms of this issue because there are no cues of the types shown in Examples 10.8.1 and 10.8.2.

Example 10.8.3

Two statements from literature reviews that are unclear as to whether they are data-based (not recommended):

First statement: While the impact of homelessness cannot be separated from poverty, sustained homelessness during childhood is a life event that has a tremendous impact throughout a child's adult life (Smith, 2003). [*Note*: It is not clear from this statement whether Smith provides statistics on the "impact of homelessness."]

Second statement: Teachers know the importance of early reading comprehension achievement to later success in school (Jones, 2002). [*Note*: It is not clear from this statement whether Jones provides statistics on how much teachers know or how many teachers have a specified degree of knowledge.]

✍ Guideline 10.9
Consider discussing the statistical support, if any, for important theories.

The importance of considering and discussing theories in your literature review has been stressed throughout this book. Theories help us to conceptually tie together a number of diverse variables. As a result, they enable us to make predictions. The ultimate test of a theory is whether empirical results confirm the predictions made on the basis of the theory. Thus, even if you are disinclined to discuss research methods and statistical results in other parts of your literature review, you should consider doing so when discussing theories that are important in helping you arrive at a synthesis on which you base your conclusions.

Indicating statistical support for a theory can be done by discussing details of research that is designed to test it. This is especially important if there are pivotal studies that have a direct bearing on the validity and usefulness of the theory. Depending on your purposes and the tone you wish to use in your review (i.e., a qualitatively oriented or quantitatively oriented tone), however, indicating statistical support can also be done by using phrases that make only general references to research and statistics such as "this theory has been thoroughly investigated," "a theory with strong empirical support is," "many researchers have found support for the XYZ theory," and "research has failed to confirm the basic tenets of the ABC theory." The author of Example 10.9.1 makes a general reference to statistical support for a theory by saying that "evidence suggests."

Note that the term "evidence suggests" in Example 10.9.1 is a relatively neutral statement in support of the theory. If the evidence was more substantial and convincing, the writer might use a stronger term such as "substantial evidence suggests" or "strong evidence suggests." If the evidence is very limited, a phrase indicating its limitation such as "some preliminary evidence suggests" might be used.

Example 10.9.1

A statement with a phrase (i.e., "evidence suggests") that informs readers that the theory has statistical support:

The duplex *theory* of hate is presented as a theory that applies to both individuals and groups. Indeed, *evidence suggests* that....[9]

Concluding Comments

The extent to which you quantify your literature review by citing statistical results is a matter of judgment. You should consider the needs of your audience and your purpose (i.e., provide a broad general overview versus a detailed discussion of findings reported in the literature). Many of you might want to strive for a balance to avoid the possible criticisms that either (a) your review is too broad and general and, hence, you have failed to fully support your conclusions or (b) your review is so riddled with a multitude of statistics that readers find it difficult to obtain a good overview from your literature review. You can avoid both of these criticisms through the judicious selection of statistics to include in your review and by following the other guidelines in this chapter.

In the next chapter, we will consider a highly mathematical method for arriving at a synthesis of research literature called a "meta-analysis." Even though the method for ultimately arriving at a synthesis is purely mathematical, a report on a meta-analysis also typically contains many of the same elements as a qualitatively oriented review. Also, you can consider incorporating a "mini" meta-analysis within a larger qualitatively oriented review, a possibility that will be discussed in the next chapter.

Exercise for Chapter 10

1. According to this chapter, is it necessary to choose between a dichotomy of "highly qualitative approach" versus "highly quantitative approach" when writing a literature review? Explain.

2. Suppose that a reviewer made a statement such as this in her literature review: "The mean for women was higher than the mean for men (Doe, 2004)." According to this chapter, what are readers likely to assume about the statistical significance of the difference between the two means?

---

[9] Sternberg (2003, p. 303).

3. Very briefly explain why you should consider pointing out the size of differences even if they are statistically significant. In other words, is it sufficient to say that a difference is statistically significant without mentioning its size? Explain.

4. In this chapter, what is named as being "one of the most common flaws in writing literature reviews"?

5. At this point, to what extent do you plan to quantify your literature review? Do you plan to use a table to report key statistics? Explain.

6. According to this chapter, is it possible to "overquantify" a literature review? Explain.

7. According to this chapter, is it acceptable to rely heavily on methodologically weak studies (and their statistics) in creating a synthesis and reaching conclusions in a literature review? If yes, what should you point out to your readers if you do this?

8. Write two terms or phrases that would help tip off your readers that a statement you are citing from the literature is data-based.

9. Is it appropriate to discuss statistics when discussing theories? Explain.

10. If you have already written your literature review, read it again to determine if there are points at which the addition of some specific statistical information would strengthen your review. If you find any, describe one and come to class prepared to discuss it.

11. In addition to the possibility of incorporating some statistics into your literature review, are there other suggestions in this chapter that you plan to use in revising the draft of your literature review? If yes, name one and come to class prepared to discuss it.

Chapter 11

Introduction to Meta-Analysis

The prefix "meta-" means "more comprehensive; transcending others." A meta-analysis is a statistical analysis that transcends others by mathematically combining the results of studies conducted by various researchers to obtain an overall result (a statistical synthesis).[1] This chapter discusses only the basics of meta-analysis. Although they may be "basic," they can be used to make an important contribution to synthesizing data on a topic.

Let us move quickly from the abstract to the specific by considering how percentages might be treated and interpreted in a meta-analysis. (See Guideline 11.1.)

⅍ Guideline 11.1

A meta-analysis of percentages reported in various studies can be conducted by calculating a weighted average of the percentages.

The raw statistics from three national polls (conducted by three different researchers) on public attitudes toward the XYZ issue are presented in Box 11A. In each case, the pollster has reported the number of people surveyed and the percentage who said "yes" when asked a question about the issue. Let us assume that the three researchers used approximately the same wording in the question. As you can see, they obtained three different percentages. Such differences are to be expected because of sampling error (each pollster used only a sample of the entire national population). Based on these three samples, what is our best estimate of the percentage of the *population* that would answer "yes" if everyone in the population were polled?

Box 11A *Results of three national polls on the XYZ issue.*

Poll 1	Poll 2	Poll 3
Number of people interviewed: 595	Number of people interviewed: 1,028	Number of people interviewed: 1,440
Percentage who answered "yes": 72%	Percentage who answered "yes": 51%	Percentage who answered "yes": 50%

To answer the question, you might be tempted to simply sum the percentages (72% + 51% + 50% = 173%) and divide the sum by the number of polls (173%/3 = 57.66%, which rounds to 58%). However, notice that Polls 2 and 3 had many more respondents than Poll 1. Hence, the results of Polls 2 and 3 are probably more reliable than Poll 1, and they should be

---

[1] An alternative meaning of "meta-" is "occurring later" or "occurring after." This meaning also applies to meta-analysis because a meta-analysis occurs after the original studies on which it is based have occurred.

given more weight in determining the average percentage across the three studies. The first step in doing this is to calculate the total number of respondents, which is done in Column 2 of Box 11B (595 + 1,028, + 1,440 = 3,063). The second step is to calculate the total number of respondents who answered "yes," which is done in Column 4 of Box 11B (428 + 524 + 720 = 1,672). At this point, we could report that 1,672 of the 3,063 respondents in the three studies answered "yes." Such a report would be a report on a meta-analysis (i.e., a statistical synthesis of the results of the three studies).

Box 11B *First steps in calculating a weighted percentage.*

Column 1	Column 2	Column 3	Column 4
	Total number of respondents.	Percentage who said "yes."	Calculate the number who said "yes" by multiplying.
Poll 1	595	72%	(595)(0.72) = 428
Poll 2	1,028	51%	(1,028)(0.51) = 524
Poll 3	1,440	50%	(1,440)(0.50) = 720
Sum of Column 2 = 3,063		**Sum of Column 4 = 1,672**	

The values of 1,672 and 3,063 can be used to calculate a single percentage for the three studies combined. Specifically, the result of dividing the *part* (1,672) by the *whole* (3,063) and multiplying by 100 will yield the percentage. Thus: $1,672/3,063 = 0.5459 \times 100 = 54.59\%$, which rounds to 55%.[2]

Notice that a value of 58% was obtained on the previous page by simply adding the three percentages and dividing by three (i.e., giving the three studies equal weight). Although it may not be obvious at first glance, by performing the calculations as we did in the previous paragraph, a *weighted* percentage (giving more weight to the studies with larger samples) of 55% was obtained. Thus, in a report on a meta-analysis, we could make a statement such as: "The combined percentage for the three studies, weighted for sample size, is 55%." If the weighting procedure is used, it should be mentioned.

A more elaborate statement regarding the statistics we have been considering and the meta-analysis that we conducted is shown in Example 11.1.1.

Example 11.1.1

Sample statement of results of the meta-analysis of percentages:

Three national polls were conducted on public attitudes toward XYZ. The results of the polls are shown in Table 1 on the next page. Note that the percentages that responded "yes" vary from 50% in the poll with the largest sample (Smith, 2004) to 72% in the poll with the smallest sample size (Doe, 2004). The average percentage, weighted to take account of differences in sample size, is 55%, which indicates that

---

[2] Note that percentages are usually reported to whole numbers in the popular media. In academic journals, they are often reported to one or two decimal places.

a majority of the population is in favor of XYZ. This percentage is based on a total sample of 3,063 respondents.

Table 1

Percentage Who Answered "Yes" on XYZ

	Doe (2004)	Jones (2004)	Smith (2004)
Percentage	72%	51%	50%
(n)	(595)	(1,028)	(1,440)

As you will see from the guidelines in the rest of this chapter and by examining Model Literature Reviews 6 and 7, a meta-analysis involves more than merely stating the statistical results of individual studies and then providing a weighted average of them. Nevertheless, you have now seen an example of the basic technique for obtaining a synthesis of percentages reported in various studies.

Note that a *major advantage* of meta-analysis is that it provides an average result that is based on a larger sample than was used in any of the individual studies on which it is based. In this case, our best estimate of 55% is based on the answers of 3,063 respondents, which is twice as large as the answer of 50% from the single poll with the largest sample (Poll 3, which had 1,440 respondents). Because national polls usually are based on about 1,500 respondents or less, the sample size in this meta-analysis (i.e., 3,063) could be described as a very large sample.

Box 11C shows examples of how the results of the three polls might be handled by writers of literature reviews with three different orientations: highly qualitative, with no mention of specific statistics; moderately quantitative, with some mention of specific statistics; and highly quantitative (a meta-analysis). Notice that "a majority" could be any value from 50.1% to 100%. Thus, at least a moderately quantitative statement of results is recommended for this discussion.

Box 11C *Examples of qualitative and quantitative statements.*

Highly qualitative (no mention of specific statistics)	**Moderately quantitative (some statistics reported)**	**Highly quantitative (meta-analysis stating combined results)**
In the three national polls on the XYZ issue, a majority answered "yes," indicating that a majority of the population is in favor of it.	In the three national polls on the XYZ issue, between 50% and 72% answered "yes," indicating that a majority of the population is in favor of it. *OR* In the three national polls on the XYZ issue, 50%, 51%, and 72% of the respondents answered "yes," indicating that a majority of the population is in favor of it.	The number of respondents and the percentages who answered "yes" in the three national polls are shown in Table 1 above. While there is wide variation in the results, the best estimate of the true population value is 55%. This value is based on an average of the results of the three poll results, weighted for differences in sample size. Thus, the best estimate is that the majority favors XYZ.

᭰ Guideline 11.2

The beginning of a meta-analysis should be similar to the beginning of a qualitatively oriented review.

Regardless of the approach (highly qualitatively oriented through highly quantitatively oriented), you should begin a literature review by establishing the importance of the topic, providing an overview of the types of literature available (i.e., describing the scope of the literature), and commenting on the quality of the body of literature (based on your evaluations of it). You should also indicate how various theories relate to your topic whenever possible. Example 11.2.1 shows the beginning of a meta-analysis reported in a journal article. Notice that it could also be the beginning of a highly qualitatively oriented literature review because the author is introducing the topic and providing some background on it, which should be done at the beginning of any type of literature review.

> **Example 11.2.1**
>
> *The beginning of a published meta-analytic review. A beginning that could also be the beginning of a qualitatively oriented literature review*:
>
> Psychologists have long debated whether emotions are universal versus whether they vary by culture. This issue has been extensively summarized elsewhere, and we do not reiterate [it] (e.g., Ekman, 1972, 1994; Izard, 1971; Mesquita & Frijda, 1992; Mesquita, Frijda, & Scherer, 1997; Russell, 1994; Scherer & Wallbott, 1994). Although many theorists have taken extreme positions and provoked lively debate, recent theoretical models have attempted to account for both universality and cultural variation by specifying which particular aspects of emotion show similarities and differences across cultural boundaries....[3]

᭰ Guideline 11.3

Name the search terms used as well as the databases that were searched.

Traditionally, those who conduct meta-analyses describe in detail how they searched the literature for relevant publications—indicating which databases they searched, whether they searched for unpublished studies such as doctoral dissertations and reports presented at scholarly meetings, and what search terms (i.e., keywords) they used (such as "anxiety" and variations on it such as "anxious"). Although this tradition is closely associated with meta-analysis, those who conduct qualitatively oriented reviews should consider adopting it because including such information in a literature review reassures readers that a thorough search has been conducted (or, alternatively, readers might see that an important term or database was overlooked in the search). In either case, readers will be better informed if they are given this information.

---

[3] Elfenbein & Ambady (2002, p. 203).

The description of the search for literature for a meta-analysis is usually quite detailed, as the excerpt in Example 11.3.1 illustrates.

Example 11.3.1

Portions of a description of the search for literature for a meta-analysis:

We used several procedures to ensure that we had included existing studies. First, we searched several electronic indexes using the keyword "trust": *PsycINFO* (1967–2000), *SocioFile* (1974–2000), *ABI/Inform* (1985–2000), and *Dissertation Abstracts* (1861–1999). The search identified over 15,500 studies that were reviewed for consideration.... Second, we examined the reference sections of books and articles that provided a narrative review of the trust literature (e.g., Dirks & Ferrin, 2001...). Third, we manually searched for studies in the following [eleven] journals from 1980 to the present: *Academy of Management Journal, Administrative Science Quarterly*.... Fourth, we gathered unpublished research by contacting approximately 90 researchers who were considered likely to have relevant data. Unpublished studies were included to minimize publication bias (Rosenthal, 1979).[4]

✤ Guideline 11.4

Discuss efforts made to overcome the "file drawer effect" (i.e., publication bias) on the outcome of a meta-analysis.

Those who conduct meta-analyses concern themselves with the "file drawer effect," also known as a "publication bias," which is mentioned in the last sentence of Example 11.3.1. The terms refer to the possibility that researchers who obtain statistically *insignificant* results may not submit them for publication (on the assumption that editors favor publishing research that has statistically significant results). Thus, researchers with insignificant results may be stashing their never-to-be-published data in a file drawer. Those who conduct meta-analyses typically mention the possibility of a publication bias (i.e., file drawer effect) and indicate whether they have searched for unpublished studies by examining theses and dissertations, and by contacting researchers who have been conducting research on the topic to see if they have filed away studies that had insignificant results, and so on. (Notice that in Example 11.3.1, the reviewers mention that they searched *Dissertation Abstracts* and contacted almost 90 researchers who might have unpublished data in an effort to overcome publication bias.)

To the extent that there is publication bias that has not been overcome when preparing the meta-analysis, the results will be inflated because the studies that are not published (and, thus, are not included in the meta-analysis) may tend to have smaller (or even negative) results that are statistically insignificant. In other words, the average resulting from a meta-analysis will be higher than it should be if only studies with strong effects (which tend to be the studies that are published) are included when averaging.

---

[4] Dirks & Ferrin (2002, p. 617).

Although a thorough search for unpublished research reports is traditional when conducting meta-analyses, those who write qualitatively oriented reviews should also consider being thorough and making efforts to uncover unpublished research reports. Whether qualitatively oriented or quantitatively oriented, a reviewer should report on these efforts, if any. See Box 11D for a summary of the traditions used in conducting meta-analyses discussed in Guidelines 11.3 and 11.4.

Box 11D   *Two traditions followed by those who conduct meta-analyses that might be followed more often by those who write qualitatively oriented reviews.*

> 1. Describe in detail how the search for related literature was conducted. See Guideline 11.3.
> 2. Consider whether there may be studies on the topic that are unpublished because the results were statistically insignificant. Attempt to locate such studies and incorporate them in the review. See Guideline 11.4.

✣ Guideline 11.5

Decide whether to exclude studies with weak methods from the meta-analysis.

A very weak study could have a strong effect on the outcome of a meta-analysis, especially if it has a large number of participants (or if it was one of only a small number of studies, such as one study out of a total of three). While a qualitatively oriented reviewer can mention a very weak study and dismiss its importance because of its weaknesses, a very weak study in a meta-analysis may count as much as a very strong study that has the same number of participants.

While excluding weak studies from a meta-analysis is a matter of some controversy, it seems better to exclude them *if* they are excluded on the basis of pre-established, objective criteria such as "All studies without a control group will be excluded." Note that deciding to exclude certain types of studies after they have been read by the reviewer may lead some readers to suspect that the reviewer may have omitted them because their results were not consistent with what the reviewer hoped to find in his or her meta-analysis.

Some writers suggest that all studies, regardless of their weaknesses, should be included in a meta-analysis. Their rationale is that a certain type of weakness in some studies might counterbalance another type of weakness in other studies when their results are all averaged. The possibility of such a "counterbalancing effect of weaknesses" seems most likely to happen when there are a relatively large number of studies. When there are only a small number, the results of the weakest study might overwhelm the results of the limited number of strong studies when results are combined.

In your literature review, you should mention whether you omitted methodologically weak studies and, if so, what criteria were used to identify those that were omitted. Also, mention whether the criteria were established prior to reading the studies, which is highly recommended.

✎ Guideline 11.6

If studies are excluded from a meta-analysis for reasons other than weak research methods, provide specific reasons for their exclusion.

When studies on the topic are excluded from a meta-analysis, readers will want to know the reasons for excluding them. By being specific about the reasons for exclusion, readers can be reassured that there was no bias (intentional or otherwise) in the final selection of studies on which the meta-analysis is based.

To illustrate this guideline, consider Example 11.6.1. The authors of the example conducted a meta-analysis of the effectiveness of computer-assisted instruction (CAI) in supporting the teaching of beginning reading. Of the several hundred publications they initially identified, only 42 were retained for inclusion in the meta-analysis. The reasons for excluding the other studies are described in the example.

Example 11.6.1

Reasons for excluding studies from a meta-analysis on the effectiveness of CAI in supporting the teaching of reading:

The first round of selections was conducted by removing the references published before 1990 on the assumption that older studies were represented in available reviews.... A subsequent selection was carried out using abstracts. One selection criterion was that the publication should report an empirical study. Position papers and publications that contained only descriptions of CAI programs or suggestions for teachers were excluded. We also eliminated studies reporting on samples of students with severe or multiple disabilities such as aphasia, deafness, or blindness. We wanted to limit our focus to the population of modal or regular students....[5]

✎ Guideline 11.7

Consider including one or more moderator variables in a meta-analysis, and provide the rationale for their selection.

A "moderator variable" is one used to form separate groups for separate analyses within a meta-analytic project. For instance, in a recently published meta-analysis of the literature on the magnitude of genetic and environmental influences on antisocial behavior, the authors conducted meta-analyses in which they included a number of moderator variables, one of which was gender. They examined the magnitude of genetic and environmental influences in separate meta-analyses for men and women, compared the two results, and found no significant differences.[6]

The rationale for including each moderator variable should be stated in the report of the meta-analysis. For instance, because a much higher proportion of men than women are

---

[5] Blok, Oostdam, Otter, & Overmaat (2002, pp. 107–108).
[6] Rhee & Waldman (2002, p. 490).

incarcerated in jails and prisons, the use of gender as a moderator variable seems justified in a meta-analysis on antisocial behavior. Example 11.7.1 shows the rationale for including undergraduate major (academic discipline) as a moderator variable in a meta-analysis of the validity of the Graduate Record Examination (GRE).

Example 11.7.1

Rationale for including type of undergraduate major (academic discipline) as a moderator variable in a meta-analysis of the validity of the GRE:

Several variables may moderate the relationship between scores on the GRE and performance in graduate school. First, the predictive validity of the GRE may vary by academic discipline. Although there are many similarities in some of the fundamental tasks required of all graduate students, there are differences in the type of training and demands of different academic areas. To investigate the impact of academic field on the predictive validity of the GRE tests, we conducted separate analyses for subsamples representing four broad disciplines: humanities, the social sciences, life sciences, and math–physical sciences.[7]

✋ Guideline 11.8
Consider incorporating a meta-analysis within a larger qualitatively oriented review.

Because certain types of literature cannot be included in a meta-analysis, reviewers should consider writing a larger qualitatively oriented review that includes all types and incorporate a meta-analysis within it.

There are three types of literature that cannot be incorporated into a meta-analysis. First, there is speculative literature, including some literature on new theories that have not been researched yet. These cannot be included because they do not contain statistics. (Remember that a meta-analysis is a synthesis of selected statistics.) Second, some research reports do not contain a sufficient number of statistics to permit their incorporation into a meta-analysis. For instance, when means are combined in meta-analyses, which we will consider in the next guideline, standard deviations must be used. If a research report provides means without standard deviations, by default, it will be excluded. Third, some research reports contain statistics that are not compatible with the majority of the quantitative research that will be combined mathematically. For example, most reports with averages will contain means, which can be easily combined mathematically. However, some reports will contain medians or modes (and no means) as averages (i.e., measures of central tendency), which might lead to the exclusion of these reports in a meta-analysis.[8] One way around this problem is to write a qualitatively oriented review that incorporates all relevant literature and

---

[7] Kuncel, Hezlett, & Ones (2001, p. 168).
[8] Methods for calculating missing statistics from those that are reported and for estimating them in various ways by making certain mathematical assumptions are beyond the scope of this book.

incorporate within it a meta-analysis of the literature that lends itself to meta-analytic techniques.

✤ Guideline 11.9
Consider conducting a meta-analysis using Cohen's statistic named *d*.

The mean is the most commonly reported average. It is obtained by adding a set of scores and dividing by the number of scores. Frequently, researchers use means to describe the average difference between two groups such as the average difference in income between high school dropouts and high school graduates.

Let us consider a concrete example that illustrates the desirability of considering Cohen's *d* when comparing means. Suppose there have been 15 experiments on the effects of computer-assisted instruction in algebra given to the experimental groups. In each study, the control group received algebra instruction without computers. At the end of each study, algebra achievement was measured. If all experimenters used the same instruments (i.e., the same algebra tests), we could simply average the means (while first weighting each one according to the number of participants such as we did with percentages near the beginning of this chapter). Unfortunately, you will typically find wide variation from study to study in how a variable is measured. For instance, in one study, the participants might be administered a 30-item test, while in another a 120-item test might be used. For just these first 2 of the 15 studies, we might have results such as those shown in Box 11E.

When considering how to calculate the weighted average of the 15 means (including the two shown in Box 11E), however, an individual conducting a meta-analysis faces an important problem: Averaging the means will give undue weight to studies with larger numbers of test items. To understand the seriousness of this problem, consider an analogy. Suppose in one study students were asked to give nickels to charity and the mean (average) number given was 7.00 (i.e., the average student gave seven nickels). Further, suppose that in another study, students were asked to give quarters, and the mean number given was 1.00 (i.e., the average student gave one quarter). If we simply average the two means, we get a grand mean of 4.00 (7.00 + 1.00 = 8.00/2 = 4.00), but this answer (i.e., 4.00) no longer refers to nickels or quarters and is not directly interpretable. It will only be interpretable if we convert it to a *common scale*. For this analogy, the obvious common scale is "number of cents given," so we convert both results to this common scale (an average of 7.00 nickels equals 35 cents and an average of 1 quarter equals 25 cents). Using this common scale, we can average the results of the two studies (35 + 25 = 60/2 = 30) and then report that the grand average for both studies is 30 cents, which readers can readily comprehend. Just as "cents" is the common scale for expressing the results of the studies in our analogy, Cohen's *d* is the common scale for expressing the magnitude of the differences when means and standard deviations are reported, which is the case in Box 11E.[9]

---

[9] Some of the material in this guideline was adapted from Patten (2004) with permission from the publisher.

Box 11E *Results of two studies to be synthesized in a meta-analysis.*

	Experimental group	Control group
Study 1 (30 test questions)	$m = 12.00$ $s = 4.00$ $n = 30$	$m = 7.00$ $s = 4.00$ $n = 30$
Study 2 (120 test questions)	$m = 80.00$ $s = 14.00$ $n = 30$	$m = 70.00$ $s = 14.00$ $n = 30$

Calculating Cohen's *d* is mathematically quite easy. For those who have not taken statistics, the difficult part will be understanding *why* Cohen's *d* expresses means that are initially expressed on different scales on a new, common scale. Let us do the easy part first (the mathematics), which should help you understand the meaning of Cohen's *d*.

To compute Cohen's *d* for each study, subtract the control group mean from the experimental group mean and divide the difference by the standard deviation of the control group. These calculations are shown in Box 11F for Study 1. Note that the subscript "$_e$" stands for "experimental group" (i.e., m_e stands for the mean of the experimental group), and the subscript "$_c$" stands for "control group." As you can see, $d = 1.25$ for Study 1. The calculation of *d* for Study 2 is shown in Box 11G, in which *d* equals 0.71. Without any additional information, you can see that Study 1 has more units of Cohen's *d* (1.25 units worth of *d*) than Study 2 (0.71 units worth of *d*).

Box 11F *Calculation of Cohen's* d *for Study 1 using statistics in Box 11E.*

	Experimental group	Control group
Study 1	$m_e = 12.00$ $s_e = 4.00$	$m_c = 7.00$ $s_c = 4.00$

Calculation of *d* for Study 1:

$$d = \frac{m_e - m_c}{s_c} = \frac{12.00 - 7.00}{4.00} = \frac{5.00}{4.00} = 1.25$$

Box 11G *Calculation of Cohen's* d *for Study 2 using statistics in Box 11E.*

	Experimental group	Control group
Study 2	$m_e = 80.00$ $s_e = 14.00$	$m_c = 70.00$ $s_c = 14.00$

Calculation of *d* for Study 2:

$$d = \frac{m_e - m_c}{s_c} = \frac{80.00 - 70.00}{14.00} = \frac{10.00}{14.00} = 0.71$$

The number of items answered correctly on the algebra tests are known as the *raw scores*. Box 11H shows the raw-score differences as well as the differences in values of *d*.

While Study 2 has a larger raw-score difference, Study 1 has a larger difference in the value of *d*. What does this mean? Simply this: When the results of the two studies are expressed on a common scale (i.e., *d*), the difference is larger in Study 1 than in Study 2. (The raw-score difference in Study 2 is larger only because there were more test items on the algebra test in Study 2 than in Study 1.)

Box 11H *Differences between the means of experimental and control groups expressed in terms of raw scores and in terms of* d.

	Raw-score difference	Difference in *d*
Study 1	5.00	1.25
Study 2	10.00	0.71

Here is the definition of *d*: *It is a scale on which the difference between two means is expressed in terms of standard deviation units.* (Remember that for each study, we divided the raw-score difference between the two means by the standard deviation of the control group.) Thus, for Study 1, the experimental group exceeded the control group by 1.25 standard deviation units, while in Study 2, the experimental group exceeded the control group by a smaller amount: 0.71 units.

The concluding step in conducting the meta-analysis is to average the two values of *d* (1.25 + 0.71 = 1.96/2 = 0.98). The interpretation is: The value of *d* for the two studies combined is 0.98. Note that an important aspect of this result is that it is based on a total of 120 participants, while the result of each individual study is based on only 60. Because larger samples yield more reliable results, we can have more confidence in the effect size of 0.98 for the two studies combined than in the individual effect sizes of 1.25 and 0.71.

Important notes: In the computational example we have just considered, the standard deviations were the same for both groups within each study (e.g., the values of the standard deviations of the experimental and control groups in Study 1 are both 4.00). See the first guideline in the next chapter if they are different. Also, in the example, both studies had the same number of participants. If there are unequal numbers, see the second and third guidelines in the next chapter for additional mathematical procedures and considerations.

✎ Guideline 11.10

Avoid mechanical rules when interpreting values of *d*.

Cohen (1992) suggested guidelines for interpreting values of *d*. Specifically, he suggested that values of about 0.20 might be said to represent small effects, values of about 0.50 might be said to represent medium effects, and values of about 0.80 might be said to represent large effects. These values have been widely cited in the social and behavioral science literature and have led some reviewers who conduct meta-analyses to apply them mechanically without considering the nature of the underlying variables and the practical implications of the results. For example, suppose the average value of *d* across four experiments on the effects of a new drug for relieving the adverse effects of chemotherapy resulted in an average value of $d = 0.20$. Suppose furthermore that in all four studies, the differences were not only in favor of the experimental group, but all four were statistically significant, indicating that the amount of relief provided by the new drug is greater than would be expected on the basis of chance alone (i.e., that it is a reliable difference).[10] Applying Cohen's guideline mechanically would result in a conclusion that the effect is "small," without recognizing that this reliable effect (however small) might be of great importance to those suffering from the effects of chemotherapy. In other words, mechanical rules cannot take into account the physical and psychological importance of a particular finding in a meta-analysis.

To avoid this pitfall, consider how the researchers who conducted the studies included in a meta-analysis interpreted their findings. No matter how small an average value of d is, consider how important the previous researchers regarded the differences they reported. To what extent do they think that the differences are important in everyday affairs? To what extent do they think they have important implications for theories?

When interpreting the value of d in a meta-analysis, also consider its strength relative to the strength of other related treatments or variables. For instance, if other drugs commonly prescribed to relieve the effects of chemotherapy have an average value of d of only 0.10, a value of d of 0.20 for the new drug would represent a great improvement. To call 0.20 "small" under this circumstance might be quite misleading.

When interpreting value of d, also keep in mind that for all practical purposes, it is expressed on a scale that ranges from 0.00 to 3.00.[11] Furthermore, the vast majority of the cases would be expected to fall between 0.00 and 1.00, which means that it is not reasonable to expect many instances where d is greater than 1.00. Thus, most interpretations of the results of meta-analyses deal with values of less than 1.00.

✎ Guideline 11.11

Describe the overall quality of the studies included in a meta-analysis.

If you have selected a topic for review on which the research is weak, the results of your meta-analysis should be interpreted in very tentative terms. On the other hand, there are topics on which there have been a large number of studies of high quality, in which case you can have more confidence in the average effect size produced by a meta-analysis. Indicating whether the studies included in the meta-analysis are of high quality will help readers interpret the results.

---

[10] A test of statistical significance determines only whether a difference is reliable (i.e., can be counted on to occur again consistently). Although larger differences are more likely to be statistically significant, small differences can also be statistically significant (i.e., a difference can be *small and reliable*).

[11] Values of d can exceed 3 00, but rarely do in practice. In addition, values of d can be negative, which is discussed in the next chapter. What is true in the positive (e.g., the vast majority are between 0.00 and 1.00) is also true in the negative (e.g., the vast majority of the cases are between 0.00 and -1.00).

Concluding Comments

Some researchers argue that a meta-analysis is superior to a highly qualitatively oriented (narrative) literature review because the statistical procedures used in a meta-analysis are "objective." However, if you consider the early guidelines in this chapter and read Model Literature Reviews 6 and 7, you will see that even those who conduct meta-analyses must make subjective judgments such as excluding studies with weak research methods, deciding which databases to search and which keywords to use in their searches, and so on. Thus, those who conduct meta-analyses should employ good judgment when deciding which studies to include and how to discuss the results, thereby introducing important subjective elements into meta-analyses.

The mathematical procedures in this chapter are presented for those who wish to conduct a basic meta-analysis, either as the heart of a highly quantitatively oriented literature review *or* as a subsection of a basically qualitatively oriented review. All college-level students need to understand the basic concepts of "effect size" and "meta-analysis" (i.e., an analysis in which effect sizes are averaged) because they will encounter research reports in their professional fields in which these are reported.

Some important additional meta-analytic techniques are discussed in the next chapter.

Exercise for Chapter 11

1. According to this chapter, a meta-analysis is an analysis that "transcends others" by doing what?

2. Suppose Researcher A found that 50% of a sample of 200 college freshmen knew that there are nine justices on the Supreme Court of the United States while Researcher B found that 60% of a sample of 400 college freshmen knew this fact. Very briefly explain why it would be inappropriate to add 50% and 60% to get 110% and divide by 2 for an average percentage of 55%.

3. According to this chapter, what is a "major advantage" of meta-analysis?

4. How should both qualitatively oriented and quantitatively oriented literature reviews (including meta-analyses) begin?

5. Are you more likely to find a detailed description of how the search for literature was conducted in a qualitatively oriented literature review *or* in a meta-analysis?

6. Those who conduct meta-analyses are often concerned about the possibility of the "file drawer effect" (also known as a "publication bias"). Very briefly define this term.

7. Guideline 11.5 indicates that a reviewer should decide whether to exclude studies with weak methods from his or her meta-analysis. If you will be conducting a meta-analysis, do you plan to exclude such studies? Explain.

8. Suppose someone was reviewing the literature on treatment programs for those who have committed physical spousal abuse. Would you recommend using gender as a moderator variable? Explain.

9. Suppose the mean for an experimental group is 50.00 (with a standard deviation of 5.00) and the mean for the control group is 45.00 (also with a standard deviation of 5.00). What is the value of d for the difference between the two groups?

10. In Question 9, the experimental group exceeded the control group by how many standard deviations?

11. According to this chapter, is it a good idea to automatically label values of d of about 0.20 as "small"? Explain.

12. According to this chapter, are those who conduct meta-analyses purely objective in their work?

13. If you will be conducting a highly qualitatively oriented review, have you learned anything in this chapter that will help you? Explain.

Chapter 12

A Closer Look at Meta-Analysis

In the previous chapter, you learned the basics of conducting and interpreting a meta-analysis. Among other things, you learned how to average percentages reported in various studies weighted to take account of different sample sizes (see Guideline 11.1). This average weighted percentage is a synthesis of results of studies on a topic on which various researchers report percentages.

You also learned one way to calculate *d*, from means and standard deviations, which you will often need to do because authors of research reports usually do not report *d*. In this chapter, you will learn alternatives for calculating *d* (see Guideline 12.1 below). In addition, you learned in Chapter 11 how to combine values of *d* in order to create a statistical synthesis (by summing the values of *d* that you calculated for various studies on a topic and dividing by the number of studies). In this chapter, you will learn a more advanced method for combining values of *d* (see Guideline 12.2 below).

Important note: This chapter was written with the assumption that you have thoroughly mastered the material in Chapter 11. Many of the concepts covered there, especially those under Guideline 11.9, need to be known in order to understand this chapter.

✋ Guideline 12.1

When calculating *d*, consider using the pooled value of the standard deviation.

Under Guideline 11.9 in the previous chapter, you learned how to calculate the value of *d*. Note that the two groups in each study in the example there had standard deviations with the same values (e.g., see Box 11E in which both of the standard deviations in Study 1 equal 4.00 and both of the standard deviations in Study 2 equal 14.00). In practice, it would be highly unusual for two standard deviations in a study to be identical. When they are different, which one should be used to calculate *d* for a given study? One answer is to use the standard deviation of the control group, which is called for in the formula for *d* in the previous chapter, in which s_c in the denominator of the formula stands for the standard deviation of the control group.

$$d = \frac{m_e - m_c}{s_c}$$

Instead of using the standard deviation of the control group, those who conduct meta-analyses often use what is called the *pooled standard deviation*, which is a special type of average of the two standard deviations reported in a study. The formula for calculating d using the pooled standard deviation is:

$$d = \frac{m_e - m_c}{s_{pooled}}$$

Obviously, to use this formula, the value of the pooled standard deviation must first be computed. The procedure for doing this is shown below for the statistics in Box 12A. Note that the subscript "e" stands for experimental group. Thus, n_e stands for the number of participants in the experimental group. Likewise, s_e represents the experimental group's standard deviation.

Box 12A *Statistics for illustrating calculation of the pooled standard deviation.*

Group	Mean	Standard deviation	Number of participants
Exp. group	$m_e = 35.00$	$s_e = 5.00$	$n_e = 50$
Control group	$m_c = 30.00$	$s_c = 9.00$	$n_c = 60$

$$sd_{pooled} = \sqrt{\frac{(n_e - 1)s_e^2 + (n_c - 1)s_c^2}{n_e + n_c - 2}} = \sqrt{\frac{(50 - 1)5.00^2 + (60 - 1)9.00^2}{50 + 60 - 2}}$$

$$= \sqrt{\frac{(49)25.00 + (59)81.00}{110 - 2}} = \sqrt{\frac{1225.00 + 4779.00}{108}} = \sqrt{\frac{6004}{108}} = \sqrt{55.59} = 7.46$$

Using this value for the pooled standard deviation, we calculate d as follows:

$$d = \frac{m_e - m_c}{s_{pooled}} = \frac{35.00 - 30.00}{7.46} = \frac{5.00}{7.46} = 0.67$$

If the standard deviation for the control group (instead of the pooled standard deviation) had been used, this result would have been obtained:

$$d = \frac{m_e - m_c}{s_c} = \frac{35.00 - 30.00}{9.00} = \frac{5.00}{9.00} = 0.56$$

As you can see, the value of d obtained by using the pooled standard deviation (i.e., 0.67) is noticeably different from the value obtained by using the standard deviation of the control group (0.56), which raises the question of which method is superior. Unfortunately, there is no simple answer. While this writer prefers using the formula with the standard deviation of the control group in the denominator,[1] probably the majority of those who publish meta-analytic studies use the pooled standard deviation. You will probably not be faulted for using either method as long as you clearly state which method you used.

---

[1] By using the standard deviation of the control group, the value of d has a clear meaning: It indicates the extent to which the experimental group exceeded the control group *in terms of the control group's standard deviation*. The meaning is less clear when using the pooled standard deviation because the pooled standard deviation does not refer to either group in particular, but rather to the average.

It is important to note that only some meta-analytic reviews deal with *experiments*. As you may know, in a classic, simple experiment there is an experimental group that is given some special treatment (such as a new drug in pill form) while a control group is given either no treatment or a neutral treatment (such as an inert pill that looks like the pill given to the experimental group). In *nonexperimental studies*, groups that receive no special treatment from the researcher are compared. For instance, a study might compare the amount of job-related anxiety reported by men and reported by women. In such a case, either group could be called Group 1 and the other Group 2. Let us say that the women are called Group 1, while the men constitute Group 2. Then, the formula for the pooled standard deviation will have "1" and "2" instead of "e" and "c" as subscripts and will look like this:

$$s_{pooled} = \sqrt{\frac{(n_1 - 1)s_1^2 + (n_2 - 1)s_2^2}{n_1 + n_2 - 2}}$$

Under this circumstance, the formula for *d* looks like this:

$$d = \frac{m_1 - m_2}{s_{pooled}}$$

✑ Guideline 12.2

Consider weighting for differences in sample size when calculating an average value of *d*.

When we considered percentages under Guideline 11.1 in the previous chapter, you also learned how to weight percentages to account for differences in sample size. That is, you learned how to give more weight to samples with more participants when calculating the average of the percentages reported in various studies. Here, you will learn how to calculate a weighted average value of *d*.

Consider the values of *d* in Box 12B. As you may recall, these indicate how many standard deviations separate the experimental and control groups. For instance, the value of *d* for Experiment 1 (i.e., 1.50) indicates that the experimental group exceeded the control group by one and one-half standard deviation units.[2]

Box 12B *Statistics for illustrating the computation of the weighted average of* d.

Experiment	Value of *d*	Number of standard deviations separating the experimental and control groups' means
Experiment 1 (*n* = 300)	1.50	one and one-half
Experiment 2 (*n* = 10)	0.20	two-tenths

---

[2] If you have taken a statistics class, you may recall that most of the cases lie near the middle in a typical distribution (such as the normal curve, where the curve is high near the middle because that is where most of the cases are). You may also recall that there are only about three standard deviation units on each side of the mean in a typical distribution. Hence, one group being 1.5 standard deviation units higher than another is quite substantial on a scale that runs from 0.00 standard deviation units to only 3.00 standard deviation units.

Notice that the results of the two experiments in Box 12B are very different (i.e., one shows an extremely large effect with a value of d of 1.50 relative to the other value of d of 0.20). Notice, too, that the sample sizes (indicated by n) are also quite different. Specifically, there was a total of 300 participants in Experiment 1 (perhaps 150 in the experimental group and 150 in the control group or some other combination such as 200 and 100 that sum to 300), while there was a total of only 10 participants in Experiment 2. If we average the two values of d, we have the result of a meta-analysis (i.e., a statistical synthesis of results across various studies). However, if we compute an average by simply summing the two values of d and dividing by the number of studies (i.e., $1.50 + 0.20 = 1.70/2 = 0.85$), we are giving both experiments the same weight (i.e., each study counts as exactly "one out of two" as a result of dividing 1.70 by 2). However, it is usually desirable to give more weight to studies with more participants. In this case, it seems desirable to give more weight to Experiment 1, which had 300 participants, than to Experiment 2, which had only 10 participants.

To calculate an average value of d that is weighted to take account of the varying numbers of participants, follow these steps:

1. Create a box such as Box 12C and write the values of d in the second column. (Note that if values of d are not reported in some research reports, you will have to calculate these values from the means and standard deviations that are reported. See Guideline 11.9 in the previous chapter and Guideline 12.1 in this chapter for the computational procedures.)

2. Multiply the values of d by the numbers of participants (e.g., 1.50×300 for Study 1) and write the answer in the last column.

3. Calculate the total number of participants (e.g., $300 + 10 = 310$).

4. Sum the last column. (In this case, the sum is 452.00.)

5. Divide the answer to step 4 by the answer to step 3 (e.g., $452.00/310 = 1.458 = 1.46$).

Thus, in this example, the weighted value of d (1.46) is very much closer to the value of 1.50 reported in Study 1 than to the value of 0.20 reported in Study 2. This is true because the calculations we just completed gave much more weight to Study 1 with 300 participants than to Study 2 with only 10 participants. In other words, in this example, Study 2 had little effect on the average value of d (for the two studies combined) because it had very few participants.

Box 12C *Preliminary steps in getting a weighted average of* d *(steps: 1. multiply* d *times* n, *2. total the number of participants, and 3. total the products in the last column).*

Study	Value of d	times	Number of participants (n)	equals	Product of $d \times n$
Study 1	1.50	×	300	=	450.00
Study 2	0.20	×	10	=	2.00
			Sum = 310		**Sum = 452.00**

If you weight for differences in sample size, it should be reported in your meta-analytic review, which can be done in a single sentence such as the one shown in Example 12.2.1.

Example 12.2.1

Sample statement indicating that the values of d *were weighted*:

The average value of *d* was weighted to account for differences in sample size.

✥ Guideline 12.3

Be cautious when there are large variations in sample sizes.

If the sample sizes vary greatly from one study to another, mention this fact in your description of the results of your meta-analysis. This is especially important if there are one or two studies with samples that are much larger than the others and you have weighted to take account of this. For instance, suppose you are reviewing a topic on which there is one study with 1,000 participants and six other studies with about 30 participants each. A weighted average value of *d* (or of percentages) will be very heavily influenced by the single study with 1,000 participants. This, in part, negates this important characteristic of meta-analysis: By averaging results across studies, we get a more reliable estimate of what is known about the topic, assuming that the various errors that inflate the results in some studies will cancel out the various errors that deflate the results in other studies. However, whatever errors exist in the study with 1,000 participants cannot be adequately cancelled out by the other six studies because they have so little influence on the average when weighting for sample size is used.

In this case, a solution is to report the values of *d* and the number of cases for each study separately (perhaps in a table). Then, report the average value of *d* for all studies. Next, report the average value of *d* for all studies *except* the one with the very large number of participants. If these two values of *d* are quite different, urge the readers of your review to use caution in interpreting the results because the first value of *d* is based largely on one study (due to the weighting), while the second value of *d* is based on a number of studies that unfortunately had small sample sizes.

✥ Guideline 12.4

Interpret negative values of *d* appropriately.

A negative value of *d* will be obtained if the larger mean is subtracted from the smaller mean in the numerator of either of the formulas for *d* shown in this chapter. There are two circumstances under which the larger value will be subtracted from the smaller value. First, when an instrument yields scores on a scale on which it is desirable to have low scores, the experimental group may have a lower mean than the control group. Consider, for instance, a self-report measure of depression on which *lower scores indicate less depression* (i.e., the fewer symptoms of depression an individual reports, the lower his or her score). In an experiment designed to reduce depression in the experimental group, we would expect lower scores for the experimental group than for the control group. If the expectation is reached in 12 studies, we might have a result such as the one shown in Example 12.4.1. Because of the nature of the instrument (with lower scores being better scores), reporting a negative value of *d* makes sense.

Example 12.4.1

A statement regarding a negative value of d:

The average value of *d* weighted for varying sample sizes for the 12 studies under review equals –0.50. This indicates that, on average, the mean depression score for the 12 experimental groups is a full one-half of a standard deviation *lower than* the average control group's score.

Second, if it is widely hypothesized that one group will score higher than another, it makes sense to subtract the second group's mean from the first group's mean when calculating *d*, even if the second group's mean is higher than the first group's, resulting in a negative value. Suppose, for instance, that it is widely hypothesized that poodles are more affectionate than collies. If a study reported the opposite with poodles having a mean of 60.00 on an affection scale while collies had a mean of 90.00 (and a pooled standard deviation of 10.00 for the two groups of dogs), we would obtain a negative value of *d* [i.e., (60.00 – 70.00)/10.00 = –1.00]. If similar results were obtained in four studies, the result of the meta-analysis could be described as shown in Example 12.4.2.

Example 12.4.2

Another statement regarding a negative value of d:

The average value of *d* weighted for varying sample sizes for the four studies under review equals –1.00. The negative value indicates that the results were the opposite of what has been widely hypothesized. In other words, the studies under consideration had an average effect size that favors collies over poodles.

✑ Guideline 12.5

Meta-analyses are often conducted by averaging correlation coefficients.

The Pearson *r* is the most commonly used correlation coefficient. It expresses the degree and direction of the linear relationship between two variables. For instance, we might administer a vocabulary test and a reading comprehension test to *one* sample of participants and calculate a Pearson *r* to determine whether vocabulary knowledge and reading comprehension are related and, if so, to what degree.[3]

The Pearson *r* is expressed on a scale from –1.00 (a perfect inverse relationship) through 0.00 (total absence of a relationship) to +1.00 (a perfect direct relationship). The

---

[3] Note that up to this point in our discussion of meta-analysis, we have considered the comparison of two groups of participants (e.g., men and women) on one variable (e.g., job-related anxiety). We use correlation when there is only one group of participants (e.g., a group of students) and two or more variables (e.g., vocabulary knowledge and reading comprehension).

value of r is interpreted by squaring it and multiplying the square by 100%. For instance, if we calculated an r of 0.72 for the relationship between height and weight, its square is 0.72 × 0.72 = 0.52 × 100% = 52%, which means that 52% of the differences in weight can be accounted for by the differences in height among the sample.

Because r is expressed on an invariant scale (i.e., it can only vary from −1.00 to +1.00), values of r are useful when considering relationships between variables measured on diverse scales (such as pounds for weight and inches for height). Thus, like d, r is a measure that is comparable from study to study in which r is reported.

Consider this example: Suppose we collect 30 studies in which scores on reading comprehension tests have been correlated with scores on math word problem tests, and values of r are reported in each. For the meta-analysis, we could report the values of r for the individual studies, perhaps in a table. For an overall, combined average (i.e., the statistical synthesis), however, we need to perform a few calculations. The steps are:[4]

1. Convert each value of r to a value of Z using Table 1 near the end of this book.

2. Multiply each value of Z by the number of participants in the study. Call this product "nZ."

3. Sum the values of nZ.

4. Divide the sum of Step 3 by the total number of participants in the studies.

5. Convert the Z found in Step 4 back to r, using Table 1 again.

To illustrate these steps, let us assume that there are only two studies with relevant values of r, which are shown in Box 12D along with other statistics. Sum the values in the last column (48.65 + 97.02 = **145.67**) and sum the number in the samples (50 + 140 = **190**). Then divide the sum of the last column by the total number in the combined samples: 145.67/190 = **0.767**. At this point, we have the weighted average value of Z (0.767). To express this as the weighted average correlation coefficient, refer to Table 1 again and read from the Z column moving left to the r column. In this case, you will find that a Z of 0.767 corresponds to an r of 0.645. Thus, we could report that the weighted average value of r across studies is 0.645, with an underlying combined sample of 190 participants.

Box 12D   *Values of* r *and corresponding values of* Z *from Table 1. Multiply values of* Z *by the numbers of subjects. Sum the last column.*

Study	Value of r	Corresponding value of Z from Table 1 near the end of the book	times	Number of participants (n)	equals	nZ (i.e., $Z \times n$)
Study 1	0.75	0.973	×	50	=	48.65
Study 2	0.60	0.693	×	140	=	97.02
				Sum = 190		**Sum = 145.67**

---

[4] The method shown here is the *approximate method*. To use the precise method, subtract 3 (a constant for all studies) from the number in each sample before multiplying by the value of Z. Then, follow the steps shown above, but perform the final division by the sum of the same sizes minus 3 for each sample. The approximate method and the precise method usually yield very similar results. For our particular sample, the result using the precise method is exactly the same as the result using the approximate method: 0.645.

♻ Guideline 12.6
A single meta-analysis can contain values of both *d* and *r*.

Some studies on a given topic may report values of *d* (or means and standard deviations, which permit the calculation of *d*) while other studies on the same topic may report values of *r*. In this circumstance, you might report the weighted average value of *d* for the studies that report *d*, and report the weighted average value of *r* for the studies that report values of *r*.

Exercise for Chapter 12

1. One formula for *d* calls for the use of the standard deviation of the control group in the denominator. What does the other formula use in the denominator?

2. Is it possible to calculate values of *d* for *nonexperimental* studies? Explain.

3. Suppose one of the studies you are including in a meta-analytic review has these statistics: Boys (mean = 30.00) and Girls (mean = 32.00). Further, suppose the pooled standard deviation equals 2.00. What is the value of *d*?

4. Suppose these statistics were reported in the studies a reviewer is including in a meta-analytic review: Study 1 (*d* = 0.30, *n* = 22), Study 2 (*d* = 0.40, *n* = 52), and Study 3 (*d* = 0.25, *n* = 12). Furthermore, suppose the reviewer summed the values of *d* and divided by the number of studies (i.e., 0.30 + 0.40 + 0.25 = 0.95/3 = 0.32) and reported that the average value of *d* equals 0.32. What other method for calculating the average value of *d* could you recommend to the reviewer?

5. Suppose one study has 1,500 participants and ten others have about 25 participants each. According to this chapter, how many average values of *d* should you report? Explain.

6. According to this chapter, there are two circumstances under which you might subtract the larger mean from the smaller mean. What is the first circumstance that is described?

7. In addition to the circumstance you named in response to Question 6, what is the other circumstance?

8. A Pearson *r* is expressed on an invariant scale that can only vary from −1.00 to what higher value?

9. The first step in calculating the average value of r in a meta-analysis is to convert the values of r to what statistic?

10. Is it acceptable to prepare a meta-analysis that includes both values of d and r?

11. If you will be conducting a meta-analysis, do you expect that you will mainly be reporting values of d or values of r? Explain.

Notes:

Chapter 13

A Closer Look at Creating a Synthesis

As you know from Chapter 1, a literature review is a *synthesis* of the literature on a topic. To create the synthesis, one must first interpret and evaluate individual pieces of literature. Then, the ideas and information they contain must be integrated and restated in order to create a new, original written work. By following the guidelines in the earlier chapters, you should now have in hand a first draft of your review, which synthesizes the literature on your topic. The guidelines in this chapter will help you refine your synthesis and make it more understandable and useful to your readers.

✍ Guideline 13.1
Consider providing an overview near the beginning of the literature review.

As you know from Chapter 8, you should begin your literature review by establishing the importance of your topic. Having done that, you might then use a major heading of "Overview" to start a section that provides a general overview of the types of literature you examined and a brief statement of your major conclusions. Note that your conclusions are the culmination of your synthesis. Example 13.1.1 shows an overview that consists of the third, fourth, and fifth paragraphs in a literature review. Note that in the two paragraphs preceding the material in the example (i.e., the first two paragraphs of the review), the reviewers introduce the topic and point out that there are "three literatures" that address their topic, which is social influences on food intake. The "literatures" are: (1) social facilitation, (2) modeling, and (3) impression management.

In Example 13.1.1, some important terms have been bolded in order to draw your attention to them. By talking about a general pattern, stating conclusions based on the *body of literature* (i.e., not based on isolated studies), by combining literature, and by presenting a new model, the reviewers are giving readers an overview of their synthesis.

Example 13.1.1

An "Overview" of a literature review presented near the beginning of the review:

Overview

Below [in the literature review], we provide a detailed narrative review of the three literatures on the effects of the presence of others on eating. Not surprisingly, each of these literatures presents some empirical inconsistencies. Still, a **general pattern** within each literature emerges quite clearly. With only a modest degree of oversimplification, we may **conclude** that (a) when people eat in groups, they tend to eat more than they do when alone (social facilitation); (b) when individuals eat in the presence of models who consistently eat a lot or a little, these individuals likewise tend to eat a lot or a little, respectively (modeling); and (c) when people eat in the presence of others who they believe are observing or evaluating them, they tend to eat less than they do when alone (impression management). **When the three literatures are combined**, then, it appears that the presence of others affects the amount eaten in every possible way. Each individual literature, however, shows substantial consistency.

Along with the narrative reviews that we present below, we discuss the explanations that have been offered in each of the three literatures. These explanations are to a greater or lesser degree inadequate to the task of fully explaining why the presence of others affects eating as it does. **When we consider the three literatures together**, the isolated explanations that have been offered for one or another of these literatures are all the more inadequate. Accordingly, we take this opportunity to **present a new, more general explanatory model** designed to account for the divergent pattern of eating across the three literatures. This new model no doubt has its own limitations, but it is a first step toward a general theory of social influences on eating.

Before we address the individual literatures, we outline our general model. We then apply it to each of the literatures in turn, after we have reviewed the empirical research and prevailing explanations.[1]

Note that in the next chapter, we will consider how to write an abstract of a review, which is usually placed just below the title and author(s)' names (not in the body of a review where an overview should be placed). Traditionally, abstracts are much shorter than overviews.

☙ Guideline 13.2
Consider providing a brief summary at the end of each section of the review.

In Chapter 9, you were urged to be generous in the use of subheadings within your literature review because they help readers understand the organization of your review and help them follow your transitions from one topic or subtopic to another. Each subheading identifies the beginning of a different section of the literature review. As illustrated in Example 13.2.1, a summary serves as a brief synthesis. Note that the first section under "Predisposing Characteristics" consists of five paragraphs, with the fifth one being a summary (with bold added for emphasis). Also, note that the second section under "Initiation: Do Stress and NA Promote Smoking?" consists of only one paragraph, and the reviewers chose not to include a formal summary of that section. However, the reviewers once again provide a summary of the third section under "Stress." Hence, this guideline should not be followed blindly; summaries should be placed at the ends of sections where you deem they are needed.

---

[1] Herman, Roth, & Polivy (2003, p. 874).

It is important to notice that these end-of-section summaries combine literature and, thus, are syntheses of the material in each section.

Example 13.2.1

Three sections of a literature review with section summaries (in bold for emphasis):
Smoking Initiation and Experimentation

Predisposing Characteristics

It has been proposed that variability in smoking status, as well as acute responses to nicotine, may be attributable to stable characteristics of smokers (Gilbert & Gilbert, 1995; O. F. Pomerleau, 1995). For example, numerous studies have found....

There is also evidence suggesting that many psychiatric disorders may be familial and that genetic factors account for a significant proportion of the variance in their etiology (Merikangas, 1995). Just as certain genetically transmitted personality traits (e.g., neuroticism, extraversion, psychoticism) are linked to smoking onset and dependence....

Another manner in which innate constitutional differences might affect the smoking-affect relationship is through initial sensitivity to nicotine. There is reason to believe that early exposure to nicotine in individuals with high innate sensitivity may produce not only aversive effects but also reinforcing consequences, including improvement in affect (O. F. Pomerleau & Pomerleau, 1984). Several findings implicate....

Studies of both rats and mice also support the hypothesis that differences in sensitivity to nicotine effects may be genetically related (Acri, Brown, Saah, & Grunberg, 1995; Marks, Stitzel, & Collins, 1989). Correspondingly, some strains of rats and mice self-administer more nicotine than other strains, although this may....

In sum, individual differences in personality (Heath, Madden, Slutske, & Martin, 1995), innate sensitivity to nicotine (O. F. Pomerleau, 1995), and psychopathology (Gilbert & Gilbert, 1995) are among some of the likely variables associated with NA that appear to predispose to smoking. Both animal and human studies also support the view that genetic differences contribute to the propensity to self-administer nicotine. Such results derive from between-subjects levels of analysis and thus point to possible etiological (within-subject) mechanisms governing smoking-affect associations. However, these results cannot be construed as validating within-subject mechanisms.

Initiation: Do Stress and NA Promote Smoking?

The pathways to becoming a smoker are complex and likely involve more than just genetic makeup. In fact, social factors, such as peer affiliations and peer socialization (e.g., Oetting & Donnermeyer, 1998), have emerged in the literature as perhaps the most potent and reliable predictors of smoking initiation and experimentation. There is also reason to believe.... It is thus critical to distinguish the processes that govern smoking initiation and experimentation from those that underlie progression to nicotine dependence (Colby, Tiffany, Shiffman, & Niaura, 2000; Kassel, 2000a; Shadel, Shiffman, Niaura, Nichter, & Abrams, 2000).

Stress

Numerous studies have found associations between various indices of psychological stress and smoking uptake. Childhood abuse and household dysfunction (Felitti et al., 1998), adverse childhood experiences (Anda et al., 1999), parental divorce (Patton et al., 1998a), negative life events (Koval & Pederson, 1999; Siqueira, Diab, Bodian, & Rolnitzky, 2000), acute and chronic stressors (Koval, Pederson, Mills, McGrady, & Carvajal, 2000), and perceived stress (Dugan, Lloyd, & Lucas, 1999; Siqueira et al., 2000) all have been found to increase the risk for smoking uptake. Byrne and Mazanov (1999) reported that the impact of different types of stressors on smoking uptake varied by gender such that relationships were generally stronger for girls, particularly with respect to family-related stress and smoking. Finally, affective distress and negative life events also appear to predict transition from experimental to regular smoking (see Hirschman et al., 1984; Koval et al., 2000; Orlando, Ellickson, & Jinnett, 2001; Siqueira et al., 2000).

In sum, there is fairly strong evidence that adolescents who experience stress (assessed in a variety of ways) are at heightened risk to begin smoking, as well as to progress to more regular smoking. Although convergent results from both cross-sectional and prospective studies suggest that stress is often an antecedent to smoking onset and not simply a consequence of smoking initiation (e.g., Gorsuch & Butler, 1976; Kandel, Kessler, & Margulies, 1978), potential third-factor causal confounds render interpretation of some studies difficult.[2]

ᴪ Guideline 13.3

Consider providing a comprehensive summary near the end of the review.

A summary of the entire review is often desirable. Ordinarily, this should be placed just before the Conclusions section of a review (see the next guideline).

ᴪ Guideline 13.4

Consider starting the Conclusions section of the literature review with a statement of the purposes of the review.

It is appropriate to state specific purposes of a review near its beginning. In long reviews, the purposes might be restated at the beginning of the Conclusions section.[3] Example 13.4.1 shows the first sentence in the Conclusions section of a lengthy review published as an article in a journal.

Example 13.4.1

A statement of purpose at the beginning of the Conclusions section of a review:

The purpose of this article was to critically review the existing practice-based and empirically based literature on executive coaching to determine (a) what has been written and therefore what is known about executive coaching, (b) whether executive coaching is an effective tool for improving individual and organizational performance, and (c) whether executive coaching is just another business fad.[4]

ᴪ Guideline 13.5

Consider speculating on possible future findings in the Conclusions section of the literature review.

Your conclusions are the final element of the synthesis of the literature on a topic. On almost all topics, there will be important aspects that have not yet been investigated or have been investigated minimally. Your readers will find it helpful if you (who at this point are an expert on the topic) speculate in the Conclusions section on what future studies might reveal.

---

[2] Kassel, Stroud, & Paronis (2003, p. 276).
[3] The final section of a literature review often has the heading "Conclusions." It is also common to use headings such as "Discussion and Conclusions" or "Summary, Discussion, and Conclusions," or some other variation on terms such as "Discussion and Implications."
[4] Kampa-Kokesch & Anderson (2001, p. 222).

Notice that the authors of Example 13.5.1 use the term "speculate," which emphasizes that the statement is speculative in nature—not a statement based on firm empirical evidence. Also, notice the use of the first person (i.e., "we"), which might be appropriate to use in a literature review if it is not so overused that it distracts from the message.[5]

Example 13.5.1

A speculative statement in the Conclusions section of a research report:

Based on available, but minimal data, **we speculate** that the key mechanisms connecting young children's health and SES include unhygienic home environments; conflictual, inconsistent family relationships; child-care quality; stressful life events; and health care access and quality. In adolescence, the role of peer groups; neighborhood environments; and emotional, attitudinal, and cognitive processes gain prominence. These mechanisms are all subject to empirical investigation. Public policies could then target more precise mechanisms once they are verified.[6]

✢ Guideline 13.6
State hypotheses and/or research purposes that are clearly derived from the literature.

Most research reports begin with literature reviews that should lead logically to the hypotheses and/or research purposes that the research examined. When writing such a review, explicitly state how these hypotheses or research purposes are related to the literature reviewed. Do not assume that readers will automatically see the connection between the literature and the hypotheses or purposes. In Example 13.6.1, the authors explicitly point out how their two hypotheses are based on "theorizing" in the literature. The first paragraph describes what is known (or is thought to be known), while the second one draws the connection between this information and the specific hypotheses tested in the study.

Example 13.6.1

Two hypotheses based explicitly on ideas found in the literature:

According to economic theory, workers make rational choices between work and leisure (e.g., Killingsworth, 1993). When workers are paid more, the opportunity costs associated with trading work for leisure also increase, motivating them to seek a new equilibrium between work and leisure by spending more time at work (Killingsworth, 1993). In short, those who are paid more rationally choose to work more because the cost of leisure is too high. Another possibility is that those who work long hours and are paid well have the resources to spend on quick leisure that does not cut too heavily into work time (e.g., a weekend skiing, going to the beach,

---

[5] Check with your instructor on whether the use of the first person is permissible. In academic writing, it is often avoided, as in this book.
[6] Chen, Matthews, & Boyce (2002, p. 322).

or going to the theatre at the end of a business trip). Either explanation leads to the same conclusion: Those who are paid more work more and pursue leisure less.

This theorizing suggests that if managers are making a rational trade-off between work and leisure, there should be a negative relationship between work hours and leisure hours and a negative relationship between total compensation and leisure hours. [Therefore, these hypotheses are consistent with the literature]:

Hypothesis 1: The more hours managers work, the fewer hours they will spend pursuing leisure activities.

Hypothesis 2: The more managers earn, the fewer hours they will spend pursuing leisure activities.[7]

✥ Guideline 13.7
State specific implications in the Conclusions section of the literature review.

Near the end of a Conclusions section, state the implications of your conclusions. The more specific the implications are, the more helpful they will be to your readers. When possible, avoid vague statements of implications such as: "Counselors should be more sensitive to the needs of individuals who are alcohol dependent."

Example 13.7.1 states implications that are quite specific in terms of what clinicians who work with individuals who are alcohol dependent should do. When possible, the implications should be based on research results (such as in Example 13.7.1). When research results are weak or absent, they can be based on theories that are well established or, if necessary, on your speculation (see Guideline 13.5).

Example 13.7.1

A statement of specific implications in the Conclusions section of a review. Implications that suggest specific actions are shown in bold:

Finally, a growing body of research suggests that AA and other 12-step approaches are an effective source of help for alcohol-involved persons. Moreover, AA is one of the few sources of help in the United States that is both widely available and free of charge (except for voluntary contributions), thus offering maximal affordability. This is an important factor to consider for the many alcohol-involved clients for whom cost is a significant consideration (Johnson & Chappel, 1994). Given the efficacy, ubiquity, and accessibility of AA and other 12-step programs, **clinicians are encouraged to consider referring clients to such programs as an adjunct to their treatment and should keep abreast of AA or other self-help meetings in their area of practice.** AA is listed in the yellow pages of phone books in the United States, and a toll-free number for this organization is often provided where schedules of local and regional AA meetings can be obtained. **It is a good idea for**

---

[7] Brett & Stroh (2003, p. 68).

clinicians to keep this information readily available. Further, as Miller and Kurtz (1994) suggested, it is a good idea for clinicians to be familiar with the ideology of AA and with truths and misconceptions regarding this approach in order to adequately prepare clients for referral. Numerous resources exist to help clinicians to work with AA in their clinical practices (Kurtz, 1997; Riordan & Walsh, 1994). Some have noted the importance of differentiating between AA attendance and AA involvement (McCrady et al., 1996). Specifically, degree of personal involvement in AA (e.g., working the steps of AA, spiritual commitment, etc.) has been shown to be associated with better alcohol-related outcomes (Montgomery et al., 1995; Morgenstern et al., 1997). **Thus, clinicians are also encouraged to work with clients not only to attend meetings but also to become more personally invested in this program. This may include using therapy time to talk about AA experiences, making suggestions about finding a sponsor or taking on leadership roles within the organization, and focusing on issues of spirituality and making amends.**[8]

Note that when a literature review is designed to be the introduction to a research report, implications are usually stated at the end of the research report (as opposed to being placed at the end of the introductory literature review) and emphasis in deriving the implications is usually on the original research results presented in the research report. Of course, the research results should be interpreted in light of the previous literature. In other words, in such a situation, there should be a literature review, followed by a report of original research, followed by a Conclusions section that includes implications based on the original research results and consideration of the literature.

Exercise for Chapter 13

1. According to this chapter, should an overview be placed near the beginning *or* near the end of a literature review?

2. According to this chapter, is it mandatory to write a summary to include at the end of each section of a literature review?

3. Example 13.2.1 illustrates that a summary serves as a brief _____.

4. A comprehensive summary should be placed just before what section of a review?

5. You should consider starting the Conclusions section of the literature review with what?

---

[8] Read, Kahler, & Stevenson (2001, p. 230).

6. You should consider speculating on what?

7. Did it surprise you to learn that speculation (when it is adequately identified as speculative) is acceptable in scientific writing? Explain.

8. Most research reports begin with what?

9. When writing a research report, you should state hypotheses and/or research purposes that are clearly derived from what?

10. What is your opinion of the following statement of implications included near the end of the Conclusions and Implications section of a research report?

    "The implication of this finding is that teachers need to be more sensitive to students' needs."

11. Assuming that the findings regarding Alcoholics Anonymous (AA) stated in Example 13.7.1 are correct, do you think that the implications are appropriate? Do you think that they are sufficiently specific? Explain.

Chapter 14

Writing Titles and Abstracts

This chapter will help you write effective titles and abstracts. A title helps readers locate reviews of interest to them. Because an abstract provides a brief summary of a literature review, it also helps readers locate relevant reviews.

✣ Guideline 14.1
A title should be brief.

Typically, the title of a literature review published in academic journals consists of about 10 to 14 words. Example 14.1.1 shows some titles of typical length.

Example 14.1.1
Titles of typical length for literature reviews published in academic journals:

The Role of Physical Exercise in Alcoholism Treatment and Recovery[1]
  –10 words

Advances in the Diagnosis and Treatment of Autism Spectrum Disorders[2]
  –10 words

The Role of Language in Training Psychologists to Work with Hispanic Clients[3]
  –12 words

If your review contains a discussion of many variables related to your topic, consider referring to the variables in groups instead of by their individual names. Example 14.1.2 illustrates this. For instance, "physical stamina, strength, and body weight" in the original title are referred to by the single term "Physical Benefits" in the improved version of the title.

Example 14.1.2
A lengthy title improved by referring to variables in groups:

Original title: Benefits of Physical Education for Primary Grade Students in Terms of Ability to Make Friends, Cooperation Among Each Other, Physical Stamina, Strength, and Body Weight

Improved title: Social and Physical Benefits of Physical Education for Primary Grade Students

---

[1] Read & Brown (2003, p. 49).
[2] Kabot, Masi, & Segal (2003, p. 26).
[3] Biever et al. (2002, p. 330).

✎ Guideline 14.2

A title should be a statement—not a complete sentence.

All the titles under the previous guideline illustrate this guideline because they do not have subjects and verbs to make them complete sentences. Note that because they are not sentences they should not end with period marks.

✎ Guideline 14.3

Avoid using a question that can be answered with a "yes" or "no" as a title.

Almost any topic being reviewed is sufficiently complex that a simple "yes" or "no" answer would be an oversimplified conclusion. In Example 14.3.1, the title in the form of a question has been improved by restating it as a statement.

Example 14.3.1

A title in the form of a question improved by restating it as a statement:

Original title: Do Depression and Anxiety Interfere with Smoking Cessation Efforts?

Improved title: The Influence of Depression and Anxiety on Smoking Cessation Efforts

✎ Guideline 14.4

Consider using a subtitle to amplify a main title.

Using a subtitle sometimes helps to create a title that is more comprehensible. Obviously, the topic of the review should be stated in the main title, and factors that amplify it should be stated in the subtitle. This is illustrated by the three titles in Example 14.4.1.

Example 14.4.1

Titles in which the main titles are amplified by subtitles:

First title: The Social Risk Hypothesis of Depressed Mood: Evolutionary, Psychosocial, and Neurobiological Perspectives[4]

Second title: Victimization and Substance Abuse Among Women: Contributing Factors, Interventions, and Implications[5]

Third title: Genetic Testing: Psychological Aspects and Implications[6]

Note that implications should be discussed in all literature reviews. Hence, it is safe to assume that implications will be discussed without its mention in a title. However, if there is emphasis on implications in the review or if new and very important implications are

---

[4] Allen & Badcock (2003, p 887).
[5] Logan, Walker, Cole, & Leukefeld (2002, p. 325).
[6] Lerman, Croyle, Tercyak, & Hamann (2002, p. 784).

presented, it would be appropriate to include the term "implications" in a title as was done in the second and third titles in Example 14.4.1.

✍ Guideline 14.5
Consider using a subtitle to indicate that the document is a review.

Consider using the terms "review," "meta-analysis," or some derivative of them in the subtitle. Using these terms will help readers who are trying to identify reviews (as opposed to reports of original research). Example 14.5.1 contains titles that follow this guideline.

Example 14.5.1
Titles with subtitles that indicate that the document is a review:

Developmental and Contextual Factors that Influence Gay Fathers' Parental Competence: A Review of the Literature[7]

Relationship of Personality to Performance Motivation: A Meta-Analytic Review[8]

The Job Satisfaction–Job Performance Relationship: A Qualitative and Quantitative Review[9]

Note that if you are writing a literature review as a class project, your instructor may prefer that you use a subtitle to amplify the main title (see the previous guideline) because he or she already knows that the document you submit to him or her is a literature review.

Another exception to this guideline is if you are writing for a journal that publishes only literature reviews (e.g., *Psychological Bulletin*). For such journals, the terms "review" and "literature review" are usually omitted from titles. Because meta-analysis is a relatively new set of techniques, however, it is customary to mention the term "meta-analysis" in subtitles, even in such journals.

✍ Guideline 14.6
An abstract should begin by naming the topic being reviewed.

Two abstracts that begin naming the topic of the review are shown in Example 14.6.1. Note that these abstracts are of about typical length.

Example 14.6.1
Two abstracts that begin by naming the topic being reviewed:

First abstract (for a qualitative review): We review research on programs designed to promote family wellness and prevent the maltreatment of children. Based on this review, we conclude that there is currently no evidence that educational programs prevent child sexual abuse. Only home visitation programs have been shown to prevent child physical abuse and neglect, and multicomponent, community-based

---

[7] Armesto (2002, p. 67).
[8] Judge & Ilies (2002, p. 797).
[9] Judge, Thoresen, Bono, & Patton (2001, p. 376).

programs have been shown to promote family wellness and prevent a number of negative outcomes for children. The most effective programs are those that address several different ecological levels of analysis, begin at birth, are long-term and intensive, are flexible, responsive, and controlled by the local community, and are based on respectful and trusting relationships between community members and staff, who are well trained and competent.[10]

Second abstract (for a quantitative review): Although the merits of parents using corporal punishment to discipline children have been argued for decades, a thorough understanding of whether and how corporal punishment affects children has not been reached. Toward this end, the author first presents the results of meta-analyses of the association between parental corporal punishment and 11 child behaviors and experiences. Parental corporal punishment was associated with all child constructs, including higher levels of immediate compliance and aggression and lower levels of moral internalization and mental health. The author then presents a process–context model to explain how parental corporal punishment might cause particular child outcomes and considers alternative explanations. The article concludes by identifying seven major remaining issues for future research.[11]

Note that the authors of the first abstract in Example 14.6.1 refer to themselves in the first person (i.e., "we"). The author of the second abstract refers to herself in the third person as "the author." An alternative to these two devices is to use the passive voice. For instance, instead of saying, "**We review** research on programs designed to promote family wellness and prevent the maltreatment of children," the authors could have used the passive voice and said, "The research on programs designed to promote family wellness and prevent the maltreatment of children **was reviewed**." Use of the passive voice is much more common than use of the first or third voices in academic writing.

✍ Guideline 14.7

An abstract should emphasize the findings and conclusions—not other elements such as how the literature was searched.

The two abstracts in Example 14.6.1 and the abstract in Example 14.8.1 illustrate this guideline.

---

[10] Nelson, Laurendeau, & Chamberland (2001, p. 1).
[11] Gershoff (2002, p. 539).

↳ Guideline 14.8

It is acceptable, but not necessary, to cite specific statistics in the abstract of a meta-analysis.

Meta-analyses produce statistics such as *d* and *r*. Including their values in an abstract can be informative. Example 14.8.1 illustrates how this can be done.

Example 14.8.1

An abstract of a meta-analytic review that includes statistics (i.e., values of d*):*

A meta-analysis was conducted on studies using a treatment–comparison group design to evaluate HIV/AIDS risk-reduction interventions for clients enrolled in drug abuse treatment programs. Overall, the interventions studied were found to have a reliable positive (weighted) effect size ($d = 0.31$), and this was unlikely to be due to publication bias. Effect sizes for specific categories of outcome variables were 0.31 for knowledge, attitudes, and beliefs; 0.26 for sexual behavior; 0.62 for risk-reduction skills; and 0.04 for injection practices. A number of potential moderators were examined. Effect sizes were negatively correlated with the presence of predominantly ethnic minority samples and positively correlated with the number of intervention techniques used, the intensity of the intervention, intervention delivery at a later stage of drug treatment or within methadone treatment, and the presence of a number of specific intervention techniques.[12]

Exercise for Chapter 14

1. According to this chapter, a title typically contains about how many words?

2. If you review many variables related to your topic, what should you consider doing in the title of your review?

3. Should a title be a complete sentence?

4. Does this chapter encourage you to use a yes–no question as the title of a review?

5. You should consider using a subtitle to do what two things?

6. An abstract should begin by naming what?

7. An abstract should emphasize what?

---

[12] Prendergast, Urada, & Podus (2001, p. 389).

8. Is it acceptable to cite specific statistics in the abstract of a meta-analysis?

9. Critique the following title of a literature review.

   "Socioeconomic Status Plays a Role in Determining Physical Health."

10. Critique the following title of a literature review.

    "Is Depression Related to HIV Risk Behaviors?"

11. Critique the following abstract of a literature review.

    "The ERIC database was searched by computer to identify all evaluations of driving-under-the-influence (DUI) school-based prevention programs. In all, a total of 15 evaluations were identified. Of these, only ten met the criterion of having a control or comparison group. These ten were carefully examined, compared, and contrasted in order to reach general conclusions regarding the effectiveness of such programs. Implications for educators and directions for future research are discussed."

Chapter 15

Citing References

A reference list should be placed at the end of the literature review under the main heading "References." As you know from Chapter 9, it is important to cross-check the references cited in the body of your review against those in your reference list at the end to make sure that they match (see Guideline 9.11). For instance, make sure that the spelling of the names in the citations in the body of your literature review are the same as in the reference list.

The most widely used method for citing references is the Harvard method. When using it, a reviewer uses the last name(s) and year of publication in the text to refer to a source. As you know from Guideline 9.10, there are two ways to do this. First, it can be done by using the surname of the author(s) in the body of a sentence, usually as the subject of a sentence, which is illustrated here:

"In a rigorous experimental study, Smith (2004) found strong support for the ABC Theory."

Second, it can be done by making the name and date parenthetical, with the surname and date in parentheses as illustrated here:

"A rigorous experimental study found strong support for the ABC Theory (Smith, 2004)."

Of the two ways, the second is usually preferred because it keeps the sentence focused on the topic and not on the name of the researcher who investigated the topic. (See Guideline 9.10 for more information and examples.)

The Harvard Method has been adapted by the American Psychological Association (APA) as the organization's style for use in their journals, books, and other publications. Their version of the method is described in great detail in the *Publication Manual of the American Psychological Association*, which is available in most college and university bookstores. If it is unavailable to you there, you can purchase it directly from APA (for information on how to do so, visit www.apa.org).

The APA's *Publication Manual* is strongly recommended, not only for learning their method of citing references, but also because it covers many difficult issues for writers such as avoiding sexist language and determining who will be listed first when there are multiple authors of a paper, and so on.

✎ Guideline 15.1

A reference list for a literature review should refer to only publications cited in the literature review.

Writers often have some materials that, for one reason or another, were not cited in their reviews. References for these uncited materials should *not* be included in the reference list at the end of a literature review.

✎ Guideline 15.2

List references alphabetically by surname, and use hanging indents to make it easy to locate surnames.

A hanging indent is created when the first line is *not* indented but the subsequent ones are indented, as in Example 15.2.1, where the surnames of the authors stand out on the left margin of the list. Note that to create a hanging indent in Microsoft Word, click on a reference with the right button, then click on "Paragraph," then click on the pull down menu (down arrow) under "Special:," which will reveal the choice "Hanging," which you should click on.

Example 15.2.1
Two references in alphabetical order with hanging indents:

Apple, D. W. (2004). A test of the XYZ phenomenon: Experimental evidence. *The Journal of New Developments, 55*, 99–104.

Boy, C. C. (2003). New evidence on the validity of the XYZ phenomenon: New perspectives and implications for counselors. *Psychological Renderings, 44*, 454–499.

✎ Guideline 15.3

Use italics appropriately, such as for titles of books and journals as well as volume numbers of journals.

As you know from basic English classes, the titles of books should be italicized. Likewise, journal titles are also italicized because in traditional nonelectronic publishing, academic libraries bind all issues of a journal published in a year with hard binding, which creates a book. For a journal article, the volume number should also be italicized in the reference list because the volume number is used to distinguish one bound volume from another. (See the next guideline for more information on this matter.)

Note that before modern word processing programs were available, it was not possible for a typist to italicize because there were no keys with italicized letters on a typewriter. Therefore, typists would <u>underline</u> any material that they wanted to have a typesetter (using typesetting equipment) subsequently set in italics. It is no longer necessary to underline because with a word processing program, it is just as easy to italicize as it is to underline. However, some instructors and style manuals prefer the traditional look of underlining in papers that are not yet published. Check with your instructor for guidance on this matter.

✍ Guideline 15.4

Provide volume numbers (but not issue numbers) for journal articles.

Each year, a journal typically publishes between four and 12 *issues*, such as the spring, summer, fall, and winter issues. All the issues for a year constitute a *volume*. All pages within a volume are sequentially numbered, regardless of the issue. For instance, if the first issue for a year ends on page 97, the second issue for that year begins on page 98. Hence, to identify a journal article, it is not necessary to refer to the issue number because the volume number and page numbers identify an article. Consider the reference in Example 15.4.1. Note that the volume number (*33*) is in italics just after the title of the journal (with a comma separating the title and volume number).[1]

Example 15.4.1

A reference to a journal article, with the title and volume number italicized:

Smith, A. B., & Doe, V. R. (2004). Another look at a new theory of disassociation: New evidence questioning its validity. *Current Trends in Sociology, 33*, 222–234.

✍ Guideline 15.5

Capitalize the first letters of proper nouns, but only the first letters of the first word in titles and subtitles of journal articles.

The first letters of proper nouns (such as authors' names and the titles of journals) should be capitalized. The title of a journal article, however, is not a proper noun and should not be capitalized in a reference list (except for the first letter of the title and subtitle, if any).[2] You can see this in Example 15.4.1 above where the letter "A" at the beginning of the main title of the article as well as the letter "N" in "New" in the subtitle are capitalized. (There are no capital letters in "look at a new theory of disassociation" in the main title or in "evidence questioning its validity" in the subtitle.)

---

[1] Note the comma between Smith's and Doe's names.
[2] Of course, when the title of an article or literature review is placed in the body of a review, the first letters of all main words should be capitalized in order to identify it.

↵ Guideline 15.6

Check for punctuation, especially for commas between elements such as authors' names and period marks at the ends of lists.

As you know from basic English, elements in a list such as a list of authors' names or a list of the elements that identify a particular journal article (i.e., title, volume number, and page numbers) should be separated by commas. Use a period mark at the end of each list. These principles are followed in Example 15.4.1 above, which shows a period mark after the publication year ["(2004)."] at the end of the list of authors' names, and at the very end after the ending page number (i.e., "222–234."). Note that the word "pages" or the abbreviation "pp." are not needed because they are always the last element in a reference.

↵ Guideline 15.7

Provide the date and URL for any reference citations to material published on the Internet.

Because material published on the Web may easily be modified from time to time (unlike the contents of journals, which are not modified, and unlike books, for which no changes are made in a given edition), it is important to indicate the date on which material from the Internet was retrieved. Also, be sure to provide the full URL (such as www.example.com/retrieve) as well as any other identifying information such as the name of the author, if known. See Example 15.7.1.

Example 15.7.1

A reference to material retrieved from the Internet:

Jones, A. A. (1999). Some new thoughts on material evidence in the XYZ matter. Retrieved January 2, 2004, from www.newexample.org/specimen

Exercise for Chapter 15

1. Suppose you located some interesting material that you did not include in your literature review. According to this chapter, should you include a reference to it in your reference list?

2. Should the reference list be arranged by date (with the newest reference listed first) *or* alphabetically by authors' surnames?

3. Should the title of a journal article be in italics (i.e., underlined if using a typewriter)?

4. Should the title of a journal be in italics (i.e., underlined if using a typewriter)?

5. In the following reference, what element is missing its italics?

> Doe, J. Y. (2004). An experimental study of the feasibility of modifying the school lunch program. *New Journal of Educational Studies and Research,* 63, 555–578.

6. The following reference to a journal article contains information that is not needed to identify the article. What information is not needed?

> Smith, J. Y. (2004). A new experiment on the feasibility of further modifying the school lunch program. *Extensive Lunch Programs Journal,* 33, Issue 52, 67–74.

7. Which word in the following reference should start with a capital letter?

> Jones, V. M., Hart, J. J., & Smith, O. W. (2003). Evidence regarding the effects of exercise on mental health: another replication. *Journal of Physical Exercise and Recreation, 21,* 102–119.

8. Should the word "pages" be placed before "67–74" in Question 6?

9. In the following reference, a period mark is missing. Where should it be placed?

> Babbitt, D. C., Doe, M. B., & Rice, B. R. (2002) A new measure of racial prejudice based on social distancing. *Journal of Social and Political Issues, 19,* 102–119.

10. In the following reference, two commas are missing. Where should they be placed?

> Banks, Q. M. Barnes, B. J. & Leland, C. C. (2003). Evidence regarding the effects of exercise on mental health: Another replication. *Journal of Physical Exercise and Recreation,* Vol. *33,* 102–119.

11. For which of the following should you include the date that you consulted the reference?
    A. Material posted on the Web.
    B. Material published in a journal.
    C. Material published in a book.

Notes:

References

Akinbami, L. J., Cheng, T. L., & Kornfeld, D. (2001). A review of teen–tot programs: Comprehensive clinical care for young parents and their children. *Adolescence, 36,* 381–393.

Allen, N. B., & Badcock, P. B. T. (2003). The social risk hypothesis of depressed mood: Evolutionary, psychosocial, and neurobiological perspectives. *Psychological Bulletin, 129,* 887–913.

American Psychological Association. (2001). *Publication Manual of the American Psychological Association* (5th ed.). Washington, DC: American Psychological Association.

Armesto, J. C. (2002). Developmental and contextual factors that influence gay fathers' parental competence: A review of literature. *Psychology of Men & Masculinity, 3,* 67–78.

Balasubramanian, S. K., & Cole, C. (2002). Consumers' search and use of nutrition information: The challenge and promise of the Nutrition Labeling and Information Act. *Journal of Marketing, 66,* 112–127.

Biever, J. L., Castano, M. T., de las Fuentes, C., Gonzalez, C., Servin-Lopez, S., Sprowls, C., & Tripp, C. G. (2002). The role of language in training psychologists to work with Hispanic clients. *Professional Psychology: Research & Practice, 33,* 330–336.

Blok, H., Oostdam, R., Otter, M. E., & Overmaat, M. (2002). Computer-assisted instruction in support of beginning reading instruction: A review. *Review of Educational Research, 72,* 101–130.

Bloomer, S. R., Sipe, T. A., & Ruedt, D. E. (2002). Child support payment and child visitation: Perspectives from nonresident fathers and resident mothers. *Journal of Sociology and Social Welfare, 29,* 77–91.

Brett, J. M., & Stroh, L. K. (2003). Working 61 plus hours a week: Why do managers do it? *Journal of Applied Psychology, 88,* 67–78.

Carlsmith, K. M., Darley, J. M., & Robinson, P. H. (2002). Why do we punish?: Deterrence and just deserts as motives for punishment. *Journal of Personality & Social Psychology, 83,* 284–299.

Chapin, M. H., & Kewman, D. G. (2001). Factors affecting employment following spinal cord injury: A qualitative study. *Rehabilitation Psychology, 46,* 400–416.

Chen, E., Matthews, K. A., & Boyce, W. T. (2002). Socioeconomic differences in children's health: How and why do these relationships change with age? *Psychological Bulletin, 128,* 295–329.

Cheng, T. (2002). Welfare recipients: How do they become independent? *Social Work Research, 26,* 159–170.

Christopherson, N., Janning, M., McConnell, E. D. (2002). Two kicks forward, one kick back: A content analysis of media discourses on the 1999 Women's World Cup Soccer Championship. *Sociology of Sport Journal, 19,* 170–188.

Cohen, J. (1992). A power primer. *Psychological Bulletin, 112,* 155–159.

Coles, R. L. (2003). Black single custodial fathers: Factors influencing the decision to parent. *Families in Society, 84,* 247–258.

Cook, F. L., Barabas, J., & Page, B. I. (2002). Invoking public opinion: Policy elites and social security. *Public Opinion Quarterly, 66,* 235–264.

Dirks, K. T., & Ferrin, D. L. (2002). Trust in leadership: Meta-analytic findings and implications for research and practice. *Journal of Applied Psychology, 87,* 611–628.

Drigotas, S. M., Rusbult, C. E., & Verette, J. (1999). Level of commitment, mutuality of commitment, and couple well-being. *Personal Relationships, 6,* 389–409.

Duggan, C. H., & Dijkers, M. (2001). Quality of life after spinal cord injury: A qualitative study. *Rehabilitation Psychology, 46,* 3–27.

Elfenbein, H. A., & Ambady, N. (2002). On the universality and cultural specificity of emotion recognition: A meta-analysis. *Psychological Bulletin, 128,* 203–235.

Elliot, L., Foster, S., & Stinson, M. (2002). Student study habits using notes from a speech-to-text support service. *Exceptional Children, 69,* 25–40.

Fischer, R. L. (2003). School-based family support: Evidence from an exploratory field study. *Families in Society, 84,* 339–347.

Frank, E., & Brandstaetter, V. (2002). Approach versus avoidance: Different types of commitment in intimate relationships. *Journal of Personality & Social Psychology, 82,* 208–221.

Franze, S. E., Foster, M., Abbott-Shim, M., McCarty, F., & Lambert, R. (2002). Describing Head Start family service workers: An examination of factors related to job satisfaction, empowerment, and multiculturalism. *Families in Society: The Journal of Contemporary Human Services, 83,* 257–264.

Gershoff, E. T. (2002). Corporal punishment by parents and associated child behaviors and experiences: A meta-analytic and theoretical review. *Psychological Bulletin, 128,* 539–579.

Greenberg, B. S., Eastin, M., Hofschire, K., Lachlan, & Brownell, K. D. (2003). Portrayals of overweight and obese individuals on commercial television. *American Journal of Public Health, 93,* 1342–1348.

Griffin, E. (1994). *A first look at communication theory* (2nd Ed.). New York: McGraw-Hill, Inc.

Grusec, J. E. (1992). Social learning theory and developmental psychology: The legacies of Robert Sears and Albert Bandura. *Developmental Psychology, 28,* 776–786.

Harris, R. A. (2001). *The plagiarism handbook: Strategies for preventing, detecting, and dealing with plagiarism.* Los Angeles: Pyrczak Publishing.

Harris, R. A. (2003). *Writing with clarity and style: A guide to rhetorical devices for contemporary writers.* Los Angeles: Pyrczak Publishing.

Hausenblas, H. A., Nigg, C. R., Downs, D. S., Fleming, D. S., & Connaughton, D. P. (2002). Perceptions of exercise stages, barrier self-efficacy, and decisional balance for middle-level school students. *Journal of Early Adolescence, 22,* 436–454.

Henderlong, J., & Lepper, M. R. (2002). The effects of praise on children's intrinsic motivation: A review and synthesis. *Psychological Bulletin, 128,* 774–795.

Herman, C. P., Roth, D. A., & Polivy, J. (2003). Effects of the presence of others on food intake: A normative interpretation. *Psychological Bulletin, 129,* 873–886.

Hionidou, V. (2002). Why do people die in famines? Evidence from three island populations. *Population Studies, 56,* 65–80.

Hunter, K. G. (2002). An application of herd theory to interest group behavior. *Administration & Society, 34*, 389–410.

Judge, T. A., & Ilies, R. (2002). Relationship of personality to performance motivation: A meta-analytic review. *Journal of Applied Psychology, 87*, 797–807.

Judge, T. A., Thoresen, C. J., Bono, J. E., & Patton, G. K. (2001). The job satisfaction–job performance relationship: A qualitative and quantitative review. *Psychological Bulletin, 127*, 376–407.

Kabot, S., Masi, W., & Segal, M. (2003). Advances in the diagnosis and treatment of autism spectrum disorders. *Professional Psychology: Research and Practice, 34*, 26–33.

Kampa-Kokesch, S., & Anderson, M. Z. (2001). Executive coaching: A comprehensive review of the literature. *Consulting Psychology Journal: Practice and Research, 53*, 205–228.

Kassel, J. D., Stroud, L. R., & Paronis, C. A. (2003). Smoking, stress, and negative affect: Correlation, causation, and context across stages of smoking. *Psychological Bulletin, 129*, 270–304.

Kegler, M. C., McCormick, L., Crawford, M., Allen, P., Spigner, C., & Ureda, J. (2002). An exploration of family influences on smoking among ethnically diverse adolescents. *Health Education & Behavior, 29*, 473–490.

Kuncel, N. R., Hezlett, S. A., & Ones, D. S. (2001). A comprehensive meta-analysis of the predictive validity of the Graduate Record Examinations: Implications for graduate student selection and performance. *Psychological Bulletin, 127*, 162–181.

Kuther, T. L. (2003). Medical decision-making and minors: Issues of consent and assent. *Adolescence, 38*, 343–358.

Lerman, C., Croyle, R. T., Tercyak, K. P., & Hamann, H. (2002). Genetic testing: Psychological aspects and implications. *Journal of Consulting & Clinical Psychology, 70*, 784–797.

Locke, E. A., & Latham, G. P. (2002). Building a practically useful theory of goal setting and task motivation. *American Psychologist, 57*, 705–717.

Logan, T. K., Walker, R., Cole, J., & Leukefeld, C. (2002). Victimization and substance abuse among women: Contributing factors, interventions, and implications. *Review of General Psychology, 6*, 325–397.

Loneck, B., Banks, S., Way, B., & Bonaparte, E. (2002). An empirical model of therapeutic process for psychiatric emergency room clients with dual disorders. *Social Work Research, 26*, 132–144.

Lupton, R. A., & Chapman, K. J. (2002). Russian and American college students' attitudes, perceptions, and tendencies towards cheating. *Educational Research, 44*, 17–27.

Lydon, J. E. (1996). Toward a theory of commitment. In C. Seligman, J. Olson, & M. Zanna (Eds.), *Values: The Eighth Ontario Symposium* (pp. 191–213). Hillsdale, NJ: Erlbaum.

McKay, J. R., Pettinati, H. M., Morrison, R., Feeley, M., Mulvaney, F. D., & Gallop, R. (2002). Relation of depression diagnoses to 2-year outcomes in cocaine-dependent patients in a randomized continuing care study. *Psychology of Addictive Behaviors, 16*, 225–235.

Merriam-Webster Unabridged Dictionary [electronic version]. (2002). Springfield, MA: Merriam Webster.

Nelson, G., Laurendeau, M. C., & Chamberland, C. (2001). A review of programs to promote family wellness and prevent the maltreatment of children. *Canadian Journal of Behavioural Science, 33,* 1–13.

Patten, M. (2004). *Understanding research methods: An overview of the essentials* (4th ed.). Glendale, CA: Pyrczak Publishing.

Pinto, R. M. (2002). Social work values, welfare reform, and immigrant citizenship conflicts. *Families in Society: The Journal of Contemporary Human Services, 83,* 85–92.

Porta, C., Handelman, E., & McGovern, P. (1999). Needlestick injuries among health care workers: A literature review. *AAOHN Journal, 47,* 237–244.

Prendergast, M. L., Urada, D., & Podus, D. (2001). Meta-analysis of HIV risk-reduction interventions within drug abuse treatment programs. *Journal of Consulting and Clinical Psychology, 69,* 389–405.

Purdie, N., Hattie, J., & Carroll, A. (2002). A review of the research on interventions for Attention Deficit Hyperactivity Disorder: What works best? *Review of Educational Research, 72,* 61–99.

Read, J. P., & Brown, R. A. (2003). The role of physical exercise in alcoholism treatment and recovery. *Professional Psychology: Research and Practice, 34,* 49–56.

Read, J. P., Kahler, C. W., & Stevenson, J. F. (2001). Bridging the gap between alcoholism treatment research and practice: Identifying what works and why. *Professional Psychology: Research and Practice, 32,* 227–238.

Rhee, S. H., & Waldman, I. D. (2002). Genetic and environmental influences on antisocial behavior: A meta-analysis of twin and adoption studies. *Psychological Bulletin, 128,* 490–529.

Rhoades, L., & Eisenberger, R. (2002). Perceived organizational support: A review of the literature. *Journal of Applied Psychology, 87,* 698–714.

Rubinstein, M. L., Halpern-Felsher, B. L., Thompson, P. J., & Millstein, S. G. (2003). Adolescents discriminate between types of smokers and related risks: Evidence from nonsmokers. *Journal of Adolescent Research, 18,* 651–663.

Schmitz, C. L., Wagner, J. D., & Menke, E. M. (2001). The interconnection of childhood poverty and homelessness: Negative impact/points of access. *Families in Society: The Journal of Contemporary Human Services, 82,* 69–77.

Segrin, C. (2003). Age moderates the relationship between social support and psychosocial problems. *Human Communication Research, 29,* 317–342.

Somers, M. J. (1995). Organizational commitment, turnover and absenteeism: An examination of direct and interaction effects. *Journal of Organizational Behavior, 16,* 49–58.

Sternberg, R. J. (2003). A duplex theory of hate: Development and application to terrorism, massacres, and genocide. *Review of General Psychology, 7,* 299–328.

Torres-Reyna, O., & Shapiro, R. Y. (2002). The polls–trends: Defense and the military. *Public Opinion Quarterly, 66,* 279–303.

Unger, J. B., Gallaher, P., Shakib, S., Ritt-Olson, A., Palmer, P. H., & Johnson, C. A. (2002). The AHIMSA Acculturation Scale: A new measure of acculturation for adolescents in a multicultural society. *Journal of Early Adolescence, 22,* 225–251.

References

Van Lange, P. A. M., Rusbult, C. E., Drigotas, S. M., Arriaga, X. B., Witcher, B. S., & Cox, C. L. (1997). Willingness to sacrifice in close relationships. *Journal of Personality and Social Psychology, 72,* 1373–1395.

Walker, J. (2003). Radiating messages: An international perspective. *Family Relations, 52,* 406–417.

Wood, S. J., Murdock, J. Y., & Cronin, M. E. (2002). Self-monitoring and at-risk middle school students. *Behavior Modification, 26,* 605–626.

Zechmeister, J. S., & Romero, C. (2002). Victim and offender accounts of interpersonal conflict: Autobiographical narratives of forgiveness and unforgiveness. *Journal of Personality & Social Psychology, 82,* 675–686.

Notes:

Appendix A

Checklist of Guidelines

Instructors may want to refer to the following checklist numbers when commenting on students' writing. Students can use this checklist to review important points as they prepare their literature reviews.

Chapter 1 Qualitative Versus Quantitative Reviews

____ 1.1   In quantitatively oriented literature reviews, precise statistical results from the literature are presented and sometimes mathematically combined.

____ 1.2   If the main thrust of a review is the mathematical combination of results of studies by various researchers, the result is called a meta-analysis or meta-analytic review.

____ 1.3   In qualitatively oriented reviews, statistical studies are often described in general terms, but precise statistical values are de-emphasized.

____ 1.4   Qualitative and quantitative reviews have many common features.

____ 1.5   Many literature reviews are a blend of qualitatively oriented and quantitatively oriented approaches.

____ 1.6   Distinguish between qualitative versus quantitative *literature reviews* and qualitative versus quantitative *empirical research*.

____ 1.7   Read both qualitatively oriented and quantitatively oriented reviews in preparation for writing a new review.

Chapter 2 Selecting a Topic for Review

____ 2.1   Consider carefully your audience's expectations and/or requirements when selecting a topic.

____ 2.2   When selecting a topic, emphasize your audience's expectations and requirements instead of your personal interests.

____ 2.3   Put possible topics *in writing*. If your professor is your audience, ask him or her to examine your written topic ideas.

____ 2.4   Consider brainstorming a list of possible topics.

____ 2.5   Consider starting by initially selecting broad topics and then narrowing them by adding delimitations.

____ 2.6   Scan titles and abstracts of articles in your topic area early in the process of selecting a topic.

____ 2.7   Consider selecting a topic on which there is theoretical literature.

____ 2.8   Consider selecting a theory as the topic for a literature review.

____ 2.9   Consider preliminary definitions of the terms in the topics you are considering.

____ 2.10   If your literature review will introduce your original empirical research, strive for a close fit between the topic(s) reviewed and the variables studied in your research.

____ 2.11   Consider your orientation and whether a topic you are considering lends itself more to qualitative or quantitative analysis.

____ 2.12   Consider reviewing the literature on instrument(s) or assessment procedure(s).

____ 2.13   Select a topic with an eye toward your future goals and activities.

Chapter 3   Searching for Literature and Refining the Topic

____ 3.1   Invest time in learning how to conduct advanced searches of a database.

____ 3.2   Familiarize yourself with the Boolean operators NOT, AND, and OR.

____ 3.3   Consider using demographics to delimit your search.

____ 3.4   Search for theoretical literature on your topic.

____ 3.5   Examine the references cited in the literature that you locate.

____ 3.6   Search databases for the names of prominent individuals who have written on your topic.

____ 3.7   Consider using the term "history" as a keyword in a database search.

____ 3.8   Consider using "definition" as a keyword in a database search.

____ 3.9   Consider using an exact phrase match.

____ 3.10   Consider using truncated terms or wildcards.

____ 3.11   Consider using the term "review" as a keyword in a database search.

____ 3.12   Consider using the term "qualitative" as a keyword in a database search.

____ 3.13   Consider restricting your search to the title and/or abstract fields.

____ 3.14   Consider restricting your search to the author field.

____ 3.15   Consider searching a citation index.

____ 3.16   Maintain a written record of how you conducted your literature search.

Chapter 4   Retrieving and Evaluating Information from the Web

____ 4.1   FedStats is a very important source of statistical information.

____ 4.2   State and local governments and their agencies often post very current statistics on the Web.

____ 4.3   Use the raw statistics from governmental agencies, not statistics filtered by individuals or groups with special interests.

____ 4.4   Consider consulting the Library of Congress's Virtual Reference Shelf on the Web.

____ 4.5   Consider accessing information posted on the Web by associations and businesses.

____   4.6   Major search engines used by the public at large often provide helpful information for use in academic literature reviews.

____   4.7   Pay attention to the extension (gov, edu, org, com, and net) in the results of Web searches.

____   4.8   Consider clicking on "cached" when opening a Web site from a search engine.

____   4.9   When you find a Web site that is very useful, consider following the links, if any, that it provides.

Chapter 5   Taking Notes and Avoiding Unintentional Plagiarism

____   5.1   Common knowledge does not need to be cited, but original expressions of it should be cited.

____   5.2   If you rephrase someone else's idea in your own words, the original source should be cited.

____   5.3   Failure to indicate clearly the beginning *and* end of summarized literature may lead to charges of plagiarism.

____   5.4   Establish criteria for the inclusion of literature in your review.

____   5.5   Give each piece of literature a unique identifier such as the surname of the first author.

____   5.6   While taking notes, consider building a table that summarizes key points in the literature you are reviewing.

____   5.7   Consider using color-coding while reading and making notes.

____   5.8   Pay special attention to definitions while taking notes.

____   5.9   Pay special attention to researchers' descriptions of the limitations of their research methodology.

____   5.10 It is misleading to read and make notes only on the abstracts of articles without disclosing the fact that you have done so.

____   5.11 Make notes on how other writers have organized the literature on your topic.

Chapter 6   Guidelines for Evaluating Sources of Literature

____   6.1   Even the most prestigious sources publish reports of flawed research.

____   6.2   Consider who sponsors a publication. Professional associations, foundations, government agencies, and for-profit companies are major sponsors.

____   6.3   Check to see whether a journal (or publisher) has an independent editorial board.

____   6.4   Check to see whether a journal uses a "blind" peer-review process when selecting manuscripts for publication. (This is also called a "juried process.")

____   6.5   Consider the institutional affiliation of the author.

____   6.6   Consider the overall quality of a journal in which an article is published.

____   6.7   Consider the typical length of articles published in a journal.

Chapter 7 Evaluating and Interpreting Research Literature

____ 7.1   Be wary of sources offering "proof," "facts," and "truth" based on research evidence.

____ 7.2   Research is almost always flawed by inadequate samples.

____ 7.3   Be cautious when a body of literature has a common sampling flaw.

____ 7.4   Research is almost always flawed by inadequate measures.

____ 7.5   Consider the reliability of measures used in research.

____ 7.6   Consider the validity of measures used in research.

____ 7.7   Consider researchers' self-critiques of their own research methods.

____ 7.8   Be cautious when researchers refer to causality.

____ 7.9   Assess the strengths of trends across studies when evaluating literature.

____ 7.10 Recognize the limitations of significance testing.

Chapter 8 Planning and Writing the First Draft

____ 8.1   Before preparing an outline, review your notes and group them according to content.

____ 8.2   When beginning to build a topic outline, consider the order in which other writers have presented material on your topic.

____ 8.3   Consider your first topic outline as a tentative one that is subject to change.

____ 8.4   Consider filling in your outline with brief notes (including unique identifiers) before beginning to write your review.

____ 8.5   Establish the importance of the topic that you are reviewing in the introductory paragraphs of your review.

____ 8.6   Avoid vague references to statistics—especially in the first paragraph of your review.

____ 8.7   Provide specific definitions of major variables early in the literature review.

____ 8.8   Write an essay that moves logically from one point to another. Do not write a string of annotations.

____ 8.9   When they are available, use more than one reference to support each point you make while avoiding very long strings of references for a single point.

____ 8.10 Write the literature review using your own words; use quotations very sparingly.

____ 8.11 Explicitly state what you think are reasonable conclusions based on the literature for each major subtopic that you cover.

____ 8.12 Consider theories and/or models when reaching conclusions.

____ 8.13 Critique the research you cite, which will help you show your readers why you have reached particular conclusions.

____   8.14   Point out gaps in the literature, explain why they are important, and mention them in your conclusions.

____   8.15   Consider concluding your review with suggestions for future research.

Chapter 9 Revising and Refining the First Draft

____   9.1   Recheck headings and subheadings, and modify them, as necessary.

____   9.2   Check to see that all your paragraphs are straightforward and reasonably short.

____   9.3   Check to see that you have used rhetorical questions very sparingly.

____   9.4   Consider using transitional terms to make one paragraph flow from the previous one.

____   9.5   If more than one paragraph is based on the same reference, use wording that makes it clear.

____   9.6   Avoid beginning your literature review with truisms.

____   9.7   Consider using a first paragraph that provides historical context *if* the context is clearly on target and interesting.

____   9.8   Remove any material that is meant to be clever, amusing, or flippant.

____   9.9   Revise to reduce the amount of anecdotal material.

____   9.10   When using the Harvard method for citation, it is often better to emphasize content over authorship.

____   9.11   Cross-check the references cited in the body of your review against those in your reference list at the end.

____   9.12   Have your first draft critiqued by others, and assume they are correct if anything is unclear to them.

Chapter 10 Blending Qualitative and Quantitative Approaches

____   10.1   Consider your audience's needs for reporting specific statistics in your literature review.

____   10.2   If you fail to state that a difference or relationship is statistically significant, your readers will assume that it is, which is acceptable if this is true.

____   10.3   Consider pointing out especially large (or strong) and especially small (or weak) differences or relationships.

____   10.4   Examine your literature review to identify vague terms that refer to quantities, and consider replacing them with specific statistics.

____   10.5   Consider summarizing key statistics in a table.

____   10.6   Avoid overburdening readers with statistics.

____   10.7   If a particular statistic is especially important, consider commenting on the quality of the study that produced it.

____   10.8   Use wording that indicates which statements are supported by data.

____   10.9   Consider discussing the statistical support, if any, for important theories.

Chapter 11   Introduction to Meta-Analysis

____ 11.1   A meta-analysis of percentages reported in various studies can be conducted by calculating a weighted average of the percentages.

____ 11.2   The beginning of a meta-analysis should be similar to the beginning of a qualitatively oriented review.

____ 11.3   Name the search terms used as well as the databases that were searched.

____ 11.4   Discuss efforts made to overcome the "file drawer effect" (i.e., publication bias) on the outcome of a meta-analysis.

____ 11.5   Decide whether to exclude studies with weak methods from the meta-analysis.

____ 11.6   If studies are excluded from a meta-analysis for reasons other than weak research methods, provide specific reasons for their exclusion.

____ 11.7   Consider including one or more moderator variables in a meta-analysis, and provide the rationale for their selection.

____ 11.8   Consider incorporating a meta-analysis within a larger qualitatively oriented review.

____ 11.9   Consider conducting a meta-analysis using Cohen's statistic named d.

____ 11.10   Avoid mechanical rules when interpreting values of d.

____ 11.11   Describe the overall quality of the studies included in a meta-analysis.

Chapter 12   A Closer Look at Meta-Analysis

____ 12.1   When calculating d, consider using the pooled value of the standard deviation.

____ 12.2   Consider weighting for differences in sample size when calculating an average value of d.

____ 12.3   Be cautious when there are large variations in sample sizes.

____ 12.4   Interpret negative values of d appropriately.

____ 12.5   Meta-analyses are often conducted by averaging correlation coefficients.

____ 12.6   A single meta-analysis can contain values of both d and r.

Chapter 13   A Closer Look at Creating a Synthesis

____ 13.1   Consider providing an overview near the beginning of the literature review.

____ 13.2   Consider providing a brief summary at the end of each section of the review.

____ 13.3   Consider providing a comprehensive summary near the end of the review.

____ 13.4   Consider starting the Conclusions section of the literature review with a statement of the purposes of the review.

____ 13.5   Consider speculating on possible future findings in the Conclusions section of the literature review.

____ 13.6   State hypotheses and/or research purposes that are clearly derived from the literature.

____ 13.7   State specific implications in the Conclusions section of the literature review.

Chapter 14   Writing Titles and Abstracts

____ 14.1   A title should be brief.

____ 14.2   A title should be a statement—not a complete sentence.

____ 14.3   Avoid using a question that can be answered with a "yes" or "no" as a title.

____ 14.4   Consider using a subtitle to amplify a main title.

____ 14.5   Consider using a subtitle to indicate that the document is a review.

____ 14.6   An abstract should begin by naming the topic being reviewed.

____ 14.7   An abstract should emphasize the findings and conclusions—not other elements such as how the literature was searched.

____ 14.8   It is acceptable, but not necessary, to cite specific statistics in the abstract of a meta-analysis.

Chapter 15   Citing References

____ 15.1   A reference list for a literature review should refer to only publications cited in the literature review.

____ 15.2   List references alphabetically by surname, and use hanging indents to make it easy to locate surnames.

____ 15.3   Use italics appropriately, such as for titles of books and journals as well as volume numbers of journals.

____ 15.4   Provide volume numbers (but not issue numbers) for journal articles.

____ 15.5   Capitalize the first letters of proper nouns, but only the first letters of the first word in titles and subtitles of journal articles.

____ 15.6   Check for punctuation, especially for commas between elements such as authors' names and period marks at the ends of lists.

____ 15.7   Provide the date and URL for any reference citations to material published on the Internet.

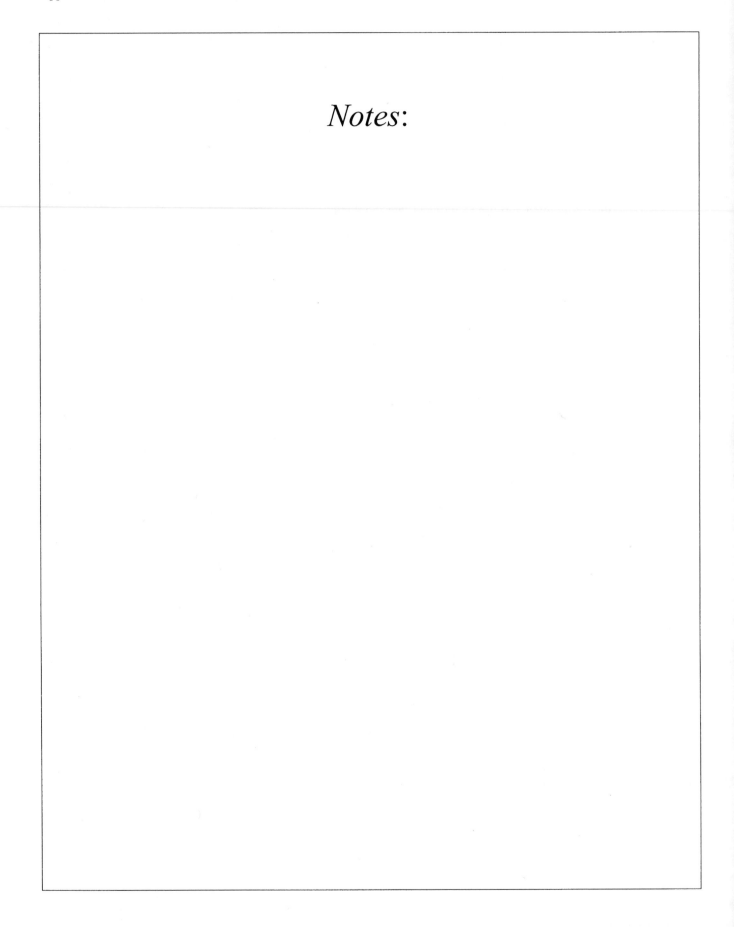

Notes:

Appendix B

Qualitative Versus Quantitative Research

Mildred L. Patten

Quantitative research is research in which the results are presented as quantities or numbers (that is, statistics) and **qualitative research** is research in which the results are trends or themes that are described in words. However, this is an oversimplification since there are many features that distinguish the two types. To understand some of the major differences, consider the following example.

Suppose a metropolitan police force is demoralized—with signs of demoralization such as high rates of absenteeism, failure to follow procedures, and so on. Furthermore, the press has raised questions about the effectiveness of the force and its leadership. In such a situation, the police commission might contract with a researcher to identify possible causes and solutions.

If a quantitative researcher is retained, she would probably begin with a review of the research literature on demoralized police departments. From the review, she would attempt to develop hypotheses to be explored in her research. This is a *deductive approach* to planning the research, that is, she is deducing from the literature possible explanations (that is, hypotheses) to be tested in the research. In contrast, a qualitative researcher would tend to use an *inductive approach* to planning the research (i.e., starting with specifics of the situation based on observations instead of starting with literature on the topic). He might, for example, begin to gather data on the specific police force in question and use the very early, preliminary findings as a basis for planning other research activities. In fact, some qualitative researchers consciously avoid considering previous research since it might color the way they look at a given situation.

When deciding what types of instruments (that is, measuring tools) to use, a quantitative researcher would tend to emphasize those that produce data that can quickly be reduced to numbers such as structured questionnaires or interview schedules with objective formats such as multiple-choice questions. In contrast, a qualitative researcher would tend to emphasize instruments that yield words such as unstructured interviews or direct, unstructured observations of police force officers and their administrators.

When deciding which members of the force to use as participants, a quantitative researcher would tend to select a large sample, which is made possible within a limited research budget by objective instruments such as an anonymous, objective questionnaire that takes little time to administer.[1] A qualitative researcher will tend to select a small sample for the reverse reason.

When conducting the research, a quantitative researcher would tend to spend little time directly interacting with the participants (largely because the nature of her instruments do not require it). A qualitative researcher, on the other hand, might spend a considerable amount of time interviewing and observing various members of the force over an extended period.

While working with the participants,[2] a qualitative researcher would be open to the possibility of making adjustments in the instruments such as reformulating questions or adding questions based on earlier responses by participants. A quantitative researcher would seldom make such adjustments.

Also, a quantitative researcher would tend to summarize all responses with statistics and seldom report on the behavior of individual participants. A qualitative researcher would tend to cite individuals' responses (such as quoting individual participants) in the results section of a report.

Finally, a quantitative researcher would tend to generalize the results to a population (i.e., conclude that what was found by studying a sample is true of the population from which the sample was drawn), while a qualitative researcher would tend to limit the conclusions to individuals who were directly studied.

---

[1] In addition, quantitative researchers will usually attempt to select a *random sample* in which all participants have an equal chance of being selected; this can be done, for example, by drawing names out of a hat. In contrast, qualitative researchers are much more likely to select a *purposive* sample of people that they believe are key informants in terms of social dynamics, leadership, etc.

[2] When the subjects of a study participate voluntarily, they are usually called "participants"—not "subjects."

Should the police commission select a quantitative or qualitative researcher? Some of the criteria that should be considered when making such a decision are:

A. Some research questions inherently lend themselves more to the quantitative or qualitative approach. For instance, "What is the impact of AIDS on the U.S. economy?" is a question that lends itself to quantitative research since the economy is usually measured with numbers. On the other hand, "What is the emotional impact of AIDS on at-risk health care workers?" is a question that lends itself more to the qualitative approach than the first question because it focuses on emotional impact—although it could be examined with either qualitative or quantitative research depending on the orientation of the researcher.

B. When little is known about a topic, qualitative research usually should be initially favored. New topics are constantly emerging in all fields: new diseases such as HIV, new crimes such as car-jacking, and new educational techniques such as putting students on the Internet. On new topics, there will be very little, if any, research literature and, perhaps, no theory with direct applications. In their absence, quantitative researchers may find it difficult to employ the deductive approach. Also, quantitative researchers might find it difficult to write structured questions about a little-known topic. In contrast, a qualitative researcher could start with broad questions and refine them during the course of the interviews as various themes and issues start to emerge. Based on the qualitative results, theories might be developed from which hypotheses could be deduced and subsequently tested by quantitative research.

C. When the participants belong to a culture that is closed or secretive, qualitative research should usually be favored. A skilled qualitative researcher who is willing to spend considerable time breaking through the barriers that keep researchers out is more likely to be successful than a quantitative researcher who tends to spend less time interacting with participants.

D. When potential participants are not available for extensive interactions or observation, the quantitative approach should be considered. For example, it might be difficult to schedule extensive interviews with chief executives of major corporations.

E. When time and funds are very limited, quantitative research might be favored. This is an arguable criterion. However, it is suggested because quantitative research can often provide a quick, inexpensive snapshot of a narrow aspect of a problem. Qualitative methods do not lend themselves to an inexpensive snapshot approach.

F. When the audience (such as legislators or funding agencies) requires "hard numbers," quantitative research should be favored or, at least, incorporated into a qualitative research project. When someone says, "Just the numbers, please," themes and trends illustrated with quotations are unlikely to impress. For such an audience, one should, when possible, start by presenting statistics. This might open the door to consideration of more qualitative considerations. Notice that implicit in this criterion is the notion that both qualitative and quantitative approaches might be used in a given research project, with each approach contributing a different type of information.

Up to this point, we have been considering quantitative and qualitative research as though they are opposites. However, some researchers conduct research that is a blend of the two approaches. For example, a quantitative researcher who uses semistructured interviews to collect data, reduces the data to statistics, but also reports quotations from participants to support the statistics, is conducting research that has some of the characteristics of both approaches.

As you can see, our hypothetical police commission needs to make a complex decision. How would you answer the question regarding the type of research the police commission should request? Arguably, a combination of both approaches might be the best answer.

Model Literature Review 1

Stereotypes Towards Stuttering

Ashley Craig
University of Technology, Sydney

Yvonne Tran
University of Technology, Sydney

Magali Craig
University of Technology, Sydney

Editorial note: The paragraphs in this literature review have been numbered to make it easy to refer to specific portions of this review during classroom discussions. The numbers are italicized superscripts, which appear at the beginning of each paragraph. All other nonitalicized superscripts, if any, refer to footnotes within the review.

This review was written as an introduction to a report on original research conducted by the authors. Only the literature review portion of the report is reprinted here. Note that Model Literature Reviews 3 and 4 were also written as introductions to reports on original research. The remaining model literature reviews in this book were written as "stand-alone" reviews—not as introductions to original research.

[1]Because stuttering is a disorder in oral communication (i.e., it occurs when a person attempts to talk), people who stutter are believed to be susceptible to negative stereotypes and social stigma. To understand this, it is important to present a brief introduction to the disorder. Stuttering is a potentially debilitating disorder that starts as soon as children begin to talk, and for at least 20% of those children, it becomes a chronic problem into old age (Allport, 1958; Craig, 2000). It is believed to be a neurological disorder that affects the neural systems involved in the motor aspects of speech (Hulstijn, Peters, & Van Lieshout, 1997). In research recently published by the investigators (Craig, Hancock, Tran, Craig, & Peters, 2002), the prevalence of stuttering over the entire lifespan (from two years to older age) was .7%, with at least a 50% higher prevalence rate of stuttering in males (2.3 to 1 male to female ratio). While the risk of stuttering is higher (2 to 4% depending on age), a .7% prevalence rate is predictable given that many children naturally recover from stuttering. A higher prevalence rate of around 1.4% was found in children (2 to 10 years), with boys having a higher prevalence of stuttering (2.3 to 3.3 to 1). In adolescence (11 to 20 years), the prevalence fell substantially to .5%, with boys much more likely to stutter (4 to 1 ratio). However, prevalence increased in adulthood to .8% (2.2 to 1 ratio), falling once again in late middle to older age (.4 %), with males again stuttering more frequently than females (1.4 to 1 ratio). Stuttering is not only potentially debilitating, it is also a prevalent disorder as a potential 2.8 million adults in the USA stutter (Craig, Hancock, Tran, Craig, & Peters, 2002).

[2]As communication is essential for social interaction, stuttering can create barriers to normal social and psychological development, raising risks of the formation of negative stereotypes. While people who stutter are not thought to be different from those who do not stutter in terms of personality or mood (Andrews & Craig, 1988; Andrews, Craig, Feyer, Hoddinott, Howie, & Neilson, 1983; Hedge, 1972; Prins, 1972), evidence suggests that living with stuttering over many years can become associated with problems such as anxiety and distress, feelings of helplessness, lowered employment opportunities, and lower-than-desired quality of life (Craig, 1990; Craig & Calver, 1991; Craig, Hancock, Tran, & Craig, in press; Fitzgerald, Djurdjic, & Maguin, 1992; Gabel, Colcord, & Petrosino, 2002; Menzies, Onslow, & Packman, 1999). Adult research has shown that people who stutter are significantly higher in trait anxiety than nonstuttering adults of similar age (Craig, 1990; Craig, Hancock, Tran, & Craig, in press). Others have shown links of stuttering to social anxiety (Kraaimaat, Janssen, & Van Dam-Baggen, 1991; Mahr & Torosian, 1999). Stein, Baird, and Walker (1996), using structured interview techniques, noted that many adults who stutter had salient difficulties with social anxiety. These authors argued that many people who stutter should be diagnosed as social phobic. Anxiety of children who stutter is not significantly different from that of nonstuttering children (Craig & Hancock, 1996;

Craig, Hancock, Chang, McCready, Shepley, McCaul, Costello, Harding, Kehran, Masel, & Reilly, 1996). Therefore, as children grow, the experience of living with chronic stuttering increases the risk of developing anxiety, raising chances that they will also develop shyness and consequently begin to avoid those social interactions essential for their development. In further support of this, research has consistently shown that children of about five years with speech disabilities like stuttering have an increased risk of anxiety disorder in early adulthood (Baker & Cantwell, 1987; Beitchman, Brownlie, Inglis, Wild, Ferguson, & Schachter, 1996; Beitchman, Wilson, Johnson, Atkinson, Young, Adlar, Escobar, & Douglas, 2001). Stuttering can be a potentially debilitating disorder.

[3]A stereotype is generally regarded as a generalization or an exaggerated belief about a person or group of persons (Allport, 1958). Problems occur when these stereotypes lead to unfair discrimination (such as denying employment to a person who stutters) or prejudice (such as believing a person who stutters is inferior). Therefore, it is important to study the extent of stereotypes towards stuttering in the community. It has been hypothesized that stereotypes may develop because there is an "element of truth" in these beliefs (Allport, 1958), suggesting that some stereotypical generalizations may have a valid basis. Assuming that people who stutter are more socially anxious, this theory suggests that nonstuttering people hold a negative stereotype towards people who stutter. This is consistent with the finding that many nonstuttering people across different professions and communities have predominately negative stereotypes about people who stutter (Cooper & Rustin, 1985; Craig & Calver, 1991; Doody, Kalinowski, Armson, & Stuart, 1993; Ham, 1990; Klassen, 2001; Silverman & Paynter, 1990). This is also believed to be the case for those who stutter (Kalinowski, Lerman, & Watt, 1987; Klassen, 2001; Lass, Dennis, Pannbacker, Schmitt, Middleton, & Schweppenheiser, 1995) as well as their parents (Crow & Cooper, 1977). The typical person who stutters is believed to be nervous and anxious, shy and self-conscious, introverted, and insecure.

[4]The origin of stereotypes is thought to arise from a natural function of human information seeking and perceiving (Fox, 1992). It is thought stereotypes assist by simplifying complex social information (Allport, 1958; Fox, 1992). Further, some suggest that people develop these stereotypes through contact (either directly or indirectly) with those who belong to the stereotyped group (Allport, 1958). Those who have had direct contact with

people who stutter (such as family, acquaintances, clinicians, and teachers) have negative stereotypes that are resistant to change (Doody, Kalinowski, Armson, & Stuart, 1993; Dorsey & Guenther, 2000; Snyder, 2001; Woods, 1978). For example, Snyder (2001) showed that clinicians were resistant to changing their negative views about stuttering even after watching a factual video on the nature of stuttering. However, Craig and Calver (1991) reported that, while employers of people who stuttered believed them to be limited in their ability to communicate and their prospects for promotion, these attitudes were reversed when their stuttering employees received successful treatment for their stuttering. The research of Klassen (2001) suggested that long-term, more intimate rather than superficial contact with a person who stutters is associated with less negative stereotypes. White and Collins (1984) extended this contact hypothesis. They suggested and showed that people attribute their own experience of stuttered speech (either their own temporary disfluent utterances or their observations of the disfluencies of others on television, etc.). Often, these experiences (actual or observed) can be perceived as stressful, and this emotional state is then inferred in people who stutter.

[5]Most research has been conducted with people who have had some direct association with people who stutter, so it is important to identify the extent and nature of stereotypes and perceptions towards stuttering by those who have never had direct contact with a person who stutters. It is assumed that such people form their beliefs about people who stutter from activities such as discussions, reading, watching television programs, or viewing popular films (such as "A Fish Called Wanda"). Furthermore, we have not been able to find any studies that have employed a randomized and stratified design to provide reliable estimates of stereotypes towards stuttering in the general population. Currently, our knowledge about stereotypes towards stuttering is largely based upon studies employing brief survey research with convenience samples (i.e., nonrandomized samples). The aim of this research was therefore to conduct a study of beliefs towards stuttering held by those who have never had direct contact with those who stutter. An additional aim was to provide data that may assist in overcoming commonly held misconceptions and negative stereotypes.

References

Allport, G. W. (1958) *The nature of prejudice* New York: Doubleday.
Andrews, G , & Craig, A. R. (1988). Prediction of outcome after treatment for stuttering. *British Journal of Psychiatry, 153,* 236–240.

Andrews, G , Craig, A R., Feyer, A M., Hoddinott, S., Howie, P., & Neilson, M (1983) Stuttering A review of research findings and theories circa 1982 *Journal of Speech and Hearing Disorders*, 48, 226–246.

Aneshensel, C S., Frerichs, R R , Clark, V , & Yokopenic, P. A. (1982). Telephone versus in-person surveys of community health status *American Journal of Public Health*, 72, 1017–1021

Australian Bureau of Statistics (1998) *Estimated resident population by age and sex in statistical local areas in NSW 30 June 1991* Sydney: Author

Baker, L , & Cantwell, D P (1987) A prospective psychiatric follow-up of children with speech/language disorders. *Journal of American Academy of Child and Adolescent Psychiatry*, 26, 546–553.

Beitchman, J. H , Brownlie, E. R., Inglis, A., Wild, J., Ferguson, B , & Schachter, D. (1996). Seven-year follow-up of speech/language impaired and control children· Psychiatric outcome *Journal of Child Psychology and Psychiatry*, 37, 961–970

Beitchman, J H , Wilson, B , Johnson, C J , Atkinson, L , Young, A , Adlar, E., Escobar, M., & Douglas, L (2001) Fourteen-year follow-up of speech/language impaired and control children Psychiatric outcome *Journal of American Academy of Child and Adolescent Psychiatry*, 40, 75–82

Bloodstein, O. (1995) *A handbook on stuttering* (5th ed) San Diego, CA Singular Publ Group

Cannell, C. F (1985) Overview· Response bias and interviewer variability in surveys In T W Beed & R J Stimson (Eds), *Survey interviewing Theory and techniques* New York. George, Allen, & Unwin. Pp. 1–23

Cooper, E B , & Rustin, L (1985) Clinician attitudes toward stuttering in the United States and Great Britain A cross-cultural study *Journal of Fluency Disorders*, 10, 1–17.

Craig, A. R. (1990) An investigation into the relationship between anxiety and stuttering *Journal of Speech and Hearing Disorders*, 55, 290–294.

Craig, A R (2000) The developmental nature and effective treatment of stuttering in children and adolescents. *Journal of Developmental and Physical Disabilities*, 12, 173–186

Craig, A. R., & Calver, P (1991) Following up on treated stutterers. Studies of perceptions of fluency and job status *Journal of Speech and Hearing Research*, 34, 279–284

Craig, A R , & Hancock, K (1996) Anxiety in children and young adolescents who stutter *Australian Journal of Human Communication Disorders*, 24, 28–38

Craig, A R , Hancock, K , Chang, E , McCready, C , Shepley, A., McCaul, A , Costello, D , Harding, S , Kehran, R , Masel, C , & Reilly, K (1996) A controlled trial for stuttering in persons aged 9 to 14 years. *Journal of Speech and Hearing Research*, 39, 808–826

Craig, A R , Hancock, K , Tran, Y., & Craig, M (in press) Anxiety levels in people who stutter· A randomised population study *Journal of Speech, Language and Hearing Research*

Craig, A. R., Hancock, K., Tran, Y , Craig, M , & Peters, K (2002) Epidemiology of stuttering in the community across the entire lifespan *Journal of Speech, Language and Hearing Research*, 45, 1097–1105

Crow, T. A , & Cooper, E B. (1977) Parental attitudes toward and knowledge of stuttering *Journal of Communication Disorders*, 10, 343–357

Dillman, D A (1978) *Mail and telephone surveys* New York. Wiley

Doody, I , Kalinowski, J., Armson, J , & Stuart, A (1993) Stereotypes of stutterers and nonstutterers in three rural communities in Newfoundland *Journal of Fluency Disorders*, 18, 363–373

Dorsey, M , & Guenther, R. K. (2000). Attitudes of professors and students toward college students who stutter *Journal of Fluency Disorders*, 25, 77–83

Fitzgerald, H. E , Djurdjic, S D , & Maguin, E. (1992). Assessment of sensitivity to interpersonal stress in stutterers *Journal of Communication Disorders*, 25, 31–42.

Fox, R (1992) Prejudice and the unfinished task *Psychological Inquiry*, 3, 194–198

Gabel, R. M , Colcord, R. D , & Petrosino, L. (2002) Self-reported anxiety of adults who do and do not stutter *Perceptual and Motor Skills*, 94, 775–784.

Ham, R E (1990) What is stuttering Variations and stereotypes *Journal of Fluency Disorders*, 15, 259–273

Hegde, M N (1972) Stuttering, neuroticism and extroversion *Behavior Research Therapy*, 10, 395–397.

Hulstijn, W , Peters, H., & Van Lieshout, P (1997) *Speech production Motor control, brain research and fluency disorders* Amsterdam Elsevier Press

Kalinowski, J. S , Lerman, J W , & Watt, J (1987) A preliminary examination of the perceptions of self and others in stutterers and nonstutterers *Journal of Fluency Disorders*, 12, 317–331

Klassen, T. R. (2001) Perceptions of people who stutter Re-assessing the negative stereotype *Perceptual and Motor Skills*, 92, 551–559.

Kraaimaat, F , Janssen, P , & Van Dam-Baggen, R (1991) Social anxiety and stuttering *Perceptual and Motor Skills*, 72, 76

Lass, N J , Dennis, M., Pannbacker, M , Schmitt, J F , Middleton, G , & Schweppenheiser, K (1995) The perceptions of stutterers by people who stutter. *Folia Phoniatrica Logopaedica*, 47, 247–251

Mahr, G. C , & Torosian, T (1999) Anxiety and social phobia *Journal of Fluency Disorders*, 24, 119–126

Menzies, R G , Onslow, M., & Packman, A. (1999) Anxiety and stuttering· Exploring a complex relationship *American Journal of Speech-Language Pathology*, 8, 3–10.

Paulsen, A S , Crowe, R. R , Noyes, R., & Pfohl, B (1988) Reliability of the telephone interview in diagnosing anxiety disorders *Archives of General Psychiatry*, 45, 62–63.

Prins, D (1972). Personality, stuttering severity, and age. *Journal of Speech and Hearing Research*, 15, 148–154

Quine, S (1985). Does the mode matter? A comparison of three modes of questionnaires completion. *Community Health Studies*, 9, 151–156

Silverman, F. H , & Paynter, K K. (1990). Impact of stuttering on perception of occupational competence. *Journal of Fluency Disorders*, 15, 87–91

Snyder, G. J (2001) Exploratory research in the measurement and modification of attitudes toward stuttering *Journal of Fluency Disorders*, 26, 149–160

Stein, M B , Baird, A , & Walker, J. R. (1996) Social phobia in adults with stuttering *American Journal of Psychiatry*, 153, 278–280

White, P A , & Collins, S C (1984) Stereotype formations by inference. A possible explanation for the "stutterer" stereotype *Journal of Speech and Hearing Research*, 27, 567–570

Woods, C. L (1978) Does the stigma shape the stutterer? *Journal of Communication Disorders*, 11, 483–487

Address correspondence to. Ashley Craig, Department of Health Sciences, UTS, P O. Box 123, Broadway, NSW Australia 2007. E-mail: a.craig@uts edu.au

From *Perceptual and Motor Skills*, 97, 235–245. Copyright © 2003 by Perceptual and Motor Skills. Reprinted with permission.

Discussion Questions for Model Literature Review 1

Editorial Note: All the model literature reviews in this book are presented as strong models. However, there are differences of opinion on the effectiveness of any particular piece of writing, even among experts. While answering the following questions, consider the guidelines in this book (as *only* guidelines, not principles) as well as your own standards for effective writing.

1. Briefly comment on the adequacy of the title of the review.

2. Does the review have a strong beginning? Does it get straight to the point? If not, have the authors used some other effective technique to begin the review?

3. Have the authors made a strong case for reviewing the topic(s) they cover? Have they shown that the topic(s) are important?

4. Is the material presented in a logical sequence? Are the headings (and subheadings, if any) appropriate and helpful?

5. Are key variables adequately defined? Are they defined at appropriate points? Explain.

6. Are there points where the references are not well integrated with each other (i.e., simply described as an annotated list)? Explain.

7. Are the strengths and weaknesses of some of the cited research described? If yes, name at least one section where this is done using paragraph numbers.

8. Have the authors made it clear what material is theirs and what is being summarized/paraphrased from other sources? Explain.

9. Are any portions of the review unclear to you? If so, identify them by paragraph number(s).

10. Are the individual paragraphs straightforward and to the point? Explain. If yes, identify one by number that you think is especially good. If no, identify one that is weak.

11. Is the conclusion/discussion at the end of the review appropriate in light of the material covered earlier?

12. On a scale from 1 (very weak) to 10 (very strong), what is your overall evaluation of the literature review? Name one or two considerations that strongly influenced your evaluation.

13. Assume that you are on the editorial board of an academic journal and that the general topic of this review is within the scope of what the journal usually publishes. Which of the following would you recommend to the editor of the journal: publish as is, publish only after minor revisions, publish only after major revisions, *or* do not publish? Briefly defend your recommendation.

Model Literature Review 2

Jamaican Child-Rearing Practices:
The Role of Corporal Punishment

Delores E. Smith
The University of Tennessee

Gail Mosby
The University of Tennessee

Editorial note: The paragraphs in this literature review have been numbered to make it easy to refer to specific portions of this review during classroom discussions. The numbers are italicized superscripts, which appear at the beginning of each paragraph. All other nonitalicized superscripts, if any, refer to footnotes within the review.

ABSTRACT

The family is the most prominent social group that exists. It prepares its members for the various roles they will perform in society. Yet, the literature has unequivocally singled out the family as the most violent social group, with parental violence against children being the most prevalent type of family violence. While societies like the United States, Japan, and Sweden have taken a hard line on physical punishment and shifted to a gentler approach to discipline, harsh disciplining of children persists elsewhere. In the Caribbean, and Jamaica in particular, child-rearing and disciplinary practices that would warrant child abuse charges in other Western societies are rampant. This article examines the child-rearing techniques of Jamaican adults and their assumed effects on child outcomes. It also examines the plausibility of the assumption that the harsh physical punishment meted out to children is partially responsible for the current social problems of that island nation. We recommend approaches to tackle the broad goals of addressing familial and societal practices that compromise children's development and well being.

[1]Parents in all societies grapple with how to raise their children in a way that prepares them for the complexities of life (Yorburg, 2002) and equips them to one day become parents themselves (Hamner & Turner, 2001). In order to accomplish this daunting task, parents rely on their own socialization into parenting, their intuitive sense of right and wrong, and their overall cultural beliefs (Hamner & Turner, 2001). The sanctions of these influences create a prerogative that confers upon parents the responsibility to guide their children to become competent, responsible, and fully functioning members of society.

[2]Culture guides parents' beliefs about child discipline, behavior management, and control. In Jamaica, a small island nation of 2.5 million people, cultural beliefs have given rise to a parenting style that has been shown to negatively affect children's psychosocial outcomes, leading to serious concerns about the psychological adjustment of Jamaican children and adolescents (Crawford-Brown, 1999; Leo-Rhynie, 1997).

[3]According to ecological theory, the overlapping influences of the various cultural environments impact the individual's development and overall well-being (Bronfenbrenner, 1979). Although there is no research specifically showing a causal link between problem behaviors and emotional well-being in Jamaica, the popular assumption is that the increase in antisocial behaviors in that society emanates from an impaired sense of self-worth and psychological maladjustment among youth. From that assumption arises speculation about the source of that impairment and its concomitant problem behaviors. The most forceful conjecture centers on cultural socialization practices, particularly child rearing (Evans & Davies, 1997; Leo-Rhynie, 1997; Sharpe, 1997).

[4]The purpose of this article is to examine the plausibility of speculations regarding harsh child-rearing practices and the psychosocial adjustment of Jamaican children and adolescents. It reviews the research literature on the effects of harsh physical punishment and offers recommendations for addressing the issue of excessive and inappropriate discipline. Recommendations are also offered for preventing and, perhaps, reversing the trend of antisocial and destructive behaviors that are thought to be linked to Jamaican child-rearing practices.

Jamaican Child-Rearing Practices

[5]The dominant Caribbean parenting style is authoritarian, an approach consistently found to thwart optimal child socioemotional outcomes in Western cultures (Baumrind, 1991). In keeping with this authoritarian style, Jamaican parenting has been characterized as highly repressive, severe, and abusive (Arnold, 1982; Leo-Rhynie, 1997; Sharpe, 1997) and the disciplining of children described as inconsistent and developmentally inappropriate (Sloley, 1999). In fact, the sparse literature on Jamaican family processes has attested to the pervasiveness of corporal punishment and other violent disciplinary measures meted out to children by adults (Phillips, 1973; Evans & Davies, 1997; Walker, Grantham-McGregor, Himes, Williams, & Duff, 1998). Flogging, the most common response of adults to perceived misbehavior in Jamaican children (Leo-Rhynie, 1997; Smith, 1989), has been vividly described. Arnold (1982) has stated, "At times the 'beating,' as it is commonly called, can be severe and bears no relevance to the age of the child nor the stage of its development" (p. 141). The flogging of children "is carried out in such a way as to appear almost brutal. The hand, a stick, a belt, a shoe, or a tamarind switch are used to beat children to ensure compliance" (Leo-Rhynie, 1997, p. 44). Discipline "becomes severely enforced through 'shouting' and 'flogging' or 'beating.' Children are punished in this way for lying, stealing, disobedience, impoliteness, and not completing their chores. 'Playing in the house,' 'crying too much,' and 'not eating the meal provided' also constitute misdemeanors that warrant a 'beating' " (Barrow, 1996, p. 400).

[6]The extent and prevalence of such harsh disciplinary measures have been examined empirically. Landmann, Grantham-McGregor, and Desai (1983) reported that 59% of the Jamaican mothers in their study indicated that they used a belt or stick to beat their children. Grant (cited in Leo-Rhynie, 1997) found that 84% of mothers of preschool children in his study admitted to beating their children. In Smith's (1989) study, 71% of rural parents and 55% of urban parents reported flogging as the most frequent response to perceived misbehavior in their children. To emphasize his point, Smith noted that spanking (a milder form of punishment) was virtually unknown, being practiced in only 3% of families. Walker et al. (1998) noted that 53% of the adolescent girls in their study reported that they had been physically punished by their parents during the previous year. In addition, children complained that adults, especially their parents, often publicly humiliated them.

[7]Baptiste, Hardy, and Lewis (1997) reported that Caribbean immigrants in the United States tended to be overrepresented among parents charged with, and convicted of, child abuse and neglect. They noted that in therapy, these parents expressed anger and confusion about the punitive measures they faced in the United States for employing "generous doses of corporal punishment" (p. 296) and other harsh disciplinary methods against their children. Further, Baptiste, Hardy, and Lewis maintained that the sanctioning of corporal punishment in the culture of origin put these parents in serious conflict with the dominant culture, leading them to feel that their authority to discipline their children as they see fit had been eroded by the laws of the United States. These dynamics take a great mental toll on these families and often lead them to, uncharacteristically, seek professional counseling (Baptiste, Hardy, & Lewis, 1997).

[8]The Jamaican practice of beating children is culturally sanctioned and extends to the larger society. Accordingly, "the sociocultural norm, 'the right to beat the child,' embraced by parents, teachers, and parent surrogates does lead to instances of abuse and neglect, and to repeated cases of abuse and the accompanying psychological damage" (Sharpe, 1997, p. 267). Evans and Davies (1997) pointed out that corporal punishment is, indeed, a convention in Jamaican schools—not only used as a means of discipline for misbehavior, it is very much a part of the pedagogical strategy. Further, numerous Jamaican newspaper stories and letters to the editor have attested to the pervasiveness of the severe corporal punishment meted out to children by teachers. For example, Clarke (2000), in a newspaper article titled "Please teacher don't beat me," related adults' recollections of extreme treatment from teachers and provided examples of the punishment meted out to schoolchildren in present-day Jamaica. One nine-year-old boy stated, "Sometimes my teacher beats me with a belt, sometimes a board.... Anytime I don't do my work, she hits me with the board, sometimes on my hand, sometimes on my head." An eleven-year-old girl related the story of her fourth-grade teacher, who beats students for coming to school or returning from lunch late and for being disobedient: "She uses a ruler, the long ones; some teachers use leather belts." Clarke also noted the case of a high school student who had to be hospitalized after being caned by a teacher.

[9]Perhaps not surprisingly, many parents agree that children should be punished in school. Clarke noted one father's remarks: "I've never seen any statistics that show that flogging doesn't work. I send my boy to

school for the teacher to take over; if she feels he should be whipped, then so be it; if he complains, he gets more at home." These dynamics have led Evans and Davies (1997) to express concern that Jamaican schools validated the use of the severe punishment that children received at home. They bemoaned the fact that "the school, charged with an important social and developmental role in society, does not act as a countervailing force to the family; rather, it reinforces a punitive, power-assertive, authoritarian approach to relationships and to resolving conflicts" (p. 19).

[10]This kind of child maltreatment is not only socially endorsed, but sometimes also legally sanctioned. A Jamaican judge, in a family court hearing, advised a father that all the child needed to correct his behavior was "two good licks" (Sargent & Harris, 1992).

Communication Patterns

[11]Authoritarian parenting is not conducive to open parent–child communication. Caribbean parents, and Jamaican parents in particular, as a rule do not engage in positive verbal interaction with children, neither do they offer warm and gentle guidance and direction. Evans and Davies (1997) contend that Caribbean parents lacked the propensity to have extended conversations or to reason with their children. Evans and Davies noted that parents often complained about their children talking too much or asking too many questions, ideas reinforced by the cultural belief that "children should be seen and not heard." Research has supported such views regarding parent–child communication. A study commissioned by the United Nations Children's Fund (UNICEF) cited poor parent–child communication, corporal punishment, and physical abuse as central to the serious social problems facing Jamaican society ("Unfriendly Parents in Jamaica," 2001; Sloley, 1999). Specifically, the study cited a serious lack of friendly communication between Jamaican parents and their children and highlighted the severe physical punishment and public humiliation meted out to children, dynamics that seriously hindered the development of positive socioemotional development. The study attributed the lack of positive communication to parents being handicapped by cultural practices that limit their ability to engage in cordial discussions with their children. The study noted: "Some of the factors central to [the country's social problems] are the lack of balanced communication between teenagers and parents, an unwillingness to engage in discussions with children, lack of information by parents, and a lack of understanding of adolescent behavior" ("Unfriendly Parents in Jamaica," 2001). According

to Arnold (1982), "They need to learn to talk 'with' their children, rather than always 'to' or 'at' [them]" (p. 144). Clearly, many Jamaican parents lack the know-how of establishing trusting and cordial relationships with their children.

Origins of Harsh Parenting Practices

[12]The etiology of such harsh disciplinary practices in the Caribbean has been pondered. Although many arguments have been forwarded, the most pervasive and often cited explanations point back to heritage, history, tradition, and socialization. Several authors have expressed the view that the extreme authoritarian style, along with the excessive discipline meted out to children, stems from the region's West African heritage combined with learned behavior, specifically from the brutality of slavery. These dynamics are bolstered by the religious sanction of "saving the rod and spoiling the child" (Arnold, 1982; Barrow, 1996; Leo-Rhynie, 1997).

[13]The psychoanalytic concept of displacement has also been forwarded as a plausible explanation. Displacement involves shifting or redirecting anger or hostility from a threatening object to a less threatening target (Freud, 1965). It is often purported that harsh, stressful social and economic conditions create anger, frustration, and hostility in low-income parents. Parents in turn displace their anger and frustration on their children by administering unjustifiable physical punishment (Arnold, 1982; Sharpe, 1997), to the point that the beating of children has become ritualized (Arnold, 1982; Barrow, 1996). Although displacement theory seems fitting at the lower income levels (Arnold, 1982), it must be questioned in light of the fact that these extreme disciplinary practices are not confined to the poor but are pervasive at all levels of society (Leo-Rhynie, 1997). One might expect parents of better social standing to have the capacity to employ nonviolent forms of discipline, such as time-out, withholding privileges, or grounding. However, cultural values and beliefs supersede personal perspectives and provide the blueprint on how children ought to be reared (Barrow, 1996; Evans & Davies, 1997).

Effects of Harsh Disciplinary Practices

[14]There is disagreement about the effects of physical punishment on children. While some researchers have noted a direct relationship between physical punishment and psychological maladjustment (Frias-Armenta, 2002; Swinford et al., 2000), others have contended that the outcomes are culture-dependent (e.g., Barrow, 1996). Still others, while not specifically refut-

ing the relationship, have maintained that the mediating role of the child's perception of the punishment as rejection by the caretaker is substantial. A study of the effects of corporal punishment in one Caribbean locale found a modest, direct relationship between physical punishment and psychological adjustment. However, the indirect impact, mediated by the child's perception of rejection by the caregiver, was significantly stronger (Rohner, Kean, & Cournoyer, 1991).

[15]More recent studies, conducted in a variety of settings and societies, have indicated that physical punishment, used even in moderation, has an adverse effect on psychosocial adjustment and behavior. Use of physical force against children has been found to predict impaired cognitive processes such as intelligence deficits and academic failure (Cicchetti & Toth, 1998), socioemotional dysfunction (Evans & Davies, 1997; Cicchetti & Toth, 1998), low empathy (Eisenberg & Fabes, 1998), hostile, aggressive, and oppositional tendencies, severe depression, conduct disorders in childhood (Frias-Armenta, 2002), and violence and criminality in adulthood (Swinford et al., 2000).

[16]These outcomes not only have deleterious consequences for the individual but for families and society as well. In one study, 66% of the boys and 50% of the girls rated as highly aggressive were from home environments where physical punishment was the preferred disciplinary approach (Headley, 1994). Other studies have documented the long-term psychiatric and behavioral outcomes of physical maltreatment in childhood. Kamsner and McCabe (2000), in a review of the literature, found evidence of a strong link between physical maltreatment in childhood and later promiscuity, prostitution, teen pregnancy, and criminality. Specifically, male felons reported significantly higher rates of child physical abuse than their noninstitutionalized peers. The review also noted significant associations between child physical abuse and adult psychiatric illnesses such as anxiety disorders (panic disorder, social phobia), posttraumatic stress disorders, and depression. Further, Kamsner and McCabe, in their own investigation, found that child physical abuse was "the dominant abuse variable to contribute significantly to the prediction of trauma-related outcomes" (p. 1255). Sharpe (1997), in addressing the issue of mental health and socialization in the Caribbean, focused on the problem of parental discipline and neglect. Based on clinical observations, she indicated that "conduct disorder and childhood depression were common among victims of abuse and that the only cases of posttraumatic stress disorders seen in the clinic were in victims of abuse" (p. 268).

[17]Heimer (1997) hypothesized that when adults use power assertive and violent disciplinary methods, they teach children that coercive force, aggression, and violence can be used to resolve conflicts and problems. Using longitudinal data, Heimer demonstrated that violent disciplinary measures against children translate into violent delinquency later in life; violence experienced in childhood accounted for 39% of the variance in subsequent violence. Similarly, Paschall, Flewelling, and Ennett (1998) found that exposure to violence put children at increased risk for violent behavior. Crawford-Brown (1999), although not specifically studying physical punishment, examined the impact of parenting on conduct disorders in Jamaican adolescents. She found a significant link between inadequate parenting and conduct disorders, with the child's perception of the parent as a negative role model as a contributing factor. While Crawford-Brown's research did not indicate the expressed features of the negative role model construct, Rice (2000) contended that parents are positive models for their children when they restrain their expressions of anger and demonstrate that hitting and other forms of violence are unacceptable. Conversely, parents become negative role models when they model aggression.

[18]In general, research has confirmed that physical force as a means of punishment increases children's vulnerability to psychosocial dysfunction. The reliance on physical punishment to control behavior inhibits children's development of internal controls, conformity to rules, and concern for the welfare of others. It also creates in children the propensity to misunderstand how power is appropriated and wielded, and teaches them to become beaters themselves (Swinford, DeMaris, Cernkovich, & Giordano, 2000). However, some studies have shown a differential effect of physical punishment along gender lines. While physical punishment predicts externalizing behaviors, such as later violence, in males (Kamsner & McCabe, 2000), internalizing effects, such as depression, suicidal ideation, anxiety, and psychosis, are more prevalent for girls (Frias-Armenta, 2002). The Jamaican context does seem to lend credence to gender differences in behavioral outcomes; the overwhelming majority of violent crimes occurring in Jamaica are committed by males (Robotham, 1999). However, there is controversy regarding the discipline meted out to each gender. Some have noted that boys are flogged more often and more severely than girls, while girls are subjected to more verbal abuse (Leo-Rhynie, 1997). Others have maintained that mothers are more restrictive of their daughters, to protect them from sexual contact with

boys and potentially deleterious outcomes (Barrow, 1996; Evans & Davies, 1997; Phillips, 1973).

Discussion

[19]Research has demonstrated that reliance on physical force as a means of discipline and punishment to control behavior leads to child maladjustment and deviancy in adolescence and beyond. The extant literature has also shown that the optimal environments for fostering healthy growth and development are a nurturing family and supportive community, both of which appear to be missing from the lives of many Jamaican youth (Arnold, 1982; Leo-Rhynie, 1997; Phillips, 1973; Sloley, 1999). Consequently, the concern expressed by the Jamaican populace about the sense of worthlessness among young people may be warranted. Harsh disciplinary practices, typical of the Jamaican culture, exact a heavy toll on children and evoke powerful and negative reactions in adolescents, with serious and far-reaching social implications. Indeed, poor socioemotional functioning has been found to be an important consequence, if not the cause, of problem behavior (Kaplan & Lin, 2000). Furthermore, healthy psychosocial functioning acts as a deterrent to conduct disorders such as drug and alcohol use and abuse, delinquency, school dropout, precocious sexual activity, violence, and criminality (Harter, 1993; Kaplan & Lin, 2000).

[20]The foregoing, then, calls into question the efficacy of traditional child-rearing practices in Jamaica. What might have been perceived as appropriate discipline is now criticized, publicly discredited, and deemed inappropriate by the media, researchers, and social science professionals, locally and abroad. It is clear, then, that harsh disciplinary practices beg for a reexamination in terms of their impact on child and adolescent outcomes. Both the public and policymakers must make the protection of children from mistreatment a priority.

Recommendations

[21]Undoubtedly, the traditional Jamaican parenting modus operandi conflicts with current knowledge. Prevailing socialization practices, guided by cultural beliefs and values, are contrary to modern thinking on child rearing (Crawford-Brown, 1999) but there is obvious resistance to change (Leo-Rhynie, 1997). Therefore, consideration should be given to culturally palatable strategies to respond to the growing needs of children and families. Indeed, educating the populace about the detrimental effects of certain practices on optimal child development would be a first step. The provision of relevant social services is also a necessity.

[22]*Parenting education.* Parenting education programs have shown promise as both a prevention and intervention tool in changing parental behavior and protecting children from physical abuse (Gomby, Culross, & Behrman, 1999). These programs not only provide critical information to families about the developmental needs of their children, but also help families learn how to meet those needs. They may also educate families on how to find resources (e.g., training) in behavior and stress management techniques. However, at present, such resources are almost nonexistent in Jamaica (N. Gordon, personal communication, February 25, 2002).

[23]Parenting education might be especially helpful to adolescent parents, considering the high rate of adolescent pregnancy in Jamaica (Wyatt, Durvasula, Guthrie, LeFranc, & Forge, 1999). Parents tend to imitate the disciplinary practices of their own childhood, thereby perpetuating a cycle of abuse and mistreatment, and their attendant psychological distress and negative behavioral outcomes (Frias-Armenta, 2002; Cicchetti & Toth, 1998). Young parents in particular may be ignorant of alternative methods of guidance and discipline. In a discussion of children's behavior management, Jamaican parents asked, "If you do not beat them [children], what do you do?" (Arnold, 1982, p. 143).

[24]We, like Arnold (1982), suggest that parent education begin in schools, where children could, beginning at an early age, be taught the basic principles of growth, development, and effective parenting. Further up the educational ladder, it is imperative that the curriculum in teachers' colleges focus on the relevant theoretical and empirical information about the long-term effects and dangers of corporal punishment on child outcomes. Training in guidance techniques and age-appropriate discipline should also be a prominent feature of teacher-training pedagogy. To break the cycle of violence against children, teachers, like parents, must be taught alternatives to corporal punishment.

[25]We also advocate the use of the media (e.g., radio and television) to educate the public by conveying practical and useful messages about best practices in child rearing. Media blitzes, similar to those employed in family planning advertisements and AIDS prevention and education, have great potential.

[26]*Counseling.* The provision of counseling programs for parents and caregivers is a prudent strategy. Anxiety, anger, and emotional pain in parents' and caregivers' own lives often lead to child mistreatment (Arnold, 1982; Sharpe, 1997); therefore, providing counseling to help manage and alleviate persistent stress in

families with children is appropriate and timely. Indeed, the severe physical punishment meted out to children might be, in part, an inappropriate displacement of adults' frustration (Sharpe, 1997). Bailey-Davidson (2001) noted that Jamaican children suffer from a wide range of psychiatric disorders and psychoses as a result of the parental abuse they suffer. Therefore, counseling and other programs to address the psychiatric needs of children, as well as families, are necessary.

[27]*Home visitation.* The institution of home visitation programs is another option for policymakers to consider. Home visitation programs, using trained professionals, seek to create change in parents' attitudes, knowledge, and parenting behaviors "by providing parents with social support; practical assistance, often in the form of case management that links families with other services; and education about parenting and/or child development" (Gomby, Culross, & Behrman, 1999, p. 7). These programs, based on the premise that "parents who feel confident in their ability to be parents, who are less stressed, and who know a variety of ways to discipline their children will be warmer and more responsive to their children and less likely to resort to physical violence" (p. 10), have shown great promise in preventing and reducing child maltreatment.

[28]*Research.* Sharpe (1997) maintained that the greatest challenge facing mental health professionals is "to map out ways in which to change those culturally influenced patterns of behavior toward children that endanger their mental health" (p. 270). Fortunately, some research on the mental health of Jamaican children (e.g., Crawford-Brown, 1999; Lambert, Lyubansky, & Achenbach, 1998) has begun to emerge, and has supported the findings of studies done in other cultures regarding the detrimental effects of certain parenting behaviors on child outcomes. However, much more is needed. For example, there is the need to better understand how Jamaican children's environments actually promote conditions of "alienation rather than connectedness and bondedness, distance in human relationships rather than deep and enduring intimacy, superficial rather than in-depth relationships, temporary rather than enduring solutions" (Burr & Christensen, 1992, p. 462). Although there is some research on the occurrence of physical punishment in the Jamaican culture, systematic examination of its effect on child outcomes is lacking. For example, some questions that beg empirical investigation include: Does the cultural sanctioning of corporal punishment protect children from the adverse socioemotional outcomes found in cultures where physical punishment is outlawed (e.g., the United States)? What is

the role of socioeconomic status? For example, do children from families of lower socioeconomic status have better outcomes despite the occurrence of physical punishment? The role of child outcomes along gender lines should also be explored.

Conclusion

[29]The development of social policies to prevent and reduce the adverse effects of the mistreatment of children is essential. Bailey-Davidson (2001) stressed the need for policymakers to focus on the prevention of violence to reduce the loss of human resources. Therefore, child mistreatment should become an issue of national importance. However, this will take the utmost commitment from both the government and private sector. Unfortunately, according to Crawford-Brown (1999), "the child welfare system in Jamaica can be described as archaic and ineffective, modeled on an English system of a bygone era" (p. 434). Modern social services employing best practices in mental health for families and children are desperately needed.

References

Arnold, E (1982) The use of corporal punishment in child-rearing in the West Indies. *Child Abuse and Neglect, 6,* 141–145

Bailey-Davidson, Y (2001, March 28) Child abuse. A perpetual problem. *The Jamaican Gleaner Online* Retrieved December 10, 2001, from http.//www.jamaicagleaner.com/gleaner/20010328/health/health4 html

Baptiste, D A, Hardy, K. V., & Lewis, L (1997). Clinical practice with Caribbean immigrant families in the United States· The intersection of emigration, immigration, culture, and race. In J L Rooparine & J. Brown (Eds.), *Caribbean families Diversity among ethnic groups* (pp. 275–303) Greenwich, CT. Ablex

Barrow, C. (1996). *Family in the Caribbean Themes and perspectives* Kingston, Jamaica: Ian Randle.

Baumrind, D. (1991) Parenting styles and adolescent development In J. Brooks-Gunn, R. Lerner, & A. C. Peterson (Eds.), *The encyclopedia of adolescence* (pp 746–758) New York· Garland

Bronfenbrenner, U (1979) *The ecology of human development.* Cambridge, MA· Harvard University Press.

Burr, W, & Christensen, C (1992). Undesirable side effects of enhancing self-esteem *Family Relations, 41,* 460–465

Cicchetti, G, & Toth, S L (1998) Perspectives on research and practice in developmental psychopathology. In W Damon (Series Ed), I. E Sigel, & K A Renninger (Vol Eds), *Handbook of child psychology Vol 4 Child psychology in practice* (5th ed , pp. 479–582). New York Wiley

Clarke, P. (2000, October 3) Please teacher don't beat me. *Jamaica Gleaner Online* Retrieved May 3, 2002, from http //www jamaicagleaner/gleaner/2000103/youth/youth1 html.

Crawford-Brown, C. (1997). The impact of parent–child socialization on the development of conduct disorder in Jamaican male adolescents. In J. L. Rooparine & J Brown (Eds), *Caribbean families Diversity among ethnic groups* (pp 205–222) Greenwich, CT: Ablex.

Crawford-Brown, C. (1999). The impact of parenting on conduct disorder in Jamaican male adolescents. *Adolescence, 34,* 417–436

Eisenberg, N., & Fabes, R. A. (1998). Prosocial development In W. Damon (Series Ed) & Nancy Eisenberg (Vol Ed), *Handbook of child psychology Vol 3 Social, emotional, and personality development* (5th ed , pp 463–552). New York. Wiley

Evans, H , & Davies, R (1997) Overview issues in childhood socialization in the Caribbean. In J L. Rooparine & J Brown (Eds), *Caribbean families Diversity among ethnic groups* (pp 1–24) Greenwich, CT: Ablex.

Freud, S. (1965). *Normality and pathology in childhood* New York International Universities Press.

Frias-Armenta, M. (2002). Long-term effects of child punishment on Mexican women A structural model. *Child Abuse and Neglect, 26,* 371–386

Gomby, D. S., Culross, P. L., & Behrman, R. E. (1999). Home visiting: Recent program evaluations—Analysis and recommendations. *The Future of Children, 9,* 26

Hamner, T. J., & Turner, P. H. (2001) *Parenting in contemporary society.* Boston: Allyn & Bacon

Harter, S. (1993) Causes and consequences of low self-esteem in children and adolescents. In R. F. Baumeister (Ed.), *Self-esteem: The puzzle of low regard* (pp. 87–116) New York: Plenum

Headley, B. (1994, August 14). The false promise of flogging. *The Sunday Gleaner,* p. 23A

Heimer, K. (1997) Socioeconomic status, subcultural definitions, and violent delinquency. *Social Forces, 75,* 799–833

Kamsner, S., & McCabe, M. P. (2000). The relationship between adult psychological adjustment and childhood sexual abuse, childhood physical abuse and family of origin characteristics. *Journal of Interpersonal Violence, 15,* 1243–1261

Kaplan, H. B., & Lin, C. (2000) Deviant identity as a moderator of the relation between negative self-feelings and deviant behavior. *Journal of Early Adolescence, 20,* 150–177.

Lambert, C. L., Lyubansky, M., & Achenbach, T. (1998). Behavioral and emotional problems among the adolescents of Jamaica and the United States: Parent, teacher, and self-reports for ages 12 to 18. *Journal of Emotional and Behavioral Disorders, 6,* 180–187.

Landmann, J., Grantham-McGregor, S. M., & Desai, P. (1983). Child rearing practices in Kingston, Jamaica. *Child Care, Health and Development, 9,* 57–71

Leo-Rhynie, E. A. (1997) Class, race, and gender issues in child rearing in the Caribbean. In J. L. Roopanrine & J. Brown (Eds.), *Caribbean families: Diversity among ethnic groups* (pp. 25–56) Greenwich, CT: Ablex

Paschall, M. J., Flewelling, R. L., & Ennett, S. T. (1998) Racial differences in violent behavior among adults: Moderating and confounding effects. *Journal of Research in Crime and Delinquency, 35,* 148–165

Phillips, A. S. (1973) *Adolescence in Jamaica.* Kingston, Jamaica: Jamaica Publishing House.

Rice, F. P. (2000) *Human development: A life-span approach.* Upper Saddle River, NJ: Prentice Hall

Robotham, D. R. (1999, August 15) Crime and public policy in Jamaica (1). *The Sunday Gleaner,* pp. 8A, 11A

Rohner, R. P., Kean, K. J., & Cournoyer, D. E. (1991) Effects of physical punishment, perceived caretaker warmth, and cultural beliefs on the psychological adjustment of children in St. Kitts, West Indies. *Journal of Marriage and the Family, 53,* 681–693

Sargent, C., & Harris, M. (1992). Gender ideology, childrearing, and child health in Jamaica. *American Ethnologist, 19,* 523–537

Sharpe, J. (1997) Mental health issues and family socialization in the Caribbean. In J. L. Roopanrine & J. Brown (Eds.), *Caribbean families: Diversity among ethnic groups.* Greenwich, CT: Ablex

Sloley, M. (1999, November 17) Parenting deficiencies outlined. *The Jamaica Gleaner Online.* Retrieved April 2, 2002, from http://www.jamaicagleaner/1999117/news/n1.html

Smith, M. G. (1962) *West Indian family structure.* Seattle: University of Washington Press.

Smith, M. G. (1989) *Poverty in Jamaica.* Kingston, Jamaica: University of the West Indies.

Swinford, S. P., DeMaris, A., Cernkovich, S. A., & Giordano, P. G. (2000) Harsh physical discipline in childhood and violence in later romantic involvements: The mediating role of problem behaviors. *Journal of Marriage and the Family, 62,* 508–519

Unfriendly Parents in Jamaica. (2001) *Jamaica Gleaner Online.* Retrieved April 6, 2002, from http://www.jamaicagleaner200005/24/news2.html

Walker, S. P., Grantham-McGregor, S. M., Himes, J. H., Williams, S., & Duff, E. M. (1998) School performance in adolescent Jamaican girls: Associations with health, social and behavioral characteristics, and risk factors for dropout. *Journal of Adolescence, 21,* 109–122

Wyatt, G., Durvasula, R., Guthrie, D., LeFranc, & Forge, N. (1999) Correlates of first intercourse among women in Jamaica. *Archives of Sexual Behavior, 28,* 139–157.

Yorburg, B. (2002) *Family realities: A global view.* New Jersey: Prentice-Hall

Address correspondence to: Delores E. Smith, Department of Child and Family Studies, The University of Tennessee, 115 Jessie Harris Building, 1215 West Cumberland Avenue, Knoxville, TN 37996 E-mail: delsmith@utk.edu

From *Adolescence, 38,* 369–381. Copyright © 2003 by Libra Publishers, Inc. Reprinted with permission

Discussion Questions for Model Literature Review 2

Editorial note: All the model literature reviews in this book are presented as strong models. However, there are differences of opinion on the effectiveness of any particular piece of writing, even among experts. While answering the following questions, consider the guidelines in this book (as *only* guidelines, not principles) as well as your own standards for effective writing.

1. Briefly comment on the adequacy of the title of the review.

2. Comment on the adequacy of the Abstract. Does it effectively summarize the essence of the review given that abstracts are restricted to 120 words or less in the journal in which this review article appeared?

3. Does the review have a strong beginning? Does it get straight to the point? If not, have the authors used some other effective technique to begin the review?

4. Have the authors made a strong case for reviewing the topic(s) they cover? Have they shown that the topic(s) are important?

5. Is the material presented in a logical sequence? Are the headings (and subheadings, if any) appropriate and helpful?

6. Are key variables adequately defined? Are they defined at appropriate points? Explain.

7. Are there points where the references are not well integrated with each other (i.e., simply described as an annotated list)? Explain.

8. Are the strengths and weaknesses of some of the cited research described? If yes, name at least one section where this is done using paragraph numbers.

9. Have the authors made it clear what material is theirs and what is being summarized/paraphrased from other sources? Explain.

10. Are any portions of the review unclear to you? If so, identify them by paragraph number(s).

11. Are the individual paragraphs straightforward and to the point? Explain. If yes, identify one by number that you think is especially good. If no, identify one that is weak.

12. Is the conclusion/discussion at the end of the review appropriate in light of the material covered earlier?

13. On a scale from 1 (very weak) to 10 (very strong), what is your overall evaluation of the literature re-view? Name one or two considerations that strongly influenced your evaluation.

14. Assume that you are on the editorial board of an academic journal and that the general topic of this review is within the scope of what the journal usu-ally publishes. Which of the following would you recommend to the editor of the journal: publish as is, publish only after minor revisions, publish only after major revisions, *or* do not publish? Briefly defend your recommendation.

Model Literature Review 3

Adolescent Mothers' Relationship with Their Children's Biological Fathers: Social Support, Social Strain, and Relationship Continuity

Christina B. Gee
George Washington University

Jean E. Rhodes
University of Massachusetts, Boston

Editorial note: The paragraphs in this literature review have been numbered to make it easy to refer to specific portions of this review during classroom discussions. The numbers are italicized superscripts at the beginning of each paragraph. All other nonitalicized superscripts, if any, refer to footnotes within the review.

This review was written as an introduction to a report on original research conducted by the authors. Only the literature review portion of the report is reprinted here. Note that Model Literature Reviews 1 and 4 were also written as introductions to reports on original research. The remaining model literature reviews in this book were written as "stand-alone" reviews—not as introductions to original research.

[1]In the United States, close to half a million adolescents give birth each year, but only 16% will marry before their child is born (Child Trends, 2001). Over the past decade, statistics such as these have increased attention, particularly among those interested in social policy, on the fathers of children born to adolescent mothers.[1] Reflecting this interest in fathers, the 1996 Personal Responsibility and Work Opportunity Reconciliation Act placed an increased emphasis on establishment of paternity and strengthening child support efforts, effectively increasing fathers' involvement in the lives of adolescent mothers and their children (Coley & Chase-Lansdale, 1998). For example, women receiving public assistance who fail to cooperate with the establishment of paternity can have their monthly cash aid reduced. Similarly, many states have initiated policies pertaining to the establishment of paternity and enforcement of child support.

[2]Given this recent attention to paternity, research that attempts to understand the role of fathers in the lives of adolescent mothers is necessary. To this end, we conducted a study that addressed three central questions. First, how does support and strain in adolescent mothers' relationships with the fathers of their children change over the first 3 years postpartum? Second, what are the factors that predict relationship continuity over the first 3 years postpartum? Third, does father support and strain predict adolescent mothers' psychological adjustment? And, if so, does maternal grandmother support serve as a protective factor?

Background

[3]The transition to motherhood represents a major developmental milestone for all women but is particularly stressful for adolescents. At the same time that they are struggling to negotiate their new, maternal roles and responsibilities, they are coping with the physical, emotional, and cognitive challenges of adolescence. Moreover, African American mothers often face additional adversities stemming from racial oppression and economic hardship. Chronic and isolated periods of economic hardship can be demoralizing to young, low-income, minority mothers and, not surprisingly, rates of depression are high in this population (Belle, 1994). For example, Hobfoll, Ritter, Lavin, Hulsizer, and Cameron (1995) found that 23.4% of low-income, urban, African American and European American mothers reported symptoms of postpartum depression, a rate that is double that found in middle-class samples (Cutrona, 1983; Gotlib, Whiffen, Wallace, & Mount, 1991; O'Hara, 1986). Further, for low-income, African American and Puerto Rican adolescent mothers, these depressive symptoms have been shown to endure chronically or

---

[1] In the current study, unless otherwise specified, "father" refers to the biological fathers of children born to adolescent mothers.

intermittently for at least 3 years postpartum (Leadbeater & Linares, 1992).

[4]Social support, particularly from adolescents' mothers and male partners, appears to play an important role in mitigating the postpartum adjustment difficulties (Leadbeater & Bishop, 1994; McLoyd, 1990). Because minority young mothers are more likely than older mothers to be living in poverty they often rely heavily on others for child care, material assistance, and support. Yet, as their reliance on others increases, so too does their vulnerability to the problematic aspects of social relationships and depression (Davis & Rhodes, 1994). Disputes about appropriate parenting and the young women's lifestyle can easily arise in the sharing of childrearing responsibilities (Davis, 2002; Davis, Rhodes, & Hamilton-Leaks, 1997), and disappointment and frustration with male partners is not uncommon (Gee & Rhodes, 1999). Moreover, young mothers with limited resources often find it difficult to reciprocate the support that they have received, creating an uncomfortable imbalance in the relationship (Belle, 1981). Indeed, Miller-Loncar, Erwin, Landry, Smith, and Swank (1998) found that lower SES mothers were less satisfied with their social networks, and relative to other ethnic groups, African American mothers had more stressful social interactions with their network members. These and other findings (e.g., Davis et al., 1997; Taylor, Henderson, & Jackson, 1991) suggest that low-income, urban African American mothers' heightened exposure to life stressors may undermine the potential benefits of social support. Of course, there is likely to be considerable variation in African American mothers' experiences in their social networks and the support and benefits that they derive. For example, some young mothers benefit greatly from the support that is provided by the father of their babies and, more generally, their social networks. Indeed, many are embedded in rich kinship networks (Snowden, 2001; Stack, 1974), and many African American families are embedded in extensive family, neighborhood- and church-based support networks (Wilson et al., 1995). Additional within-group research is needed to better understand the conditions under which support from key providers is available (and beneficial) to African American mothers.

Father Involvement

[5]Male partners (including fathers) are one of the primary social resources to adolescent mothers, and the support that they provide during the postpartum adjustment period is often critical to the adolescents' well-being (Colletta, Hadler, & Gregg, 1981; de Anda & Be-cerra, 1984; Stack, 1974). Approximately half of adolescent mothers identify a male partner as someone who provides social support (e.g., Gee & Rhodes, 1999; Thompson, 1986; Thompson & Peebles-Wilkins, 1992), and this support is often rated as being as important as support provided by their mothers (de Anda & Becerra, 1984; Gee & Rhodes, 1999; Spieker & Bensley, 1994; Thompson & Peebles-Wilkins, 1992). Several cross-sectional studies suggest that the child's father and maternal grandmother provide approximately equal amounts of support throughout pregnancy and early motherhood (de Anda & Becerra, 1984; Spieker & Bensley, 1994; Thompson & Peebles-Wilkins, 1992). Moreover, their support has been associated with adolescent mothers' greater overall life satisfaction (Unger & Wandersman, 1988), lower psychological distress (Thompson, 1986; Thompson & Peebles-Wilkins, 1992), and higher levels of self-esteem (Thompson & Peebles-Wilkins, 1992). Furthermore, evidence suggests that father support may contribute to less angry and punitive parenting on the part of adolescent mothers (Crockenberg, 1987).

[6]Other studies, however, present a less positive view of father support. Father support has been associated with diminished parenting skills (Shapiro & Mangelsdorf, 1994) and reduced academic achievement for African American and European American adolescent mothers (Unger & Cooley, 1992). Adolescent mothers often cite problems with their male partners ranging from disappointment over unmet expectations for financial and child care assistance to serious conflicts, difficult break-ups, and physical and sexual assault (Belle, 1981; Leadbeater & Linares, 1992; Leadbeater & Way, 2001; Leadbeater, Way, & Raden, 1996). These problems in relationships with fathers, in turn, have been associated with heightened depressive symptoms among adolescent mothers (Gee & Rhodes, 1999).

[7]Taken together, the studies cited above suggest that male partners influence young mothers' psychological adjustment. In some cases, they provide support and comfort, whereas in others they contribute to distress and heightened adjustment difficulties. Despite their potential influence, few studies have provided detailed examinations of their role in adolescent mothers' lives.

[8]Clarifying the association between father involvement and adolescent mothers' psychological adjustment is important for several reasons. As stated above, research has found high rates of depression among low-income, minority mothers (e.g., Belle, Doucet, Harris, Miller, & Tan, 2000). Maternal stress and depression can take a toll on young mothers' parent-

ing skills; depressed adolescent mothers have been rated as less competent in their parenting of infants than their nondepressed counterparts (Gelfand, Teti, & Fox, 1992). They have been found to exhibit more negative and intrusive touch (Malphurs, Raag, Field, Pickens, & Pelaez-Nogueras, 1996), more controlling and less responsive interactions (Cassidy, Zoccolillo, & Hughes, 1996; Downey & Coyne, 1990), and more negative feeding interactions with their infants (Panzarine, Slater, & Sharps, 1995).

[9]As might be expected, exposure to poverty and maternal depression put children of adolescent mothers at disproportionate risk for cognitive impairment, social–emotional problems, and early and pervasive school failure (Belle et al., 2000). Leadbeater and Bishop (1994), for example, have documented robust associations between minority adolescent mothers' depression and their reports of preschool children's behavior problems over time. Moreover, the incidence of developmental delay and behavior problems in these children increases as they get older (Furstenberg, Brooks-Gunn, & Morgan, 1987). For these reasons, it is critical that we understand the associations between father involvement and adolescent mother psychological adjustment.

[10]A first step toward this end is for research on fathers to include more detailed assessments of father involvement. Most of the existing research and corresponding policy has focused on fathers' financial contributions, relying largely on census reports of child support payments. Nonetheless, qualitative studies have found that financial contributions to adolescent mothers may be higher than reported by the census because of irregular or unreported contributions (Coley & Chase-Lansdale, 1998; Stier & Tienda, 1993). Thus, this focus on financial support is incomplete, given the range of potentially influential types of support that fathers provide. In addition, many studies have included only global indices of support (e.g., satisfaction), and few have looked at social strain (e.g., criticism, disappointment) and its influence (Rook, 1990, 1998).

Continuity of Father Involvement

[11]Despite the apparent importance of fathers in adolescent mothers' lives, these relationships appear to weaken over time (Rivara, Sweeny, & Henderson, 1986). For example, adolescent mothers report that support from their male partners (i.e., boyfriends, biological fathers) decreases over the first postpartum year (Gee & Rhodes, 1999; Wasserman, Brunelli, & Rauh, 1990). In addition, during the course of the first couple of years postpartum, some adolescent mothers remain in roman-

tic relationships with fathers whereas others terminate these relationships. For example, Unger and Wandersman (1988) reported that 50% of African American adolescent mothers in their study were no longer involved with their child's father, and 40% had a new boyfriend at 8 months postpartum. Comparable rates of father involvement (51% involved at 18 months postpartum) were found in a study of predominantly lower income, European American adolescent mothers (Cutrona, Hessling, Bacon, & Russell, 1998). Further, Leadbeater and Way's (2001) longitudinal study of low-income, inner-city, minority mothers indicated that although 26% of adolescent mothers reported close (defined as frequent and emotionally positive contact) relationships with their child's father at 3 years postpartum, this percentage declined to 12% at 6 years postpartum.

[12]Studies that document the decline of father involvement over time have prompted researchers to begin to study factors that predict continuous involvement on the part of the father. A growing body of research suggests the quality of the father's relationship with the mother early on in the pregnancy is an important predictor of continuity. Cutrona et al.'s (1998) study of lower income, European American adolescent mothers found that fathers were more likely to remain involved if their relationship with the adolescent mother was intimate and supportive during the weeks immediately following the baby's birth. Similarly, Gavin et al. (2002) found that, among low-income, urban, African American mothers, the strongest predictor of father involvement during the postpartum period was the quality of his relationship with his baby's mother. Also supporting these findings, Coley and Chase-Lansdale (1999) found that, regardless of romantic involvement, a strong or harmonious relationship with mothers increased the likelihood of urban African American fathers' involvement with their children.

[13]Along the same vein, the formation of a romantic relationship with a new male partner may also affect the likelihood of continued father involvement. Again, the research is mixed on this issue. Whereas some research suggests that biological fathers may become less involved when new partners are involved (Cutrona et al., 1998), other research has found that new partners do not necessarily deter fathers from providing support (Coley & Chase-Lansdale, 1999). Additional research examining predictors of romantic relationship continuity among adolescent mothers is clearly necessary.

[14]Finally, another potentially important influence on the longevity of the adolescent mother–father relationship is the child's maternal grandmother.[2] Maternal grandmothers sometimes serve as gatekeepers, or regulatory agents, who can either facilitate or prevent fathers from seeing adolescent mothers (Furstenberg, 1995). In support of the gatekeeping hypothesis, Gavin et al. (2002) found that fathers of children born to African American adolescent mothers were more involved when maternal grandmothers reported positive relationships with fathers.

Maternal Grandmother Support

[15]Most previous studies have not examined the child's father and maternal grandmother simultaneously; thus, the interaction between maternal grandmother support and father strain has not been examined. The protective influence of close family members may be especially salient for African American adolescent mothers who often continue to live at home after the birth of their baby (e.g., Apfel & Seitz, 1996; Chase-Lansdale, Gordon, Coley, Wakschlag, & Brooks-Gunn, 1999; Unger & Wandersman, 1988; Wasserman et al., 1990). Co-residence is particularly likely for African American adolescent mothers, who are often embedded in extensive networks of kinship support (Stack, 1974). Indeed, even when living apart, young African American mothers often obtain considerable help from immediate and extended family members (Apfel & Seitz, 1991), and for approximately half of low-income, African American adolescent mothers, a significant amount of parenting support from their mothers continues until 6 years postpartum (Apfel & Seitz, 1996).

[16]Although some studies suggest that maternal grandmothers can be a source of strain (Belle, 1981; Bogat, Caldwell, Guzman, Galasso, & Davidson, 1998; Rhodes & Woods, 1995), research consistently indicates that grandmothers' support is positively associated with adolescent mothers' psychological well-being, academic attainment, financial status, disciplinary practices, and responsive mothering behavior (Cooley & Unger, 1991; Spieker & Bensley, 1994; Unger & Cooley, 1992). Further, qualitative research indicates that receipt of financial and child care support from the maternal grandmother is associated with greater educational achievement (Cooley & Unger, 1991; Furstenberg, Brooks-Gunn, & Morgan, 1987) and better psychological well-being for adolescent mothers (e.g., Panzarine, 1986).

---

[2] In the current study, unless otherwise specified, "grandmother" refers to the mother of the adolescent mother.

Summary

[17]The existing research suggests that, at least initially, fathers are involved in the lives of adolescent mothers and their children and that their influence has costs and benefits. In light of their potential influence, as well as the policies that promote long-term involvement, it is important to identify factors that predict relationship continuity. Unfortunately, despite some notable exceptions (e.g., Furstenberg & Harris, 1993; Leadbeater & Way, 2001), the majority of the research specifically examining father involvement is cross-sectional and tends to be collected only immediately postpartum. Given the limitations of cross-sectional data, it is unclear how adolescent mothers' relationships with fathers change over time and what factors predict continued involvement.

References

Apfel, N H., & Seitz, V (1991) Four models of adolescent mother–grandmother relationships in Black inner-city families Family Relations Interdisciplinary Journal of Applied Family Studies, 40, 421–429.

Apfel, N. H., & Seitz, V (1996) African American adolescent mothers, their families, and their daughters: A longitudinal perspective over twelve years. In B J Leadbeater & N Way (Eds), Urban girls Resisting stereotypes, creating identities (pp. 149–172). New York. New York University Press

Belle, D (1981, April). The social network as a source of both stress and support to low-income mothers (Paper presented at the biennial meeting of the Society for Research on Child Development, Boston)

Belle, D (1994). Attempting to comprehend the lives of low-income women. In C. E. Franz & A J Stewart (Eds), Women creating lives Identities, resilience, and resistance (pp 37–50) Boulder, CO. Westview Press

Belle, D., Doucet, J , Harris, J , Miller, J., & Tan, E. (2000) Who is rich? Who is happy? American Psychologist, 55, 1160–1161

Bogat, G A., Caldwell, R A , Guzman, B , Galasso, L., & Davidson, W S (1998) Structure and stability of maternal support among pregnant and parenting adolescents Journal of Community Psychology, 26, 549–568

Cassidy, B , Zoccolillo, M., & Hughes, S. (1996) Psychopathology in adolescent mothers and its effects on mother–infant interactions A pilot study Canadian Journal of Psychiatry, 41, 379–384

Chase-Lansdale, P. L , Gordon, R. A , Coley, R. L , Wakschlag, L , & Brooks-Gunn, J (1999) Young African-American multigenerational families in poverty The contexts, exchanges, and processes of their lives In E M Hetherington (Ed), Coping with divorce, single parenting, and remarriage A risk and resiliency perspective Mahwah, NJ Erlbaum

Child Trends (2001) Facts at a glance Washington, DC: Author

Coley, R L , & Chase-Lansdale, P. L (1998) Adolescent pregnancy and parenthood· Recent evidence and future directions. American Psychologist, 53, 152–166

Coley, R L., & Chase-Lansdale, P L (1999). Stability and change in paternal involvement of urban African-American fathers Journal of Family Psychology, 13, 416–435.

Colletta, N D., Hadler, S , & Gregg, C H (1981). How adolescents cope with the problems of early motherhood Adolescence, 16, 499–512.

Cooley, M L., & Unger, D G (1991) The role of family support in determining developmental outcomes in children of teen mothers. Child Psychiatry and Human Development, 21, 217–233.

Crockenberg, S. B (1987) Predictors and correlates of anger toward and punitive control of toddlers by adolescent mothers Child Development, 58, 964–975

Cutrona, C E (1983) Causal attributions and perinatal depression. Journal of Abnormal Psychology, 92, 161–172.

Cutrona, C E , Hessling, R M , Bacon, P L , & Russell, D W (1998) Predictors and correlates of continuing involvement with the baby's father among adolescent mothers Journal of Family Psychology, 12, 369–387

Davis, A. A. (2002) Younger and older African American adolescent mothers' relationships with their mothers and female peers Journal of Adolescent Research, 17, 491–508

Davis, A A , & Rhodes, J. E (1994) African-American mothers and their mothers An analysis of supportive and problematic interactions. Journal of Community Psychology, 22, 12–20.

Davis, A A , Rhodes, J E , & Hamilton-Leaks, J (1997) When both parents may be a source of support and problems. An analysis of pregnant and parenting female

African American adolescents' relationships with their mothers and fathers *Journal of Research on Adolescence, 7*, 331–348

de Anda, D., & Becerra, R. M (1984) Social support networks for adolescent mothers *Journal of Social Casework, 65*, 172–181.

Downey, G., & Coyne, J C (1990) Children of depressed parents An integrative review *Psychological Bulletin, 108*, 50–76

Furstenberg, F. F. Jr. (1995). Fathering in the inner city· Paternal participation and public policy In W Marsiglio (Ed), *Fatherhood Contemporary theory, research, and social policy* London. Sage

Furstenberg, F. F, Brooks-Gunn, J , & Morgan, S. P (1987). *Adolescent mothers in later life* Cambridge, England Cambridge University Press.

Furstenberg, F F, & Harris, K M (1993) When and why fathers matter Impacts of father involvement on the children of adolescent mothers In A. Lawson & D. Rhodes (Eds.), *The politics of pregnancy* (pp 189–215) New Haven, CT Yale University Press

Gavin, L. E, Black, M M, Minor, S, Abel, Y, Papas, M A , & Bentley, M E (2002) Young, disadvantaged fathers' involvement with their infants· An ecological perspective *Journal of Adolescent Health, 31*, 266–276

Gee, C B, & Rhodes, J E (1999). Postpartum transitions in adolescent mothers' romantic and maternal relationships *Merrill-Palmer Quarterly, 45*, 512–532

Gelfand, D M, Teti, D M, & Fox, C R. (1992) Sources of parenting stress for depressed and nondepressed mothers of infants *Journal of Clinical Child Psychology, 21*, 262–272

Gotlib, I H, Whiffen, V E, Wallace, P M, & Mount, J. H (1991) Prospective investigation of post-partum depression: Factors involved in onset and recovery *Journal of Abnormal Psychology, 100*, 122–132

Hobfoll, S., Ritter, C., Lavin, J., Hulsizer, M R , & Cameron, R P. (1995) Depression prevalence and incidence among inner-city pregnant and postpartum women. *Journal of Consulting and Clinical Psychology, 63*, 445–453.

Leadbeater, B J , & Bishop, S. J (1994) Predictors of behavior problems in preschool children of inner-city Afro-American and Puerto Rican adolescent mothers. *Child Development, 65*, 638–648

Leadbeater, B J , & Linares, O (1992) Depressive symptoms in Black and Puerto Rican adolescent mothers in the first three years postpartum *Development and Psychopathology, 4*, 451–468.

Leadbeater, B J , & Way, N. (2001) *Growing up fast Transitions to early adulthood of inner-city adolescent mothers* Mahwah, NJ Erlbaum

Leadbeater, B J R, Way, N, & Raden, A (1996) Why not marry your baby's father? Answers from African-American and Hispanic adolescent mothers In B J R Leadbeater & N. Way (Eds), *Urban girls Resisting stereotypes, creating identities* New York New York University Press

Malphurs, J. E., Raag, T, Field, T., Pickens, J, & Pelaez-Nogueras, M (1996) Touch by intrusive and withdrawn mothers with depressive symptoms *Early Development and Parenting, 5*, 111–115.

McLoyd, V. C. (1990). The impact of economic hardship on Black families and children Psychological distress, parenting, and socioemotional development *Child Development, 61*, 311–346.

Miller-Loncar, C L, Erwin, L. J, Landry, S H, Smith, K E, & Swank, P R (1998) Characteristics of social support networks of low socioeconomic status African American, Anglo American, and Mexican American mothers of full term and preterm infants. *Journal of Community Psychology, 26*, 131–143

O'Hara, M W (1986) Social support, life events, and depression during pregnancy and the puerperium *Archives of General Psychiatry, 43*, 569–573

Panzarine, S. (1986) Stressors, coping, and social supports of adolescent mothers *Journal of Adolescent Health Care, 7*, 153–161

Panzarine, S, Slater, E, & Sharps, P. (1995) Coping, social support, and depressive symptoms in adolescent mothers *Journal of Adolescent Health, 17*, 113–119.

Rhodes, J E, & Woods, M. (1995) Comfort and conflict in the relationships of pregnant, minority adolescents. Social support as a moderator of social strain *Journal of Community Psychology, 23*, 74–84

Rivara, F. P., Sweeny, P., & Henderson, B. F (1986) Black teenage fathers What happens after the child is born? *Pediatrics, 17*, 151–158

Rook, K S (1990) Parallels in the study of social support and social strain *Journal of Social and Clinical Psychology, 9*, 118–132.

Rook, K S (1998) Investigating the positive and negative sides of personal relationships· Through a lens darkly? In B J Spitzberg & W. R. Cupach, (Eds.), *The dark side of close relationships* (pp 369–393) Mahwah, NJ Erlbaum

Shapiro, J R, & Mangelsdorf, S C. (1994) The determinants of parenting competence in adolescent mothers *Journal of Youth and Adolescence, 23*, 621–641

Snowden, L (2001) Social embeddedness and psychological well-being among African Americans and Whites. *American Journal of Community Psychology, 29*, 519–536.

Spieker, S. J, & Bensley, L (1994). Roles of living arrangements and grandmother social support in adolescent mothering and infant attachment *Developmental Psychology, 30*, 102–111.

Stack, C (1974) *All our kin Strategies for survival in a Black community* New York. Harper & Row

Stier, H., & Tienda, M (1993). Are men marginal to the family? Insights from Chicago's inner city In J C Hood (Ed), *Men, work, and family* (pp. 23–44) Newbury Park, CA Sage

Taylor, J , Henderson, D., & Jackson, B. B. (1991) A holistic model for understanding and predicting depressive symptoms in African American women *Journal of Community Psychology, 19*, 306–320

Thompson, M (1986) The influence of supportive relations on the psychological well-being of teenage mothers *Social Forces, 64*, 1006–1024.

Thompson, M, & Peebles-Wilkins, W. (1992) The impact of formal, informal, and societal support networks on the psychological well-being of Black adolescent mothers *Social Work, 37*, 322–328

Unger, D G, & Cooley, M. (1992). Partner and grandmother contact in Black and White teen parent families *Journal of Adolescent Health, 13*, 546–552

Unger, D G., & Wandersman, L. P. (1988) The relationship of family and partner support to the adjustment of adolescent mothers *Child Development, 59*, 1056–1060

Wasserman, G A., Brunelli, S A, & Rauh, V. A. (1990) Social support and the living arrangements of adolescent and adult mothers *Journal of Adolescent Research, 5*, 54–66

Wilson, M N., Greene-Bates, C, McKim, L, Simmons, F, Askew, T, Curry-El, J , & Hinton, I. D (1995) African American family life The dynamics of interactions, relationships, and roles. In M. N Wilson (Ed), *African American family life Its structural and ecological aspects* (pp 5–21) San Francisco· Jossey Bass.

Address correspondence to: Christina B. Gee, Department of Psychology, George Washington University, 2125 G Street NW, Washington, DC 20052. E-mail. cgee@gwu.edu

From *Journal of Family Psychology, 17*, 370–383 Copyright © 2003 by the American Psychological Association. Reprinted with permission.

Discussion Questions for
Model Literature Review 3

Editorial Note: All the model literature reviews in this book are presented as strong models. However, there are differences of opinion on the effectiveness of any particular piece of writing, even among experts. While answering the following questions, consider the guidelines in this book (as *only* guidelines, not principles) as well as your own standards for effective writing.

1. Briefly comment on the adequacy of the title of the review.

2. Does the review have a strong beginning? Does it get straight to the point? If not, have the authors used some other effective technique to begin the review?

3. Have the authors made a strong case for reviewing the topic(s) they cover? Have they shown that the topic(s) are important?

4. Is the material presented in a logical sequence? Are the headings (and subheadings, if any) appropriate and helpful?

5. Are key variables adequately defined? Are they defined at appropriate points? Explain.

6. Are there points where the references are not well integrated with each other (i.e., simply described as an annotated list)? Explain.

7. Are the strengths and weaknesses of some of the cited research described? If yes, name at least one section where this is done using paragraph numbers.

8. Have the authors made it clear what material is theirs and what is being summarized/paraphrased from other sources? Explain.

9. Are any portions of the review unclear to you? If so, identify them by paragraph number(s).

10. Are the individual paragraphs straightforward and to the point? Explain. If yes, identify one by number that you think is especially good. If no, identify one that is weak.

11. Is the conclusion/discussion at the end of the review appropriate in light of the material covered earlier?

12. On a scale from 1 (very weak) to 10 (very strong), what is your overall evaluation of the literature review? Name one or two considerations that strongly influenced your evaluation.

13. Assume that you are on the editorial board of an academic journal and that the general topic of this review is within the scope of what the journal usually publishes. Which of the following would you recommend to the editor of the journal: publish as is, publish only after minor revisions, publish only after major revisions, or do not publish? Briefly defend your recommendation.

Model Literature Review 4

The Performance of Narcissists Rises and Falls with Perceived Opportunity for Glory

Harry M. Wallace
Case Western Reserve University

Roy F. Baumeister
Case Western Reserve University

Editorial note: The paragraphs in this literature review have been numbered to make it easy to refer to specific portions of this review during classroom discussions. The numbers are italicized superscripts, which appear at the beginning of each paragraph. All other nonitalicized superscripts, if any, refer to footnotes within the review.

This review was written as an introduction to a report on original research conducted by the authors. Only the literature review portion of the report is reprinted here. Note that Model Literature Reviews 1 and 3 were also written as introductions to reports on original research. The remaining model literature reviews in this book were written as "stand-alone" reviews—not as introductions to original research.

[1]Andre, a pass receiver for his football team, has a reputation as a flashy player who makes difficult, spectacular plays at crucial times in important games. When the stakes are high and the spotlight is bright, Andre is at his best. Andre has also developed a reputation as a malcontent who complains when the ball is not thrown to him. On one infamous occasion, Andre nearly started a fight with his quarterback for throwing the ball to another player—even though the pass was caught for a touchdown that won the game. Andre also has a penchant for blowing easy plays, especially during practice and in games that are relatively insignificant. One of his teammates once explained to a reporter, "Andre is a real pain in the neck. He's chronically late to practice, he struts around like he's God's gift to football, and I don't think I've ever seen him throw a decent block for another player. But when the game is on the line, we're all happy to have Andre on our team." Why does Andre only perform well when the circumstances are most challenging? What can account for Andre's lack of consideration for his coach and fellow teammates? The present research offers an explanation: Andre might be a narcissist.[1]

[2]The present investigation examines the effects of narcissism on task performance. We hypothesized that narcissism can be either advantageous or detrimental to performance, depending on the situational context. Specifically, we reasoned that the effects of narcissism on task performance should be moderated by perceived self-enhancement opportunity. Narcissists crave opportunities for self-enhancement, and some tasks offer more self-enhancement value than others. Narcissists should perform well when task success will be taken as an impressive sign of personal superiority. However, when task success will be unimpressive, narcissists should perform relatively poorly. In comparison, the performance of people with low levels of narcissism should be less affected by perceived self-enhancement opportunity.

Narcissism and Performance

[3]In Greek mythology, Narcissus was a young man who fell in love with his own reflection in a pool and ultimately perished as a result of his self-absorption. In the terminology of modern clinical psychology, such excessive and dysfunctional self-love is characteristic of people with narcissistic personality disorder (see *Diagnostic and Statistical Manual of Mental Disorders*, 4th ed. [*DSM-IV*]; American Psychiatric Association, 1994). According to *DSM-IV* classification, people with narcissistic personality disorder exhibit an exaggerated sense of self-importance and uniqueness, arrogance, an unreasonable sense of entitlement, exploitative tendencies, empathy deficits, and a need for excessive admiration.

[4]The concept of narcissism has been extended from the restricted domain of mental illness to encompass many tendencies among ostensibly normal individuals.

---

[1] We use the terms *narcissists* and *high narcissists* to refer to people with relatively high scores on the Narcissistic Personality Inventory (NPI; Raskin & Hall, 1979; Raskin & Terry, 1988), a measure of subclinical narcissism. The term *low narcissists* refers to people with relatively low scores on the NPI.

Empirical research on subclinical narcissism has flourished since the creation of the NPI (Raskin & Hall, 1979; Raskin & Terry, 1988), a self-report questionnaire that has become the standard measure of narcissism in normal populations. Empirical research using the NPI has shown that narcissistic people think highly of themselves and their abilities (Emmons, 1984; Gabriel, Critelli, & Ee, 1994; John & Robins, 1994; Raskin, Novacek, & Hogan, 1991a; Robins & Beer, 2001). This research also shows that narcissists have unusually high self-expectations (Farwell & Wohlwend-Lloyd, 1998) and an exaggerated sense of personal control over their world (Dhavale, 2000; Watson, Sawrie, & Biderman, 1991). High levels of self-confidence and self-efficacy have been linked with high achievement in past research (e.g., Bandura, 1977; Baumeister, Hamilton, & Tice, 1985; Feather, 1966, 1968; Tuckman & Sexton, 1992; see Pajares, 1997, for a review), so it is plausible that narcissism could facilitate performance success.

[5]To be sure, one might expect a positive correlation between performance and narcissism even if narcissism did not produce self-fulfilling expectancies of success. Performance success could foster narcissism. A history of performance success should gradually boost one's self-regard (Felson, 1993), which could fuel the development of narcissism. High performers might continue to perform well even as their levels of narcissism grow.

[6]Thus, there are good theoretical grounds for predicting that narcissists might outperform other people in general. Past studies examining possible links between narcissism and performance have produced conflicting results, however. Gabriel et al. (1994) found that narcissism was positively correlated with self-reported intelligence, but they found no correlation between narcissism and actual performance on an intelligence test. John and Robins (1994) found that narcissistic participants thought they performed quite well on a group interaction task, but observer evaluations indicated that narcissists performed no better or worse than others. Robins and John (1997) asked study participants to present a convincing oral argument to a group of people. People with high scores on narcissism rated their performances much higher than low scorers rated their performances. However, objective measures revealed no difference in the quality of presentations given by high and low narcissists. Raskin (1980) found that narcissism was positively correlated with both self-reported creativity and performance on an objective creativity test. Farwell and Wohlwend-Lloyd (1998) conducted two studies in which narcissistic students were more likely than their peers to overestimate their future and current course

grades. Narcissism and course grades were positively correlated in one study, but no correlation between narcissism and course grades was found in the other study. In sum, past research has demonstrated that narcissists consider themselves to be exceptional performers, but the actual performance of narcissists in past studies has often been no better than that of other people.

The Importance of
Self-Enhancement Opportunity

[7]The preceding section reveals a discrepancy. Theoretical grounds and narcissists' self-appraisals suggest that narcissism ought to improve performance, but most studies of actual performance quality have failed to find any benefit of narcissism. One possible explanation for this discrepancy is that narcissism simply makes mediocre performers think they are superior to others. The failure of confidence and self-fulfilling expectancies of success to produce any actual performance improvement would be somewhat surprising, but otherwise this explanation could account for the discrepancy between subjective and objective benefits.

[8]The present investigation, however, is based on a more complex theory about the effects of narcissism on performance. We reasoned that the performance level of narcissists might rise or fall depending on the situational opportunity for self-enhancement. We define a performance situation as having high self-enhancement opportunity to the extent that successful performance will be interpreted as an indication that the performer has impressively high levels of skills, talents, or other desirable traits. In other words, self-enhancement opportunity denotes the degree to which one can potentially win glory by performing well.

[9]Most people seek to self-enhance to some degree, but narcissists are especially zealous in their pursuit of personal glory (e.g., Campbell, Reeder, Sedikides, & Elliot, 2000; John & Robins, 1994; Morf & Rhodewalt, 2001; Robins & Beer, 2001). Because narcissists are so obsessed with self-enhancement, they should be keenly aware that some performance tasks offer more potential for self-enhancement than others. When narcissists perceive that a performance task offers no opportunity for self-enhancement, their motivation to perform that task should be reduced, and their performance may suffer.

[10]At least three factors determine whether a performance is self-enhancing for the performer: (a) the quality of the performance, (b) audience characteristics, and (c) the diagnosticity of the performance task. The first factor is obvious: The self-enhancement value of performance increases with the quality of the perform-

ance. There is no glory to be gained by performing at a low level. The self-enhancement potential of a performance is also influenced by audience characteristics. A great public performance should be more self-enhancing than an equally great private performance. Moreover, a great performance witnessed by people whose opinions are valued by the performer should be more self-enhancing than a great performance witnessed by people the performer does not respect. Still, even a successful performance in front of a respected audience may not necessarily be self-enhancing. For the performance to be self-enhancing, it must be diagnostic of special achievement. Task success is not diagnostic of achievement when success is assumed or expected. Thus, challenging tasks offer more potential for self-enhancement than unchallenging tasks.

The Impact of Challenge Level

[11]When the task goal is introduced as a difficult challenge that people rarely achieve, narcissists should view this performance task as an excellent opportunity to demonstrate their superiority over others. Just as the mythical Narcissus was obsessed with observing his own reflected beauty, modern-day narcissists crave chances to observe their reflected greatness (Robins & John, 1997). As discussed earlier, difficult goal achievement is more diagnostic of exceptional ability than easy goal achievement. Narcissists' motivation to achieve difficult goals should be especially strong because they are more concerned with self-enhancement than other people (e.g., Campbell et al., 2000; John & Robins, 1994; Paulhus, 1998). Furthermore, narcissists' inflated self-views should give them confidence that they can succeed at tasks at which most others have failed. This combination of high motivation and high self-confidence should help their performance on challenging tasks. In contrast, high performance on an unchallenging task is not indicative of high ability, so narcissists may have relatively little motivation to exert themselves on such tasks. Narcissists' high self-expectations could even be detrimental to performance on unchallenging tasks. If narcissists believe task success is common, they may take it for granted.

[12]People who are not narcissistic are less concerned about self-enhancement than narcissists, so their motivation and performance should be less affected by the self-enhancement opportunity presented by the task goal. If the difficulty of a challenge has any effect on the performance of low narcissists, the effect should be in the opposite direction of the predicted effect of challenge level on the performance of narcissists. The motivation

of low narcissists should vary little as a function of challenge level, but their confidence and performance could suffer if they consider the task goal to be too challenging. When the task goal is unchallenging, low narcissists should have some confidence in their ability to succeed, but they should be less likely than narcissists to assume success.

[13]One reason why past studies have found no evidence of a relationship between narcissism and performance may be that the performance goals used in these studies were not challenging or unchallenging enough to reveal performance differences based on levels of narcissism. Although no previous research has directly addressed the relationship among narcissism, task challenge, and performance, past research on achievement motivation provides indirect support for the present hypotheses. Atkinson (1958) and Kukla (1972, 1974) demonstrated that confidence in one's abilities helps performance on difficult tasks and hurts performance on easy tasks. This performance pattern is apparently a function of motivation: Meyer (1987) found that people with very high self-rated ability reported that they would invest more effort on tasks of high difficulty than on tasks of low difficulty, whereas people with very low self-rated ability reported that they would invest more effort on tasks of low difficulty than on tasks of high difficulty. In addition, Trope (1979) found that persons with high perceived ability have a particularly strong preference for tasks of high diagnosticity, and, as he noted, difficult tasks are especially diagnostic for high ability levels. Narcissists clearly think highly of their abilities, so they should prefer to invest more effort on highly difficult tasks.

The Impact of Audience Evaluation

[14]The self-enhancement value of high performance should increase when an audience observes the performance. In general, people are more motivated to perform when others can evaluate their individual performance. For example, people exert less individual effort toward a group goal when the individual contributions of group members are unidentifiable, a phenomenon known as social loafing (e.g., Latane, Williams, & Harkins, 1979; Williams, Harkins, & Latane, 1981; see Karau & Williams, 1993, for a review). On collective group tasks, where the performances of individual group members are indistinguishable, potential for individual self-enhancement is limited because the glory associated with exceptional group performance is diffused among group members. If narcissists are strongly motivated to self-enhance, as past research suggests, they should be

far more motivated to perform individual tasks than collective tasks. Thus, narcissists' self-serving orientation could lead them to exhibit more social loafing than less narcissistic people exhibit.

[15]The relationship between narcissism and social loafing has not been explored, but recent research has shown that people who perceive themselves as better than others are more prone to social loafing than those who consider themselves average (Charbonnier, Huguet, Brauer, & Monteil, 1998; Huguet, Charbonnier, & Monteil, 1999). In addition, Sanna (1992) found that people with high self-efficacy performed well when their performance was being evaluated but that they performed poorly when they did not expect their performance to be evaluated. People with low self-efficacy showed the opposite pattern of performance. Narcissists consistently rate themselves as better than others (e.g., Farwell & Wohlwend-Lloyd, 1998; Gabriel et al., 1994; John & Robins, 1994; Raskin, 1980; Robins & John, 1997), and they have high self-efficacy (e.g., Farwell & Wohlwend-Lloyd, 1998; Watson et al., 1991), so they too should perform best in the presence of an evaluative audience.

Present Investigation

[16]In the present research, we examined the impact of self-enhancement opportunity on performance in four experiments. The central hypothesis was that objective performance quality depends on an interaction of narcissism and self-enhancement opportunity. More precisely, we expected that high narcissists would perform better when the opportunity for self-enhancement was high and salient than when no such opportunity was present, whereas low narcissists would exhibit either no difference or the opposite pattern.

References

American Psychiatric Association (1994). *Diagnostic and statistical manual of mental disorders* (4th ed) Washington, DC· Author.

Atkinson, J. W. (1958) Towards experimental analysis of human motivation in terms of motives, expectancies, and incentives (In J W Atkinson (Ed.), *Motives in fantasy, action, and society A method of assessment and study* (pp 288–305) Princeton, NJ Nostrand)

Bandura, A (1977) Self-efficacy: Toward a unifying theory of behavioral change *Psychological Review, 84,* 191–215

Baumeister, R. F., Hamilton, J. C, & Tice, D. M. (1985) Public versus private expectancy of success Confidence booster or performance pressure? *Journal of Personality and Social Psychology, 48,* 1447–1457

Campbell, W K, Reeder, G. D., Sedikides, C, & Elliot, A J (2000) Narcissism and comparative self-enhancement strategies. *Journal of Research in Personality, 34,* 329–347.

Charbonnier, E, Huguet, P., Brauer, M, & Monteil, J. (1998) Social loafing and self-beliefs: People's collective effort depends on the extent to which they distinguish themselves as better than others. *Social Behavior and Personality, 26,* 329–340

Dhavale, D. (2000) *Narcissism and irrational positive beliefs* (Unpublished master's thesis, Case Western Reserve University)

Emmons, R A (1984). Factor analysis and construct validity of the Narcissistic Personality Inventory. *Journal of Personality Assessment, 48,* 291–300

Farwell, L, & Wohlwend-Lloyd, R (1998). Narcissistic processes Optimistic expectations, favorable self-evaluations, and self-enhancing attributions. *Journal of Personality, 66,* 65–83.

Feather, N. T. (1966) Effects of prior success and failure on expectations of success and subsequent performance. *Journal of Personality and Social Psychology, 3,* 287–298

Feather, N T (1968) Change in confidence following success or failure as a predictor of subsequent performance. *Journal of Personality and Social Psychology, 13,* 129–144

Felson, R B. (1993). The (somewhat) social self How others affect self-appraisals (In J Suls [Ed], *The self in social perspective* [Vol 4, pp 1–26]. Hillsdale, NJ Erlbaum.)

Gabriel, M T, Critelli, J W., & Ee, J. S. (1994) Narcissistic illusions in self-evaluations of intelligence and attractiveness *Journal of Personality, 62,* 143–155

Huguet, P., Charbonnier, E, & Monteil, J (1999). Productivity loss in performance groups: People who see themselves as average do not engage in social loafing *Group Dynamics Theory, Research, and Practice, 3,* 118–131

John, O. P., & Robins, R. W. (1994). Accuracy and bias in self-perception Individual differences in self-enhancement and the role of narcissism *Journal of Personality and Social Psychology, 66,* 206–219

Karau, S J, & Williams, K. D (1993) Social loafing A meta-analytic review and theoretical integration. *Journal of Personality and Social Psychology, 65,* 681–706

Kukla, A (1972) Foundations of an attributional theory of performance *Psychological Review, 79,* 454–470

Kukla, A (1974). Performance as a function of resultant achievement motivation (perceived ability) and perceived difficulty *Journal of Research in Personality, 7,* 374–383

Latane, B, Williams, K, & Harkins, S. (1979) Many hands make light the work The causes and consequences of social loafing *Journal of Personality and Social Psychology, 37,* 822–832

Meyer, W. U. (1987). Perceived ability and achievement related behavior. (In F. Halisch & J Kuhl (Eds.), *Motivation, intention, and volition* (pp 73–86) Berlin, Germany Springer-Verlag.)

Morf, C C, & Rhodewalt, F (2001) Unraveling the paradoxes of narcissism· A dynamic self-regulatory processing model. *Psychological Inquiry, 12,* 177–196.

Pajares, F. (1997). Current directions in self-efficacy research (In M L Maehr & P R Pintrich (Eds), *Advances in motivation and achievement* (Vol. 10, pp 1–49) Greenwich, CT· JAI Press)

Paulhus, D. L. (1998). Interpersonal and intrapsychic adaptiveness of trait self-enhancement: A mixed blessing? *Journal of Personality and Social Psychology, 74,* 1197–1208

Raskin, R N (1980). Narcissism and creativity Are they related? *Psychological Reports, 46,* 55–60

Raskin, R N., & Hall, C S (1979) A narcissistic personality inventory *Psychological Reports, 45,* 590.

Raskin, R, Novacek, J, & Hogan, R (1991a) Narcissism, self-esteem, and defensive self-enhancement. *Journal of Personality, 59,* 19–38.

Raskin, R., & Terry, H. (1988). A principle-components analysis of the Narcissistic Personality Inventory and further evidence of its construct validity. *Journal of Personality and Social Psychology, 54,* 890–902.

Robins, R W, & Beer, J S (2001) Positive illusions about the self Short-term benefits and long-term costs. *Journal of Personality and Social Psychology, 80,* 340–352

Robins, R W, & John, O P. (1997) Effects of visual perspective and narcissism on self-perception. Is seeing believing? *Psychological Science, 8,* 37–42.

Sanna, L J (1992) Self-efficacy theory Implications for social facilitation and social loafing. *Journal of Personality and Social Psychology, 62,* 774–786

Trope, Y. (1979) Uncertainty-reducing properties of achievement tasks. *Journal of Personality and Social Psychology, 37,* 1505–1518

Tuckman, B W., & Sexton, T L (1992). Self-believers are self-motivated, self-doubters are not. *Personality and Individual Differences, 13,* 425–428

Watson, P. J., Sawrie, S. M., & Biderman, M. D. (1991). Personal control, assumptive worlds, and narcissism. *Journal of Social Behavior and Personality, 6,* 929–941.

Williams, K, Harkins, S, & Latane, B (1981) Identifiability as a deterrent to social loafing Two cheering experiments *Journal of Personality and Social Psychology, 40,* 303–311

Note· This research was part of Harry M. Wallace's doctoral dissertation, completed under the supervision of Roy F. Baumeister. Portions of this research were presented at the meetings of the Society for Personality and Social Psychology, February 2000, 2001, and 2002, Nashville, Tennessee, San Antonio, Texas, and Savannah, Georgia, respectively, and at the meeting of the American Psychological Society, June 2000, Miami Beach, Florida. We thank Kimberly Charlton, Elizabeth Fink, Kara Hultin, and

Heather McGinness for helping to conduct these studies. We thank Kate Catanese, Natalie Ciarocco, Julie Exline, Jon Faber, Dave Kolb, and Dianne Tice for their comments on drafts of this article and Jean Twenge and Kathleen Vohs for their statistical advice. We especially thank Keith Campbell for his valuable insights and statistical guidance.

Address correspondence to: Harry M. Wallace, Department of Psychology, University of Florida, Gainesville, FL, 32611-2250. Electronic mail may be sent to hwallace@ufl.edu

Discussion Questions for Model Literature Review 4

Editorial note: All the model literature reviews in this book are presented as strong models. However, there are differences of opinion on the effectiveness of any particular piece of writing, even among experts. While answering the following questions, consider the guidelines in this book (as *only* guidelines, not principles) as well as your own standards for effective writing.

1. Briefly comment on the adequacy of the title of the review.

2. Does the review have a strong beginning? Does it get straight to the point? If not, have the authors used some other effective technique to begin the review?

3. Have the authors made a strong case for reviewing the topic(s) they cover? Have they shown that the topic(s) are important?

4. Is the material presented in a logical sequence? Are the headings (and subheadings, if any) appropriate and helpful?

5. Are key variables adequately defined? Are they defined at appropriate points? Explain.

6. Are there points where the references are not well integrated with each other (i.e., simply described as an annotated list)? Explain.

7. Are the strengths and weaknesses of some of the cited research described? If yes, name at least one section where this is done using paragraph numbers.

8. Have the authors made it clear what material is theirs and what is being summarized/paraphrased from other sources? Explain.

9. Are any portions of the review unclear to you? If so, identify them by paragraph number(s).

10. Are the individual paragraphs straightforward and to the point? Explain. If yes, identify one by number that you think is especially good. If no, identify one that is weak.

11. Is the conclusion/discussion at the end of the review appropriate in light of the material covered earlier?

12. On a scale from 1 (very weak) to 10 (very strong), what is your overall evaluation of the literature review? Name one or two considerations that strongly influenced your evaluation.

13. Assume that you are on the editorial board of an academic journal and that the general topic of this review is within the scope of what the journal usually publishes. Which of the following would you recommend to the editor of the journal: publish as is, publish only after minor revisions, publish only after major revisions, *or* do not publish? Briefly defend your recommendation.

Model Literature Review 5

The Inherent Limits of Predicting School Violence

Edward P. Mulvey
University of Pittsburgh

Elizabeth Cauffman
University of Pittsburgh

Editorial note: The paragraphs in this literature review have been numbered to make it easy to refer to specific portions of this review during classroom discussions. The numbers are italicized superscripts, which appear at the beginning of each paragraph. All other nonitalicized superscripts, if any, refer to footnotes within the review.

ABSTRACT

The recent media hype over school shootings has led to demands for methods of identifying school shooters before they act. Despite the fact that schools remain one of the safest places for youths to be, schools are beginning to adopt identification systems to determine which students could be future killers. The methods used to accomplish this not only are unproven but are inherently limited in usefulness and often do more harm than good for both the children and the school setting. The authors' goals in the present article are to place school shootings in perspective relative to other risks of violence that children face and to provide a reasonable and scientifically defensible approach to improving the safety of schools.

[1]School violence, having been dubbed a crisis, permeates the national consciousness and media outlets. This concern, moreover, has gone beyond simple statements and speculations. A heightened awareness of the potential tragedy of a school-related violent incident has prompted school administrators, law enforcement professionals, and mental health professionals to put into place methods for identifying and intervening proactively with potentially violent students and situations. Many communities have seen curriculum changes, the adoption of "safe school" policies, new weapons-reporting requirements, and increased efforts to refer problem students to mental health professionals. For example, several years ago, New York City spent over 28 million dollars on metal detectors (Kemper, 1993), and numerous school districts have implemented mandatory school uniform policies to cut down on gang identification (Stephens, 1998). After the shooting at Columbine High School, the principal distributed a memorandum requesting students to report on other students whom they deemed to be demonstrating maladaptive behavior (e.g., dressing oddly, being loners; Aronson, 2000). Currently, professionals seem open to trying just about anything to combat the perceived dangers of school violence.

[2]In the midst of these activities, it is important to note that such policy changes are fueled primarily by graphic images of children killing and being killed at school rather than by actual numbers indicating an epidemic of violence. Data from the National Crime Victimization Survey and the School Crime Supplement, for example, suggest that there is virtually no difference between the rates of criminal victimization in schools in 1989 and the rates of victimization in 1995 (Snyder & Sickmund, 1999). Other examinations of the figures regarding adolescent deaths indicate that violent deaths are a rare event, with less than 1% of the homicides and suicides among school-age children occurring in or around school grounds (Kachur et al., 1996). Moreover, the rate of violent crimes committed by juveniles remains low during the school day, but it spikes at the close of the school day and declines throughout the evening hours (Snyder & Sickmund, 1999), indicating that school hours are probably the safest time of the day for adolescents.

[3]Yet, somehow, the images of the violence at Columbine, Padukah, and Santee are more persistent than the realities of the situations connected with the 99% of school-age victims who meet their fate when school is not in session. That students are very unlikely to be assaulted in the school setting and that urban adolescents are safer in their schools than on their way to or from school do not emerge as key points in most discussions of school violence. As Joseph Stalin, of all people, noted in another time, "A single death is a tragedy, a million deaths is a statistic" (as quoted in Bartlett, 1980, p. 766).

Unfortunately, there now may have been enough tragedies to precipitate action.

[4]An attractive strategy for addressing school violence is to increase efforts at early detection of and intervention with adolescents who are likely to commit these horrible acts. One of the most common reactions to the adolescents who opened fire in Padukah, Columbine, or Santee is to ask, "How could someone not have known that this adolescent was in trouble?" The problem, of course, is that it is not often clear exactly what to look for, who should have looked for it, or what should have been done if someone had seen something. Indeed, in postmortems of these situations, one often picks up signs of distress or despair in these adolescents, but one is rarely sure if the level or types of indicators found would have been enough to make even a vigilant and caring adult do something markedly different than what was done. After all, for every killer youth, there are many others with the same behaviors or attitudes who never come close to killing their classmates.

[5]The inability to see clear markers of trouble in these cases should reveal something. It should make clear the daunting nature of the identification task taken on by many school administrators and mental health professionals. Identification of adolescents who are at high risk for committing serious, public acts of violence poses many inherent challenges; considering these can lead psychologists to think more realistically about where to direct their energies for interventions for school violence.

The Characteristics of Adolescent Violence and the Identification Process

[6]The first challenge facing any system for identifying adolescents who could commit serious acts of violence in school is that the behavior being predicted is a rare event. There are severe restrictions on the ability of any predictive strategy (even if reasonably accurate) to identify true positives for a low base-rate behavior without also identifying a large number of false positives (Hart, Webster, & Menzies, 1993; Meehl, 1954). Identification of large numbers of false positives is not a problem if such identification causes no harm (Morris & Miller, 1985), but the ratio of true positives to false positives matters greatly if all identified individuals are stigmatized or if their opportunities are limited. One way to avoid the low base-rate problem is to expand the definition of the violent outcome being predicted, effectively converting many false positives into true positives. If one includes bullying, threats, and fistfights in the definition of school violence, the base rate increases dramatically, and the ability to predict who might be involved in these activities may increase. According to the Centers for Disease Control and Prevention's 1997 Youth Risk Behavior Surveillance System, 37% of high school students said they had been in a physical fight during the past school year (Centers for Disease Control and Prevention, 1997); approximately 80% of youths have indicated that they engage in some form of bullying behavior such as pushing, teasing, or threatening others (Bosworth, Espelage, & Simon, 1999). With this expanded definition, however, comes a blurring of the behavior being examined and a good chance that the processes behind these behaviors will become more heterogeneous. Taken to extremes, this approach amounts to dealing with a problem that is hard to solve by choosing to solve a different problem. If the identified problems are too broadly defined, the intervention strategy is reduced to meeting the needs of the general pool of troubled adolescents found in any school, and the hardto-solve problem of identifying potentially violent adolescents is dealt with by choosing to solve the problem of disruptive students.

[7]The second major obstacle to identifying students who are likely to be involved in serious school violence is that the event being predicted is usually embedded in a social and transactional sequence of events. One thing that is clear about youth violence in general and seemingly about many of the recent tragedies is that this behavior has a heavy social component (Staub & Rosenthal, 1994). Youths who engage in criminal behavior, both violent and nonviolent, are not usually loners. For example, 60% of juvenile offenders who committed assault were with peers at the time, and 90% of juvenile offenders who committed robbery were with adolescent peers (Zimring, 1981, 1998). Moreover, youths who are aggressive not only seek each other out but also form coercive cliques (Cairns, Cairns, Neckerman, Gest, & Gariepy, 1988; Coie & Dodge, 1998), which in turn provide a training ground for subsequent delinquent behaviors (Parker & Asher, 1987; Patterson, Reid, & Dishion, 1992). Predictably, then, it appears that for both lethal and nonlethal incidents, school violence is more likely to occur in larger rather than smaller schools and in "unowned" areas such as hallways, dining areas, and parking lots (Astor, Meyer, & Behre, 1999). Furthermore, violent events in the schools are part of a chain of actions and reactions, often among numerous other individuals (e.g., taunting peers, disinterested girlfriends or boyfriends, uninterested parents; see Fagan & Wilkinson, 1998), and bystanders appear to be a critical component of the escalation of disputes into violence

(Decker, 1996; Tedeschi & Felson, 1994). Previous research has shown that these events do not occur in a vacuum and that there are numerous rationales for and pathways to the violent act. Identification based only on the characteristics of an individual neglects these highly salient social and transactional aspects of school violence.

[8]The third major obstacle to the task of identification is that the individuals being assessed are adolescents whose characters are often not yet fully formed. Research in the areas of physical development (Buchanan, Eccles, & Becker, 1992), psychosocial development (Cauffman & Steinberg, 2000; Steinberg & Cauffman, 1996), and even brain development (Baird et al., 1999; Giedd et al., 1999; Sowell, Thompson, Holmes, Jernigan, & Toga, 1999) suggests that adolescents are still changing and that their characters are not yet fully formed. Assessing adolescents, therefore, presents the formidable challenge of trying to capture a rapidly changing process with few trustworthy markers. Diagnostic systems for adolescents are not as well developed as those for adult disorders, many disorders do not emerge clearly until young adulthood, and the diagnostic tools used to assess adults are often of questionable value when applied to adolescents. Despite these limitations, adult diagnoses or concepts periodically have been applied to children, adolescents, or both without taking into account important developmental factors that may affect the applicability or validity of these constructs (for a review, see Achenbach, 1995). For example, some characteristics that are viewed as risk factors for psychopathy among adults (e.g., impulsivity, little concern for future consequences) are common and transitory aspects of normal adolescent development and may be easily misinterpreted when using standard approaches (Edens, Skeem, Cruise, & Cauffman, 2001). These realities make assessments of adolescents by mental health professionals using tools designed for adults difficult to interpret meaningfully.

[9]Finally, it is not clear what interventions are likely to work with violence-prone adolescents. Part of the reason for identifying an adolescent who is at high risk for serious violence is to prevent the occurrence of an incident. This can be done either by imposing restrictions on the adolescent (e.g., enforcing some schedule or activity restrictions) or by altering the processes within the adolescent or in his or her life that might be contributing to the violence (e.g., enrolling the adolescent in an anger-management group). Unfortunately, most of the single-focus interventions for violent adolescents have demonstrated limited effectiveness (McCord, Widom, &

Crowell, 2001; U.S. Department of Health and Human Services, 2001), and the most successful interventions with antisocial adolescents work in multiple community settings and focus on building specific skills (Lipsey & Wilson, 1998). Schools can certainly provide valuable prevention programs, such as social skills training, but these settings are not generally well equipped to deliver individualized, broadly based services to small numbers of identified students.

Recasting the Problem as Risk Management

[10]This dismal picture does not justify inaction. The limits of identification and intervention are real and substantial, but they should be used to inform people about reasonable strategies rather than discourage them from facing the problem. They highlight the need for professionals to take a realistic view of what might be accomplished through the development of early identification systems and to focus planning and programming in a way that increases the likelihood of success.

[11]Perhaps the first step is to approach the problem as one of ongoing risk assessment rather than prediction. A great deal can be learned in this regard from the progress that has been made over the past 20 years regarding management of violence in mentally ill adults (see Borum, 1996; Otto, 1992). In this area, as in the area of school violence, the goal is to predict and prevent rare, socially embedded violence for which little effective intervention technology exists. Trends in preventing violence in mentally ill adults, however, have been moving away from framing the problem as one of predicting an event and toward the approach of managing risk (Heilbrun, 1997). Ongoing risk assessment and management have replaced prediction of dangerousness, a shift with subtle but important implications for policy, practice, and research (Skeem & Mulvey, in press).

[12]This new approach recognizes that violence risk is a dynamic, rather than static, process. Although it is possible to sort individuals into high- and low-risk groups generally, the task of managing risk effectively requires an ongoing evaluation of the factors that increase or decrease the likelihood of a violent incident in individuals at relatively high risk already (Monahan & Steadman, 1996; Mulvey & Lidz, 1998). A risk management approach thus starts out much like a more traditional predictive strategy by using available indicators of generalized risk for adolescents and some structured data-collection scheme to sort individuals into a high- or low-risk status. This identification process, however, is only the first step toward avoiding violent incidents. The

next step is to monitor the ongoing changes in the lives of these individuals for transitions or turning points that may further increase the likelihood of violence.

[13]Framing the problem in this way might well change the focus of school violence programs. Rather than developing more elaborate and potentially discriminatory or arbitrary approaches to choosing those who might be at highest risk, researchers could direct more resources into ongoing involvement with the group of individuals who are clearly high risk. The natural reaction in the face of disastrous violence in schools is to look for a system that can pick out the people who may react similarly in the future. The reality of prediction, however, is that this is a largely futile task. The fuzziness of the categories, the base rate of the behavior being predicted, and the timeframe to which the prediction applies must always compromise any identification scheme for schoolyard killers. Therefore, rather than being used to make a marginal improvement in a sorting algorithm to identify troubled students, resources may well be better spent monitoring the activities of those students who would be identified under just about any risk-assessment method.

Need for a Focus on School Environment

[14]Although easier to do than accurately modeling individual behavior using a violence-prediction machine, keeping abreast of the ongoing activities of troubled and troubling adolescents is no easy feat. Now, as always, the best source of information about the activities of students in a school is other students. A long line of research has demonstrated that students are well aware of the problem children in their own classrooms (for a review, see Hartup, 1992). For example, since the advent of sociometric research in 1934, researchers have been able to identify which youths are liked or disliked by their peers, as well as future delinquent behaviors among youths (Rubin, Bukowski, & Parker, 1998). Ignoring this potentially rich source of information in favor of structured psychological assessment places unwarranted faith in the powers of individual assessment. Peers and teachers who talk with problem students can often provide the most useful information about when such students are in trouble.

[15]For such information to flow from students to administrators requires an atmosphere where sharing in good faith is respected and honored. Giving information about the problems that another student is having or about threats or scary activities going on in a school environment can occur only if students feel that they are (and will remain) safe and that a reasoned response will

result from their reporting. Getting accurate information about the activities of high-risk students on an ongoing basis, therefore, rests heavily on establishing and maintaining a supportive school environment.

[16]Ironically, many schools appear to be taking the opposite approach. Instead of working to foster a sense of belonging, schools are implementing zero-tolerance policies that virtually guarantee an unreasoned response to any reported problem. For example, when a student is expelled or suspended for carrying aspirin (in violation of a zero-tolerance drug policy), that student is likely to hold the school administration in contempt. It is also likely that other students will withhold information from the administration to avoid such disproportionate punishments. This change in school atmosphere is all too real. For example, in a *New York Times* op-ed piece written by a high school student from Littleton, Colorado, the student remarked as follows:

[17]High school students in Littleton now have a new excuse to get out of class for a few extra minutes: the lockdown drill.... Apart from the lockdown drills, there have been few changes in security procedures. The greatest change has been the increase of paranoia. For example, a few weeks after the shooting I was working on a graph assignment with a friend. We arranged the points on the graph to spell out a humorous but inappropriate message. A month earlier, my friend would have said, "The teacher's going to be mad." This time he said, "If we turn this in, we'll be expelled." There's the difference. (Black, 2001, p. A23)

[18]Empirical evidence, meanwhile, seems to support the contention that promoting healthy relationships and environments is more effective for reducing school misconduct and crime than instituting punitive penalties (Nettles, Mucherah, & Jones, 2000). For example, a study of 7th-, 8th-, and 9th-grade students found that commitment to school and belief in the fairness and consistent enforcement of school rules are the most important elements in reducing school crime (Jenkins, 1997). Similarly, the National Longitudinal Study of Adolescent Health found that among a nationally representative sample of 7th–12th graders, attachment to family and school served as protective factors against violence (Franke, 2000), a result consistent with earlier research indicating that adolescents with a low commitment to school are at increased risk of engaging in violent behavior (Cernkovich & Giordano, 1992; Farrington, 1991). Also, a study of school-based violence-prevention interventions found that between 1993 and 1997, elementary schools that focused on the broader school environment appeared successful in changing violence-related behavior (Howard, Flora, & Griffin,

1999). Finally, the most powerful predictor of adolescent well being is a feeling of connection to school (Resnick et al., 1997), and students who feel close to others, fairly treated, and vested in school are less likely to engage in risky behaviors than those who do not (Resnick et al., 1997). Each of these studies suggests that a key factor in preventing school violence is students' positive relations to their school environments. Students who are committed to school, feel that they belong, and trust the administration are less likely to commit violent acts than those who are uninvolved, alienated, or distrustful.

Conclusion

[19]In sum, preventing violent incidents in school does not require either more sophisticated methods for assessing students individually or a magical, uniform method for intervening with them for a short while after they have been identified. It seems instead to rest largely on developing a positive and supportive organizational climate in a school. A crucial component of any school violence program is thus a school environment where ongoing activities and problems of students are discussed, rather than tallied with structured assessment instruments. Such an environment promotes ongoing risk management, which can be achieved only with the support and involvement of those closest to the indicators of trouble.

[20]It is also worth noting that school violence is rarely just about what happens in school. Gun-related violence outside the school is a better predictor of weapon-related victimization at or during travel to and from school than is the dangerousness of the school environment itself (Sheley, McGee, & Wright, 1995), and neighborhood conditions such as poverty, population turnover, and crime rates are the strongest predictors of school violence (Laub & Lauritsen, 1998). Community incidents are carried into the school environment, just as the effects of the school day's events linger on after dismissal.

[21]Although connecting schools with families and communities is often given as a mantra for school reform, it is worth chanting once more when discussing interventions to prevent school violence. The indicators of trouble for violence-prone adolescents can come from a variety of sources, and often, the only way one can obtain a clear picture of what is moving an adolescent toward violence is by looking at the adolescent's world from the broadest perspective. Strategies designed to address school violence must recognize the interdependence of school violence with neighborhood and family conditions.

[22]This call for an emphasis on organizational issues for the prevention of school violence reflects a recognition that there will never be a technology that matches the desire to find and control the uncontrollable events of life. Violence of the sort seen recently in schools is horrific and compels society to reestablish order in the face of chaos. Unfortunately, the technology of predicting rare events will always be a poor substitute for solid human relations and sound organizational management. Establishing school environments where students feel connected and trusted will build the critical link between those who often know when trouble is brewing and those who can act to prevent it.

References

Achenbach, T M (1995) Developmental issues in assessment, taxonomy, and diagnosis of child and adolescent psychopathology. In D Cicchetti & D J. Cohen (Eds), *Developmental psychopathology, Vol 1 Theory and methods* (pp. 57–80) New York. Wiley.

Aronson, E (2000). *Nobody left to hate Teach compassion after Columbine* New York Worth

Astor, R., Meyer, H , & Behre, W (1999). Unowned places and times: Maps and interviews about violence in high schools *American Educational Research Journal, 36,* 3–42.

Baird, A , Gruber, S , Fein, D., Maas, L., Steingard, R , Renshaw, P , Cohen, B , & Yurgelun-Todd, D (1999). Functional magnetic resonance imaging of facial affect recognition in children and adolescents *Journal of the American Academy of Child and Adolescent Psychiatry, 38,* 195–199.

Bartlett, J (1980) *Bartlett's familiar quotations* (15th ed) Boston. Little, Brown

Black, N. (2001, March 8) After a shooting *The New York Times,* p A23

Borum, R. (1996) Improving the clinical practice of violence risk assessment Technology, guidelines, and training. *American Psychologist, 51,* 945–948

Bosworth, K , Espelage, D , & Simon, T (1999) Factors associated with bullying behavior in middle school students. *Journal of Early Adolescence, 19,* 341–362

Buchanan, C M , Eccles, J. S., & Becker, J. B (1992) Are adolescents victims of raging hormones? Evidence for activational effects of hormones on moods and behavior at adolescence *Psychological Bulletin, 111,* 62–107.

Cairns, R., Cairns, B , Neckerman, H , Gest, S , & Gariepy, J (1988). Social networks and aggressive behavior: Peer support or peer rejection? *Developmental Psychology, 24,* 815–823

Cauffman, E , & Steinberg, L. (2000). (Im)maturity of judgment in adolescence Why adolescents may be less culpable than adults. *Behavioral Sciences and the Law, 18,* 741–760.

Centers for Disease Control and Prevention. (1997) Rates of homicide, suicide, and firearm-related death among children—26 industrialized countries. *Morbidity and Mortality Weekly Report, 46,* 101–105

Cernkovich, S A , & Giordano, P. C (1992) School bonding, race, and delinquency *Criminology, 31,* 261–291

Coie, J , & Dodge, K (1998) Aggression and antisocial behavior. In W. Damon & N Eisenberg (Eds.), *Handbook of child psychology* (pp 779–862) New York. Wiley

Decker, S (1996) Reconstructing homicide events The role of witnesses in fatal encounters *Journal of Criminal Justice, 23,* 439–450.

Edens, J , Skeem, J , Cruise, K , & Cauffman, E (2001) The assessment of juvenile psychopathy and its association with violence A critical review *Behavioral Sciences and the Law, 19,* 53–80

Fagan, J., & Wilkinson, D (1998) Social contexts and functions of adolescent violence. In D Elliott, B Hamburg, & K Williams (Eds), *Violence in American schools* (pp 55–93) New York Cambridge University Press

Farrington, D. (1991) Childhood aggression and adult violence: Early precursors and later life outcomes. In D. Pepper & K Rubin (Eds), *The development and treatment of childhood aggression* (pp. 5–29). Hillsdale, NJ Erlbaum

Franke, T (2000) The role of attachment as a protective factor in adolescent violent behavior. *Adolescent and Family Health, 1,* 40–51

Giedd, J , Blumenthal, J , Jeffries, N , Castellanos, F , Liu, H., Zijdenbos, A , Paus, T., Evans, A , & Rapoport, J (1999) Brain development during childhood and adolescence A longitudinal MRI study *Nature Neuroscience, 2,* 861–863.

Hart, S D , Webster, C. D , & Menzies, R. J. (1993) A note on portraying the accuracy of violence predictions. *Law and Human Behavior, 17,* 695–700

Hartup, W (1992) Peer relations in early and middle childhood In V B Van Hasselt & M Hersen (Eds), *Handbook of social development A lifespan perspective* (pp 257–281) New York Plenum.

Heilbrun, K (1997) Prediction versus management models relevant to risk assessment The importance of legal decision-making context *Law and Human Behavior, 21,* 347–359

Howard, K., Flora, J., & Griffin, M. (1999) Violence-prevention programs in schools State of the science and implications for future research *Applied and Preventive Psychology, 8,* 197–215

Jenkins, P (1997). School delinquency and the school social bond. *Journal of Research in Crime and Delinquency, 34,* 337–367

Kachur, S P , Stennies, G , Powell, K , Modzeleski, W , Stephens, R , Murphy, R , Kresnow, M , Sleet, D , & Lowry, R (1996) School-associated deaths in the United States, 1992–1994 *JAMA, 275,* 1729–1733

Kemper, P (1993, Fall) Disarming youth *California School Boards Journal, 25–33*

Laub, J , & Lauritsen, J (1998). The interdependence of school violence with neighborhood and family conditions. In D Elliott, B Hamburg, & K Williams (Eds), *Violence in American schools* (pp 55–93) New York Cambridge University Press

Lipsey, M , & Wilson, D (1998) Effective intervention for serious juvenile offenders. A synthesis of research In R. Loeber & D. Farrington (Eds.), *Serious and violent juvenile offenders Risk factors and successful interventions* (pp 313–345). Thousand Oaks, CA· Sage

McCord, J , Widom, C S , & Crowell, N A (Eds) (2001) *Juvenile crime, juvenile justice* Washington, DC. National Academy Press.

Meehl, P E (1954) *Clinical versus statistical prediction A theoretical analysis and a review of the evidence* Minneapolis University of Minnesota Press

Monahan, J , & Steadman, H (1996) Violent storms and violent people How meteorology can inform risk communication in mental health law *American Psychologist, 51,* 931–938

Morris, N , & Miller, M. (1985). Predictions of dangerousness In M Tonry & N. Morris (Eds), *Crime and justice An annual review of research* (Vol 6, pp 1–50). Chicago University of Chicago Press

Mulvey, E P , & Lidz, C W (1998). The clinical prediction of violence as a conditional judgment *Social Psychiatry and Psychiatric Epidemiology, 33,* 107–113

Nettles, S , Mucherah, W , & Jones, D (2000) Understanding resilience. The role of social resources *Journal of Education for Students Placed at Risk, 5,* 47–60

Otto, R K. (1992) Prediction of dangerous behavior. A review and analysis of "second-generation" research *Forensic Reports, 5,* 103–133

Parker, J , & Asher, S (1987). Peer relations and later personal adjustment Are low-accepted children at risk? *Psychological Bulletin, 102,* 357–389

Patterson, G , Reid, J , & Dishion, T (1992) *Antisocial boys* Eugene, OR Castalia

Resnick, M , Bearman, P , Blum, R , Bauman, K , Harris, K , Jones, J , Tabor, J , Beuhring, T , Sieving, R , Shew, M , Ireland, M , Bearinger, L , & Udry, R. (1997) Protecting adolescents from harm Findings from the National Longitudinal Study on Adolescent Health *JAMA, 278,* 823–832.

Rubin, K , Bukowski, W., & Parker, J (1998) Peer interactions, relationships, and groups. In W. Damon & N Eisenberg (Eds), *Handbook of child psychology* (pp 619–700) New York: Wiley.

Sheley, J., McGee, Z , & Wright, J (1995) Gun-related violence in and around inner-city schools. *American Journal of Diseases of Children, 146,* 677–682.

Skeem, J., & Mulvey, E. (in press) Assessing the violence potential of mentally disordered offenders being treated in the community In A Buchanan (Ed), *Care of the mentally disordered offender in the community* Oxford, England. Oxford University Press

Snyder, H., & Sickmund, M. (1999) *Juvenile offenders and victims 1999 national report* Washington, DC: Office of Juvenile Justice and Delinquency Prevention

Sowell, E , Thompson, P , Holmes, C , Jernigan, T., & Toga, A (1999) In vivo evidence for post-adolescent brain maturation in frontal and striatal regions *Nature Neuroscience, 2,* 859–861

Staub, E., & Rosenthal, L. (1994) Mob violence Cultural–societal sources, instigators, group processes, and participants In L Eron & J. Gentry (Eds), *Reason to hope A psychosocial perspective on violence and youth* (pp. 281–313) Washington, DC. American Psychological Association

Steinberg, L , & Cauffman, E (1996). Maturity of judgment in adolescence· Psychosocial factors in adolescent decision making *Law and Human Behavior, 20,* 249–272

Stephens, R (1998) Safe school planning In D Elliott, B Hamburg, & K Williams (Eds), *Violence in American schools* (pp 253–289) New York· Cambridge University Press

Tedeschi, J , & Felson, R (1994) *Violence, aggression, and coercive actions* Washington, DC American Psychological Association

U S. Department of Health and Human Services (2001) *Youth violence A report of the Surgeon General* Washington, DC: Author.

Zimring, F. (1981) Kids, groups, and crime. Some implications of a well-known secret. *Journal of Criminal Law and Criminology, 72,* 867

Zimring, F. (1998). *American youth violence* New York Oxford University Press.

Address correspondence to Edward P. Mulvey, Law and Psychiatry Program, Western Psychiatric Institute and Clinic, University of Pittsburgh, 3811 O'Hara Street, Pittsburgh, PA 15213 E-mail· mulveyep@msx upmc.edu

From *American Psychologist, 56,* 797–802. Copyright © 2001 by the American Psychological Association. Reprinted with permission.

Discussion Questions for Model Literature Review 5

Editorial note: All the model literature reviews in this book are presented as strong models. However, there are differences of opinion on the effectiveness of any particular piece of writing, even among experts. While answering the following questions, consider the guidelines in this book (as *only* guidelines, not principles) as well as your own standards for effective writing.

1. Briefly comment on the adequacy of the title of the review.

2. Comment on the adequacy of the Abstract. Does it effectively summarize the essence of the review given that abstracts are restricted to 120 words or less in the journal in which this review article appeared?

3. Does the review have a strong beginning? Does it get straight to the point? If not, have the authors used some other effective technique to begin the review?

4. Have the authors made a strong case for reviewing the topic(s) they cover? Have they shown that the topic(s) are important?

5. Is the material presented in a logical sequence? Are the headings (and subheadings, if any) appropriate and helpful?

6. Are key variables adequately defined? Are they defined at appropriate points? Explain.

7. Are there points where the references are not well integrated with each other (i.e., simply described as an annotated list)? Explain.

8. Are the strengths and weaknesses of some of the cited research described? If yes, name at least one section where this is done using paragraph numbers.

9. Have the authors made it clear what material is theirs and what is being summarized/paraphrased from other sources? Explain.

10. Are any portions of the review unclear to you? If so, identify them by paragraph number(s).

11. Are the individual paragraphs straightforward and to the point? Explain. If yes, identify one by number that you think is especially good. If no, identify one that is weak.

12. Is the conclusion/discussion at the end of the review appropriate in light of the material covered earlier?

13. On a scale from 1 (very weak) to 10 (very strong), what is your overall evaluation of the literature review? Name one or two considerations that strongly influenced your evaluation.

14. Assume that you are on the editorial board of an academic journal and that the general topic of this review is within the scope of what the journal usually publishes. Which of the following would you recommend to the editor of the journal: publish as is, publish only after minor revisions, publish only after major revisions, *or* do not publish? Briefly defend your recommendation.

Model Literature Review 6

Research on Religion-Accommodative
Counseling: Review and Meta-Analysis

Michael E. McCullough
National Institute for Healthcare Research

Editorial note: The paragraphs in this literature review have been numbered to make it easy to refer to specific portions of this review during classroom discussions. The numbers are italicized superscripts, which appear at the beginning of each paragraph. All other nonitalicized superscripts, if any, refer to footnotes within the review.

ABSTRACT

The present meta-analysis examined data from 5 studies ($N = 111$) that compared the efficacy of standard approaches to counseling for depression with religion-accommodative approaches. There was no evidence that the religion-accommodative approaches were more or less efficacious than the standard approaches. Findings suggest that the choice to use religious approaches with religious clients is probably more a matter of client preference than a matter of differential efficacy. However, additional research is needed to examine whether religion-accommodative approaches yield differential treatment satisfaction or differential improvements in spiritual well-being or facilitate relapse prevention. Given the importance of religion to many potential consumers of psychological services, counseling psychologists should devote greater attention to religion-accommodative counseling in future studies.

[1]The United States is a highly religious country; 92% of its population are affiliated with a religion (Kosmin & Lachman, 1993). According to a 1995 survey, 96% of Americans believe in God or a universal spirit, 42% indicate that they attend a religious worship service weekly or almost weekly, 67% indicate that they are members of a church or synagogue, and 60% indicate that religion is "important" or "very important" in their lives (Gallup, 1995).

[2]In addition, many scholars acknowledge that certain forms of religious involvement are associated with better functioning on a variety of measures of mental health. Reviews of this research (e.g., Bergin, 1991; Bergin, Masters, & Richards, 1987; Larson et al., 1992; Pargament, 1997; Schumaker, 1992; Worthington, Kurusu, McCullough, & Sandage, 1996) suggested that several forms of religious involvement (including intrinsic religious motivation, attendance at religious worship, receiving coping support from one's religious faith or religious congregation, and positive religious attributions for life events) are positively associated with a variety of measures of mental health. For example, various measures of religious involvement appear to be related to lower degrees of depressive symptoms in adults (Bienenfeld, Koenig, Larson, & Sherrill, 1997; Ellison,

1995; Kendler, Gardner, & Prescott, 1997) and children (Miller, Warner, Wickramaratne, & Weissman, 1997) and less suicide (e.g., Comstock & Partridge, 1972; Kark et al., 1996; Wandrei, 1985).

[3]Koenig, George, and Peterson (1998) reported that depressed people scoring high on measures of intrinsic religiousness were significantly more likely to experience a remission of depression during nearly a 1-year follow-up than were depressed people with lower intrinsic religiousness, even after controlling for 30 potential demographic, psychosocial, and medical confounds. Other studies have shown that religious involvement, as gauged through single-item measures of frequency of religious worship and private prayer as well as more complex measures of religious coping, is related to positive psychological outcomes after major life events (e.g., Pargament et al., 1990; Pargament et al., 1994; Pargament, Smith, & Brant, 1995). This is the case even though several patterns of religious belief and religious coping (e.g., the belief that one's misfortunes are a punishment from God) are associated with greater psychological distress (Pargament, 1997).

Religion in Counseling and Psychotherapy

[4]Some scholars (e.g., Bergin, 1991; Payne, Bergin,

Table 1
Sample Sizes, Effect Sizes, and 95% Confidence Intervals (CI) for the Studies Included in the Meta-Analysis

Study	Religion-accommodative treatment n	Standard treatment n	Effect size (d_+)	95% CI
Propst (1980)	7	10	+0.41	−0.56/+1.39
Pecheur & Edwards (1984)	7	7	+0.53	−0.53/+1.60
Propst et al. (1992)	19	19	+0.51	−0.14/+1.15
W. B. Johnson & Ridley (1992a)	5	5	+0.29	−0.96/+1.53
W. B. Johnson et al. (1994)	16	16	−0.51	−1.22/+0.19

& Loftus, 1992; Richards & Bergin, 1997; Shafranske, 1996; Worthington et al., 1996) posited that considering clients' religiousness while designing treatment plans might have an important effect on the efficacy of treatment. Surveys of psychiatrists (Neeleman & King, 1993), psychologists (Bergin & Jensen, 1988; Shafranske & Malony, 1990), and mental health counselors (Kelly, 1995) also indicate that many mental health professionals believe that religious and spiritual values can and should be thoughtfully addressed in the course of mental health treatment. Moreover, a variety of analogue and clinical studies (e.g., Houts & Graham, 1986; T. A. Kelly & Strupp, 1992; Lewis & Lewis, 1985; McCullough & Worthington, 1995; McCullough, Worthington, Maxey, & Rachal, 1997; Morrow, Worthington, & McCullough, 1993) indicate that clients' religious beliefs can influence both (a) the conclusions of clinicians' structured psychological assessments and (b) the process of psychotherapy (cf. Luborsky et al., 1980).

Evidence from Comparative Efficacy Studies

[5]Given the existing research on religion and mental health, an important question for counseling psychologists is whether supporting clients' religious beliefs and values in a structured treatment package yield clinical benefits that are equal to or greater than standard methods of psychological practice. Several empirical studies have addressed this issue. Although the findings of studies that have examined such questions have been reviewed in narrative fashion elsewhere (e.g., W. B. Johnson, 1993; Matthews et al., 1998; Worthington et al., 1996), no researchers have used meta-analytic methods to estimate quantitatively the differential efficacy of such treatments. Meta-analytic reviews that compare religious approaches to counseling with standard approaches to counseling are one of three meta-analytic strategies that can be used to examine whether a given therapeutic approach has therapeutic efficacy (Wampold, 1997).

[6]In the present article, I review the existing research on such religious approaches to counseling using quantitative methods of research synthesis (e.g., Cooper & Hedges, 1994; Hunter & Schmidt, 1990) to estimate the differential efficacy of religious approaches in comparison to standard forms of counseling for depressed religious clients.

Method

Literature Search

[7]The *PsycLIT*, *PsycINFO*, *Medline*, *ERIC*, and *Dissertation Abstracts* electronic databases were searched through August 1998 for published and unpublished studies that examined the differential efficacy of a religion-accommodative approach to counseling in comparison to a standard approach to counseling. The reference sections of relevant articles were searched for other studies that would be relevant to this review. This search process continued until no new studies were revealed. In addition, several experts in the field of religion and mental health were contacted to identify unpublished studies.

[8]Studies had to meet four criteria to be included in the meta-analytic sample: They had to (a) compare a religion-accommodative approach to counseling to a standard approach to counseling; (b) randomly assign patients to treatments; (c) involve patients who were suffering from a specific set of psychological symptoms (e.g., anxiety or depression); and (d) offer equal amounts of treatment to clients in the religion-accommodative and standard treatments. Five published studies and one unpublished dissertation (W. B. Johnson, 1991), which was later reported in W. B. Johnson, DeVries, Ridley, Pettorini, and Peterson (1994) met these inclusion criteria. Several studies that investigated religious approaches to psychological treatment (e.g., Azhar & Varma, 1995a, 1995b; Azhar, Varma, & Dharap, 1994; Carlson, Bacaseta, & Simanton, 1988; Richards, Owen, & Stein, 1993; Rye & Pargament, 1997; Toh & Tan, 1997) were obtained, but these studies failed to meet all four inclusion criteria. Thus, they were omitted from the

meta-analytic sample. A single rater determined which studies met inclusion criteria. This rater's decisions were made without reference to the results or discussion sections of the articles.

[9]The resulting meta-analytic sample included five studies representing data from 111 counseling clients. Descriptions of study populations, measures used, and effect size estimates (with 95% confidence intervals) are given in Table 1.

The Studies

[10]Researchers interested in accommodative forms of religious counseling have taken standard cognitive–behavioral protocols or specific techniques, such as cognitive restructuring (Beck, Rush, Shaw, & Emery, 1979), cognitive coping skills (Meichenbaum, 1985), and appeals to rational thinking (e.g., Ellis & Grieger, 1977), and have developed religion-friendly rationales for and versions of such protocols or techniques (W. B. Johnson & Ridley, 1992b). These adapted protocols or techniques are thought to be theoretically equivalent to standard cognitive–behavioral techniques (Propst, 1996), but more amenable to the religious world view and religious language that religious clients use to understand their lives and their problems. The five studies are described in greater detail next.

[11]*Propst (1980).* Propst (1980) examined the differential efficacy of a manualized, religion-accommodative approach to cognitive restructuring and imagery modification. Volunteers who scored in the mild or moderate range of depression on the Beck Depression Inventory (BDI; Beck, Ward, Mendelson, Mock, & Erbaugh, 1961) and in at least the moderate range on the King and Hunt (1972) religion scales were randomly assigned to one of two treatments. The standard treatment was an integration of Beck's (1976) cognitive therapy for depression and Meichenbaum's (1973) cognitive–behavior modification. During eight 1-hr sessions conducted over 4 weeks, clients were trained to observe their cognitions and imagery during depressed moods. After clients were convinced of the links between their moods, thoughts, and images, they practiced cognitive restructuring skills for modifying their thoughts and images using imagery and positive self-statements (e.g., "I can see myself in the future coping with that particular situation"). Ten of 11 clients assigned to this condition completed it.

[12]In the religion-accommodative treatment, clients completed the same therapeutic protocol as that used in the standard treatment. The only difference is that participants were trained to replace their negative cogni-

tions and imagery with religious images (e.g., "I can visualize Christ going with me into that difficult situation in the future as I try to cope"). Seven of 9 clients assigned to this condition completed the treatment.

[13]*Pecheur & Edwards (1984).* Pecheur and Edwards (1984) assessed the differential efficacy of Beck et al.'s (1979) cognitive therapy for depression and a religion-accommodative version of the same therapy. Clients were students from a Christian college who met research diagnostic criteria for major depressive disorder. They also scored in the depressed range on the BDI, the Hamilton Rating Scale for Depression (HRSD; Hamilton, 1960), and a single-item visual analogue scale. In the standard treatment, clients completed eight 50-min sessions of cognitive behavior modification. All 7 clients who were assigned to this treatment completed it.

[14]In the religion-accommodative treatment, clients completed the standard cognitive therapy tasks specified in Beck et al. (1979); however, challenges to negative cognitions were placed in a religious context. For example, rather than replacing negative views of self with statements such as "Our self-acceptance and self-worth are not lost or lessened when we fail," the religion-accommodative approach trained clients to use self-statements such as, "God loves, accepts, and *values us just as we are.*" This treatment was also administered according to a manual, which appears in Pecheur (1980).

[15]*Propst, Ostrom, Watkins, Dean, & Mashburn (1992).* Propst et al. (1992) compared the efficacy of Beck et al.'s (1979) cognitive therapy for depression with a manualized, religion-accommodative version of the same therapy (see Propst, 1988). Clients were recruited from the community and scored at least 14 on the 28-item version of the HRSD. They also scored at least in the moderate range on standard measures of religious commitment (e.g., Allport & Ross, 1967; King & Hunt, 1972). Clients in the standard treatment completed 18 sessions of individual cognitive therapy for depression. All 19 clients enrolled in this condition completed it.

[16]In the religion-accommodative treatment, clients completed 18 sessions of cognitive therapy that challenged negative cognitions and images by replacing them with positive thoughts and imagery of a religious nature, as in Propst (1980). All 19 clients enrolled in this condition completed it.

[17]*W. B. Johnson & Ridley (1992a).* W. B. Johnson and Ridley (1992a) compared the efficacy of rational-emotive therapy (RET), using Walen, DiGiuseppe, and Wessler's (1980) treatment manual, with a manualized, religion-accommodative version of the same therapy.

Clients were theology students and local church members who scored in at least the mildly depressed range on the BDI. They also scored in the "intrinsic" range on a standard measure of religious motivation (Allport & Ross, 1967), suggesting that their religious faith was highly internalized. In the standard RET condition, clients completed six 50-min sessions in 3 weeks, including homework sessions and in-session rehearsal of rational-emotive techniques. All 5 clients assigned to this condition completed it.

[18]In the religion-accommodative treatment, three explicitly Christian treatment components were added. First, clients were directed to dispute irrational beliefs using explicitly Christian beliefs, as in Propst (1980). Second, clients were encouraged to use Christian prayer, thoughts, and imagery in their homework assignments. Third, counselors used brief prayers at the end of each session. All 5 clients assigned to this condition completed it.

[19]*W. B. Johnson et al. (1994).* W. B. Johnson et al. (1994) compared the efficacy of standard RET and a religion-accommodative form of RET, as in W. B. Johnson and Ridley (1992a). Selection criteria were almost identical to those reported in W. B. Johnson and Ridley (1992a). The standard RET condition was an eight-session protocol delivered over 8 weeks, and was based on two popular RET treatment manuals (Ellis & Dryden, 1987; Walen et al., 1980). All 16 clients assigned to this condition completed it.

[20]The religion-accommodative treatment was based on two treatment manuals discussing Christian versions of RET (Backus, 1985; Thurman, 1989). Although the basic structure of RET was kept intact, clients were encouraged to dispute irrational beliefs based on scriptural beliefs and biblical examples. Homework assignments also used biblical examples and beliefs. All 16 clients assigned to this condition completed it.

Effect Size Estimates

[21]Effect sizes and homogeneity statistics were calculated from means and standard deviations using the DSTAT statistical software, Version 1.10 (B. T. Johnson, 1989), using the formulas prescribed by Hedges and Olkin (1985). Effect sizes were based on the difference between the mean of clients in the standard counseling condition and the mean of clients in the religion-accommodative conditions. This difference was divided by the pooled standard deviation of clients in both conditions. All effect size estimates, expressed as d_+ values, are corrected for the bias that is present in uncorrected g values, as recommended by Hedges and Olkin (1985).

Effect sizes can be interpreted as the increased amount of symptom reduction afforded to participants in the religion-accommodative condition, expressed in standard deviation units. In calculating aggregate effect size estimates, individual effect sizes were weighted by the inverse of their sampling error variance, so that studies with larger samples were given greater weight in the calculation of d_+ (Hedges & Olkin, 1985).

[22]The Q statistic was also used to estimate the degree of variability among the effect sizes. The Q statistic is basically a goodness-of-fit statistic with a roughly χ^2 distribution that enables a test of the hypothesis that all observed effect sizes were drawn from the same population. Significant Q values imply a heterogeneous set of effect sizes (Hunter & Schmidt, 1990).

Handling Multiple Dependent Measures

[23]All five studies used the BDI as a dependent measure of depression. Although two of the studies also used the HRSD or a single-item visual analogue measure of depression, or both (Pecheur & Edwards, 1984; Propst et al., 1992), effect size estimates were based exclusively on the BDI for three reasons. First, the BDI has been shown to produce conservative effect size estimates in comparison to rating scales that are completed by clinicians, such as the HRSD (Lambert, Hatch, Kingston, & Edwards, 1986). Second, single-item visual analogue measures of depression (e.g., Aitken, 1969) appear to contain remarkably little true score variance (Faravelli, Albanesi, & Poli, 1986). Third, the aggregation of data across multiple dependent measures requires knowing their intercorrelations, which were not available for all five studies. Thus, the individual and mean effect size estimates reported here can be considered to be somewhat conservative.

Handling Data from Multiple Follow-Up Periods

[24]All five studies collected follow-up data within 1 week of the termination of the trial. Although three of the studies (W. B. Johnson et al., 1994; Pecheur & Edwards, 1984; Propst et al., 1992) also reported follow-up data collected between 1 and 3 months after the termination of the trial, and one study (Propst et al., 1992) reported an effect size for a 24-month follow-up, we based our effect size estimates only on the data from the 1-week follow-up.

Other Problems with Coding Effect Sizes

[25]Some studies reported data on additional experimental conditions, including self-monitoring and therapist contact conditions (Propst, 1980), waiting list control conditions (Pecheur & Edwards, 1984; Propst et al.,

1992), and pastoral counseling conditions (Propst et al., 1992). Because none of these conditions were relevant to the central goal of this study, these data were neither coded nor included in the present meta-analytic study.

[26]Two other problems arose in coding effect sizes. First, although Propst (1980) reported posttreatment means on the BDI for both conditions, standard deviations were not reported. On the basis of the assumption that the other four studies in the present meta-analysis would yield similar pooled standard deviations for the BDI, a mean standard deviation for posttest scores on the BDI from these studies (5.81) was used as an imputed standard deviation for Propst (1980). This imputed standard deviation produced a nonsignificant test statistic for the comparison of the religious and standard counseling conditions, as Propst (1980) reported, giving us confidence that our imputed standard deviation was not wholly inaccurate.

[27]Second, Propst et al.'s (1992) results reported treatment effects separately for religious and nonreligious therapists, which was an independent factor in their experimental design. To collapse treatment effects across levels of the therapist religiousness factor, means and standard deviations obtained for religious and nonreligious therapists within each of the two religious counseling conditions were pooled before calculating an effect size for the treatments.

Corrections of Findings for Unreliability in Dependent Measures

[28]Scholars in meta-analysis advise that effect size estimates be corrected for biases (Hunter & Schmidt, 1990, 1994). One of the easiest biases to correct is attenuation resulting from unreliability in the dependent variable. This bias can be corrected by dividing observed effect sizes and standard errors by the square root of the internal consistency of the dependent variable. Because meta-analytic estimates of the BDI's internal consistency were readily available (Beck, Steer, & Garbin, 1988, estimated its internal consistency at $\alpha = .86$), the observed mean effect size and its confidence interval (CI) were divided by the square root of .86, or .927. Corrections for attenuation resulting from unreliability of the dependent variable produce increased effect size estimates but also a proportionate increase in confidence intervals; thus, a nonsignificant effect size will not become significant as a result of this correction (Hunter & Schmidt, 1994).

Estimating Clinical Significance

[29]We were also interested in whether religion-accommodative and standard approaches to counseling yielded clinically significant differences in efficacy (Jacobson & Revenstorf, 1988; Jacobson & Truax, 1991). Thus, we calculated meta-analytic summaries of clinical significance for two studies that reported clinical significance data (using BDI > 9 as a cutoff for "mild clinical depression"; Kendall, Hollon, Beck, Hammen, & Ingram, 1987).

Results

Observed Mean Effect Size and Attenuation-Corrected Effect Size

[30]The mean effect size for the difference between religious and standard counseling during the 1-week follow-up period (number of effect sizes = 5, $N = 111$) was $d_+ = +0.18$ (95% CI: $-.20/+0.56$), indicating that clients in religion-accommodative counseling had slightly lower BDI scores at 1-week follow-up than did clients in standard counseling conditions. This effect size was not reliably different from zero ($p = .34$). The five effect sizes that contributed to this mean effect size were homogeneous, $Q(4) = 5.38$, $p > .10$. The mean effect size after correcting the effects for attenuation resulting from unreliability was $d_+ = +0.20$ (95% CI: $-0.19/+0.61$).

Differences in Clinical Significance

[31]Two studies (W. B. Johnson & Ridley, 1992a; Propst, 1980) reported the percentage of participants in the religious and standard psychotherapy conditions who manifested evidence of at least mild clinical depression (BDI scores > 9) during the 1-week follow-up period. Aggregation of these data indicated that, among the 20 religion-accommodative counseling clients in the two studies, 4 (20%) were still at least mildly depressed at the end of treatment. Among the 26 standard counseling clients in the two studies, 9 (34.6%) were at least mildly depressed when treatment ended. This difference in clinical significance was not statistically significant, $\chi^2(1, N = 46) = 1.19$, $p > .10$.

Discussion

[32]The goal of the present study was to review the existing empirical evidence regarding the comparative efficacy of religion-accommodative approaches to counseling depressed religious clients. These data suggest that, in the immediate period after completion of counseling, religious approaches to counseling do not have any significant superiority to standard approaches to counseling. Given that the differences in efficacy of most bonafide treatments are surprisingly small (e.g., Lambert & Bergin, 1994; Wampold, 1997), the existing

literature on psychotherapy outcomes would have portended the present meta-analytic results. These findings corroborate some narrative reviews that claim equal efficacy for religion-accommodative and standard approaches to counseling (e.g., Worthington et al., 1996), and help to resolve the inconsistencies that others have observed among these studies (e.g., W. B. Johnson, 1993; Matthews et al., 1998).

[33]Although it is true that the religious approaches to counseling were no more effective than the standard approaches to counseling, it is equally true that they were no less effective than the standard approaches to counseling. Thus, the decision to use religion-accommodative approaches might be most wisely based not on the results of comparative clinical trials, which tend to find no differences among well-manualized treatments, but rather on the basis of patient choice (see Wampold, 1997). Not every religious client would prefer or respond favorably to a religion-accommodative approach to counseling. Indeed, the available evidence suggests that all but the most highly religious clients would prefer an approach to counseling that deals with religious issues only peripherally rather than focally (Wyatt & Johnson, 1990; see Worthington et al., 1996, for review).

[34]On the other hand, many religious clients—especially very conservative Christian clients—would indeed be attracted to a counseling approach (or counselor) precisely because the counseling approach (or the counselor) maintained that the clients' system of religious values were at the core of effective psychological change (Worthington et al., 1996). The research reviewed herein indicates that no empirical basis exists for withholding such religion-accommodative treatment from depressed religious clients who desire such a treatment approach.

The Last Word?

[35]There is inherent danger in publishing meta-analytic results. Because of their ability to provide precise-looking point estimates and short CIs (especially when the observed effect size estimates are relatively heterogeneous), meta-analytic summaries can be perceived to be the last word in evaluating research questions. It would be unfortunate if the present results were interpreted as the last word in evaluating the efficacy of religious approaches to counseling, however, because interesting and important questions remain.

[36]For example, although religion-accommodative approaches to counseling do not appear to be differentially efficacious in reducing symptoms (at least depres-

sive symptoms), they might produce differential treatment satisfaction among some religious clients. Also, comparative studies of religion-accommodative therapy are needed with longer follow-up periods. It is possible that religion-accommodative approaches might prove to be superior to standard treatments in longer term follow-up periods, particularly in helping clients from relapsing, for example, back into depressive episodes. The differential effects of religion-accommodative and standard approaches to treatment also need to be investigated for a wider variety of disorders, including anxiety, anger, alcohol and drug problems, and marital and family problems. As well, although religion-accommodative and standard approaches to counseling do not appear to influence clients' religiousness or religious values differentially (Worthington et al., 1996), it is possible that religion-accommodative counseling yields differential improvements in religious clients' spiritual well-being.

[37]Finally, on a technical note, it should be noted that the studies in this body of literature currently have been seriously underpowered (i.e., in all cases fewer than 20 clients per treatment). This literature would benefit enormously from as few as three or four very high-quality, large-sample (i.e., 30 or more clients per condition) studies that investigated these questions in greater detail. W. B. Johnson (1993) provided other helpful methodological recommendations to which research on religion-accommodative counseling should adhere.

Limitations

[38]The stability of meta-analytic findings comes from the number of studies included in the meta-analysis as well as the number of participants in the constituent studies. Thus, the findings from meta-analyses with small numbers of studies, such as the present study, are more easily overturned than meta-analyses that include larger numbers of studies. Although meta-analytic methods can be used to synthesize the results of as few as two studies (for examples of small-k meta-analyses, see Allison & Faith, 1996; Benschop et al., 1998; Kirsch, Montgomery, & Sapirstein, 1995; Uchino, Cacioppo, & Kiecolt-Glaser, 1996), our findings would obviously be considered more trustworthy if more studies had been available.

[39]A second limitation of the present findings relates to the nature of the meta-analytic sample. The five studies reviewed herein all investigated religion-accommodative counseling with depressed Christian clients. We can only speculate whether the present pattern of results would generalize to different religious

populations or to people with different sets of presenting problems. Obviously, research is needed to fill in such gaps.

Conclusion

[40]A variety of empirical data now suggest that certain forms of religious involvement can help prevent the onset of psychological difficulties and enhance effective coping with stressors. In addition, the majority of mental health professionals and the general public believe that patients' religious beliefs should be adequately assessed and taken into consideration in mental health treatment. Moreover, data indicate that patients' religious commitments can play a substantial role in counseling processes (Worthington et al., 1996). Data from the present study also indicate that religious approaches to counseling can be as effective as standard approaches to counseling depressed persons. Thus, for some clients, particularly very religious Christian clients, religion-accommodative approaches to counseling could be, quite literally, the treatment of choice. It is hoped that the present study will encourage counseling psychologists to examine whether religion-accommodative approaches yield similar or even superior benefits on other important metrics of therapeutic change and with other common difficulties in living.

References

Aitken, R. C. B. (1969). Measurement of feeling using visual analogue scales *Proceedings of the Royal Society of Medicine*, 62, 989–993

Allison, D B , & Faith, M. S. (1996) Hypnosis as an adjunct to cognitive-behavioral psychotherapy for obesity A meta-analytic reappraisal *Journal of Consulting and Clinical Psychology*, 64, 513–516

Allport, G W , & Ross, J M. (1967) Personal religious orientation and prejudice *Journal of Personality and Social Psychology*, 5, 432–443

Azhar, M. Z , & Varma, S L. (1995a). Religious psychotherapy in depressive patients *Psychotherapy and Psychosomatics*, 63, 165–168.

Azhar, M. Z , & Varma, S L. (1995b). Religious psychotherapy as management of bereavement *Acta Psychiatrica Scandinavica*, 91, 233–235

Azhar, M. Z , Varma, S. L , & Dharap, A. S. (1994) Religious psychotherapy in anxiety disorder patients. *Acta Psychiatrica Scandinavica*, 90, 1–3

Backus, W (1985). *Telling the truth to troubled people* Minneapolis, MN: Bethany House.

Beck, A T. (1976) *Cognitive therapy and the emotional disorders* New York. International University Press.

Beck, A T , Rush, A J , Shaw, B. F , & Emery, G. (1979). *Cognitive therapy of depression*. New York· Guilford Press.

Beck, A T., Steer, R. A., & Garbin, M G (1988) Psychometric properties of the Beck Depression Inventory Twenty-five years of evaluation *Clinical Psychology Review*, 8, 77–100

Beck, A. T , Ward, C H , Mendelson, M , Mock, J. E , & Erbaugh, J. K (1961) An inventory for measuring depression *Archives of General Psychiatry*, 4, 561–571.

Benschop, R. J., Geenen, R , Mills, P J , Nahboff, B D , Kiecolt-Glaser, J. K., Herbert, T B , van der Pompe, G., Miller, G , Matthews, K. A., Godaert, G L R , Gilmore, S. L., Glaser, R , Heijnen, C J , Dopp, J M , Bijlsma, J W. J., Solomon, G. F , & Cacioppo, J. T (1998) Cardiovascular and immune responses to acute psychological stress in young and old women A meta-analysis. *Psychosomatic Medicine*, 60, 290–296

Bergin, A E (1991) Values and religious issues in psychotherapy and mental health. *American Psychologist*, 46, 394–403

Bergin, A E , & Jensen, J. P (1988). Mental health values of professional therapists A national interdisciplinary survey. *Professional Psychology Research and Practice*, 19, 290–297

Bergin, A E , Masters, K S , & Richards, P S (1987) Religiousness and mental health reconsidered A study of an intrinsically religious sample *Journal of Counseling Psychology*, 34, 197–204.

Bienenfeld, D , Koenig, H G , Larson, D. B , & Sherrill, K. A (1997) Psychosocial predictors of mental health in a population of elderly women. *American Journal of Geriatric Psychiatry*, 5, 43–53.

Carlson, C. R , Bacaseta, P. E., & Simanton, D. A. (1988) A controlled evaluation of devotional meditation and progressive relaxation. *Journal of Psychology and Theology*, 16, 362–368.

Comstock, G. W., & Partridge, K B. (1972) Church attendance and health *Journal of Chronic Disease*, 25, 665–672.

Cooper, H., & Hedges, L V. (1994) *Handbook of research synthesis* New York Russell Sage Foundation

DeVries, R., Ridley, C R , Pettorini, D , & Peterson, D R (1994) The comparative efficacy of Christian and secular rational-emotive therapy with Christian clients *Journal of Psychology and Theology*, 22, 130–140

Edwards, K. J. (1984) A comparison of secular and religious versions of cognitive therapy with depressed Christian college students. *Journal of Psychology and Theology*, 12, 45–54

Ellis, A , & Dryden, W (1987) *The practice of rational-emotive therapy* New York Springer

Ellis, A , & Grieger, R. (1977). *Handbook of rational-emotive therapy*. New York. Springer.

Ellison, C. G (1995) Race, religious involvement, and depressive symptomatology in a southeastern U.S. community. *Social Science and Medicine*, 40, 1561–1572

Faravelli, C., Albanesi, G , & Poli, E (1986) Assessment of depression· A comparison of rating scales *Journal of Affective Disorders*, 11, 245–253

Gallup, G (1995) *The Gallup Poll Public opinion 1995*. Wilmington, DE· Scholarly Resources

Hamilton, M. (1960) A rating scale for depression. *Journal of Neurology, Neurosurgery, and Psychiatry*, 23, 56–62

Hedges, L V., & Olkin, I (1985) *Statistical methods for meta-analysis*. Orlando, FL. Academic Press

Houts, A C., & Graham, K. (1986). Can religion make you crazy? Impact of client and therapist religious values on clinical judgments *Journal of Consulting and Clinical Psychology*, 54, 267–271.

Hunter, J E , & Schmidt, F L (1990) *Methods of meta-analysis Correcting error and bias in research findings* Newbury Park, CA Sage.

Hunter, J. E , & Schmidt, F. L. (1994) Correcting for sources of artificial variation across studies. In H Cooper & L. V. Hedges (Eds.), *Handbook of research synthesis* (pp. 323–336) New York Russell Sage Foundation.

Jacobson, N. S., & Revenstorf, D. (1988). Statistics for assessing the clinical significance of psychotherapy techniques Issues, problems, and new developments *Behavioral Assessment*, 10, 133–145.

Jacobson, N. S., & Truax, P. (1991) Clinical significance A statistical approach to defining meaningful change in psychotherapy research *Journal of Consulting and Clinical Psychology*, 59, 12–19.

Johnson, B. T. (1989). *DSTAT Software for the meta-analytic review of research literatures* Hillsdale, NJ. Erlbaum

Johnson, W B (1991) *The comparative efficacy of religious and nonreligious rational-emotive therapy with religious clients*. Unpublished doctoral dissertation, Fuller Graduate School of Psychology, Pasadena, CA.

Johnson, W. B. (1993) Outcome research and religious psychotherapies Where are we and where are we going? *Journal of Psychology and Theology*, 21, 297–308.

Johnson, W. B , & Ridley, C. R. (1992b) Sources of gain in Christian counseling and psychotherapy *The Counseling Psychologist*, 20, 159–175.

Kark, J. D., Shemi, G , Friedlander, Y , Martin, O., Manor, O , & Blondheim, S. H (1996). Does religious observance promote health? Mortality in secular vs religious kibbutzim in Israel *American Journal of Public Health*, 86, 341–346.

Kelly, E. W. (1995). Counselor values: A national survey. *Journal of Counseling and Development*, 73, 648–653

Kelly, T. A., & Strupp, H H. (1992) Patient and therapist values in psychotherapy: Perceived changes, assimilation, similarity, and outcome *Journal of Consulting and Clinical Psychology*, 60, 34–40

Kendall, P C , Hollon, S. D., Beck, A T , Hammen, C. L , & Ingram, R. E. (1987) Issues and recommendations regarding use of the Beck Depression Inventory. *Cognitive Therapy and Research*, 11, 289–299.

Kendler, K S , Gardner, C. O , & Prescott, C. A (1997). Religion, psychopathology, and substance use and abuse: A multimeasure, genetic-epidemiologic study *American Journal of Psychiatry*, 154, 322–329.

King, M. A , & Hunt, R. A (1972) Measuring the religious variable· A replication *Journal for the Scientific Study of Religion*, 11, 240–251.

Kirsch, I , Montgomery, G., & Sapirstein, G. (1995) Hypnosis as an adjunct to cognitive-behavioral psychotherapy. A meta-analysis. *Journal of Consulting and Clinical Psychology*, 63, 214–220

Koenig, H. G , George, L. K., & Peterson, B. L. (1998). Religiosity and remission of depression in medically ill older patients *American Journal of Psychiatry*, 155, 536–542

Kosmin, B A., & Lachman, S P (1993) *One nation under God Religion in contemporary American society*. New York Harmony.

Lambert, M. J , & Bergin, A. E. (1994). The effectiveness of psychotherapy In A E Bergin & S. L Garfield (Eds), *Handbook of psychotherapy and behavior change*

(4th ed , pp 143–189) New York Wiley

Lambert, M J., Hatch, D R, Kingston, M. D., & Edwards, B. C (1986) Zung, Beck, and Hamilton rating scales as measures of treatment outcome. A meta-analytic comparison *Journal of Consulting and Clinical Psychology*, *54*, 54–59.

Larson, D. B , Sherrill, K. A., Lyons, J. S., Craigie, F C , Thielman, S B , Greenwold, M. A , & Larson, S S (1992) Associations between dimensions of religious commitment and mental health reported in the *American Journal of Psychiatry* and *Archives of General Psychiatry*: 1978–1989. *American Journal of Psychiatry*, *149*, 557–559

Lewis, K N , & Lewis, D A (1985). Impact of religious affiliation on therapists' judgments of patients *Journal of Consulting and Clinical Psychology*, *53*, 926–932

Luborsky, L., Mintz, J., Auerbach, A , Cristoph, P , Bachrach, H , Todd, T , Johnson, M , Cohen, M , & O'Brien, C. P. (1980) Predicting the outcome of psychotherapy: Findings of the Penn Psychotherapy Project *Archives of General Psychiatry*, *37*, 471–481

Matthews, D A , McCullough, M. E , Larson, D B , Koenig, H. G , Swyers, J. P., & Milano, M G. (1998) Religious commitment and health A review of the research and implications for family medicine. *Archives of Family Medicine*, *7*, 118–124.

McCullough, M. E., & Worthington, E L (1995) College students' perceptions of a psychotherapist's treatment of a religious issue Partial replication and extension *Journal of Counseling and Development*, *73*, 626–634

McCullough, M. E., Worthington, E. L , Maxey, J , & Rachal, K C (1997). Gender in the context of supportive and challenging religious counseling interventions *Journal of Counseling Psychology*, *44*, 80–88.

Meichenbaum, D. (1973) *Therapist manual for cognitive behavior modification.* Unpublished manuscript, University of Waterloo, Ontario, Canada

Meichenbaum, D. (1985) *Stress inoculation training.* New York. Pergamon Press.

Miller, L., Warner, V , Wickramaratne, P , & Weissman, M (1997) Religiosity and depression Ten-year follow-up of depressed mothers and offspring. *Journal of the American Academy of Child and Adolescent Psychiatry*, *36*, 1416–1425.

Morrow, D , Worthington, E L , & McCullough, M. E. (1993) Observers' perceptions of a psychotherapist's treatment of a religious issue *Journal of Counseling and Development*, *71*, 452–456.

Neeleman, J , & King, M B (1993) Psychiatrists' religious attitudes in relation to their clinical practice. A survey of 231 psychiatrists *Acta Psychiatrica Scandinavica*, *88*, 420–424.

Ostrom, R , Watkins, P , Dean, T , & Mashburn, D. (1992). Comparative efficacy of religious and nonreligious cognitive-behavioral therapy for the treatment of clinical depression in religious individuals *Journal of Consulting and Clinical Psychology*, *60*, 94–103.

Pargament, K I (1997) *The psychology of religion and coping* New York. Guilford Press

Pargament, K. I., Ensing, D S , Falgout, K , Olsen, H , Reilly, B., Van Haitsma, K , & Warren, R. (1990) God help me· I. Religious coping efforts as predictors of the outcomes to significant life events *American Journal of Community Psychology*, *18*, 793–824.

Pargament, K I , Ishler, K., Dubow, E , Stanik, P , Rouiller, R , Crowe, P , Cullman, E , Albert, M , & Royster, B J (1994). Methods of religious coping with the Gulf War Cross-sectional and longitudinal analyses *Journal for the Scientific Study of Religion*, *33*, 347–361.

Pargament, K I , Smith, B , & Brant, C (1995, November). *Religious and nonreligious coping methods with the 1993 Midwest flood.* Paper presented at the meeting of the Society for the Scientific Study of Religion, St Louis, MO

Payne, I. R , Bergin, A E , & Loftus, P. E. (1992). A review of attempts to integrate spiritual and standard psychotherapy techniques *Journal of Psychotherapy Integration*, *2*, 171–192.

Pecheur, D. (1980) *A comparison of the efficacy of secular and religious cognitive behavior modification in the treatment of depressed Christian college students* Unpublished doctoral dissertation, Rosemead School of Psychology, La Mirada, CA

Propst, R L (1980) The comparative efficacy of religious and nonreligious imagery for the treatment of mild depression in religious individuals *Cognitive Therapy and Research*, *4*, 167–178

Propst, R L (1988) *Psychotherapy in a religious framework.* New York Human Sciences Press.

Propst, R. L (1996) Cognitive-behavioral therapy and the religious person In E P Shafranske (Ed.), *Religion in the clinical practice of psychology* (pp 391–408). Washington, DC: American Psychological Association

Richards, P S , & Bergin, A. E. (1997). *A spiritual strategy for counseling and psychotherapy* Washington, DC American Psychological Association.

Richards, P S , Owen, L , & Stein, S. (1993). A religiously oriented group counseling intervention for self-defeating perfectionism: A pilot study *Counseling and Values*, *37*, 96–104

Ridley, C. R (1992a) Brief Christian and non-Christian rational-emotive therapy with depressed Christian clients. An exploratory study. *Counseling and Values*, *36*, 220–229.

Rye, M S , & Pargament, K. I. (1997, August) *Forgiveness and romantic relationships in college* Paper presented at the 105th Annual Convention of the American Psychological Association, Chicago

Schumaker, J. F. (1992) *Religion and mental health*. New York. Oxford University Press.

Shafranske, E. P (1996). *Religion and the clinical practice of psychology*. Washington, DC: American Psychological Association.

Shafranske, E. P., & Malony, H. N. (1990). Clinical psychologists' religious and spiritual orientations and their practice of psychotherapy. *Psychotherapy*, *27*, 72–78.

Thurman, C. (1989). *The lies we believe* Nashville, TN. Thomas Nelson

Toh, Y , & Tan, S Y (1997). The effectiveness of church-based lay counselors: A controlled outcome study *Journal of Psychology and Christianity*, *16*, 260–267.

Uchino, B. N , Cacioppo, J T., & Kiecolt-Glaser, J K (1996). The relationship between social support and physiological processes. A review with emphasis on underlying mechanisms and implications for health. *Psychological Bulletin*, *119*, 488–531.

Walen, S R , DiGiuseppe, R., & Wessler, R (1980) *A practitioner's guide to rational emotive therapy* New York Oxford University Press.

Wampold, B E. (1997). Methodological problems in identifying efficacious psychotherapies *Psychotherapy Research*, *7*, 21–43

Wandrei, K. E. (1985) Identifying potential suicides among high-risk women *Social Work*, *30*, 511–517

Worthington, E L , Kurusu, T. A., McCullough, M E , & Sandage, S. J (1996) Empirical research on religion and psychotherapeutic processes and outcomes A ten-year review and research prospectus. *Psychological Bulletin*, *119*, 448–487.

Wyatt, S. C , & Johnson, R. W. (1990). The influence of counselors' religious values on clients' perceptions of the counselor *Journal of Psychology and Theology*, *18*, 158–165.

Address correspondence to: Michael E McCullough, National Institute for Healthcare Research, 6110 Executive Boulevard, Suite 908, Rockville, MD 20852. Electronic mail may be sent to Mike@nihr.org

Discussion Questions for Model Literature Review 6

Editorial note: All the model literature reviews in this book are presented as strong models. However, there are differences of opinion on the effectiveness of any particular piece of writing, even among experts. While answering the following questions, consider the guidelines in this book (as *only* guidelines, not principles) as well as your own standards for effective writing.

1. Briefly comment on the adequacy of the title of the review.

2. Comment on the adequacy of the Abstract. Does it effectively summarize the essence of the review given that abstracts are restricted to 120 words or less in the journal in which this review article appeared?

3. Does the review have a strong beginning? Does it get straight to the point? If not, has the author used some other effective technique to begin the review?

4. Has the author made a strong case for reviewing the topic(s) he covers? Has the author shown that the topic(s) are important?

5. Is the material presented in a logical sequence? Are the headings (and subheadings, if any) appropriate and helpful?

6. Are key variables adequately defined? Are they defined at appropriate points? Explain.

7. Are there points where the references are not well integrated with each other (i.e., simply described as an annotated list)? Explain.

8. Are the strengths and weaknesses of some of the cited research described? If yes, name at least one section where this is done using paragraph numbers.

9. Has the author made it clear what material is his and what is being summarized/paraphrased from other sources? Explain.

10. Are any portions of the review unclear to you? If so, identify them by paragraph number(s).

11. Are the individual paragraphs straightforward and to the point? Explain. If yes, identify one by number that you think is especially good. If no, identify one that is weak.

12. Is the conclusion/discussion at the end of the review appropriate in light of the material covered earlier?

13. On a scale from 1 (very weak) to 10 (very strong), what is your overall evaluation of the literature review? Name one or two considerations that strongly influenced your evaluation.

14. Assume that you are on the editorial board of an academic journal and that the general topic of this review is within the scope of what the journal usually publishes. Which of the following would you recommend to the editor of the journal: publish as is, publish only after minor revisions, publish only after major revisions, *or* do not publish? Briefly defend your recommendation.

Model Literature Review 7

Risk Propensity Differences Between Entrepreneurs and Managers: A Meta-Analytic Review

Wayne H. Stewart
Clemson University

Philip L. Roth
Clemson University

Editorial note: The paragraphs in this literature review have been numbered to make it easy to refer to specific portions of this review during classroom discussions. The numbers are italicized superscripts at the beginning of each paragraph. All other nonitalicized superscripts, if any, refer to footnotes within the review.

ABSTRACT

Research examining the relative risk-taking propensities of entrepreneurs and managers has produced conflicting findings and no consensus, posing an impediment to theory development. To overcome the limitations of narrative reviews, the authors used psychometric meta-analysis to mathematically cumulate the literature concerning risk propensity differences between entrepreneurs and managers. Results indicate that the risk propensity of entrepreneurs is greater than that of managers. Moreover, there are larger differences between entrepreneurs whose primary goal is venture growth versus those whose focus is on producing family income. Results also underscore the importance of precise construct definitions and rigorous measurement.

[1]Recent meta-analyses in applied psychology have strongly supported the importance of personality traits in understanding and predicting organizational outcomes such as job performance, training success, and salary (e.g., Barrick & Mount, 1991; Hough, Eaton, Dunnette, Kamp, & McCloy, 1990), challenging years of thought that personality does not significantly influence behavior. Although most of these analyses have focused on performance-related outcomes in larger, well-established organizations, there are also implications for entrepreneurs and their emerging organizations. The role of personality in entrepreneurial career choice and in entrepreneurial cognition, important in the development of a theory of the entrepreneur (J. W. Carland, Hoy, Boulton, & Carland, 1984; Johnson, 1990), has received substantial research attention. A prime example is entrepreneurial risk-taking propensity, a research stream emanating from Cantillion's early-18th-century conceptualization of entrepreneurial risk bearing. While scholars have been speculating on the role of risk in entrepreneurial behavior for over 300 years, the empirical evidence concerning the hypothesis that entrepreneurs have a greater risk propensity than do managers has been plagued by methodological limitations, and the results appear inconsistent.

[2]Because of contradictory results in the primary studies, reviews of the literature (e.g., Brockhaus & Horwitz, 1986; Chell, 1985; Perry, 1990) have frequently concluded that entrepreneurs do not have a distinctive risk propensity compared with managers. These narrative summaries, however, are prone to major methodological limitations, such as not mathematically cumulating results, lack of attention to sampling error, and measurement reliability concerns. To date, there has been no rigorous assessment that satisfactorily incorporates these methodological complexities in examining differences in the risk propensities of entrepreneurs and managers. As a result, divergent theoretical positions and discordant empirical findings have culminated in confusion in the entrepreneurial risk propensity literature, and in an impasse in theory development associated with dispositions and entrepreneurial risk behavior. The cumulation of the existing literature is the first step toward clarifying the role of risk-taking propensity in entrepreneurial behavior and stimulating future research. Thus, our purpose is to meta-analyze the literature concerning the comparative risk propensities of entrepreneurs and to pinpoint where research is needed.

Risk Propensity and the Entrepreneur

[3]In classic decision theory, risk is often viewed as a function of the variation in the distribution of possible

outcomes, the associated outcome likelihoods, and their subjective values (cf. March & Shapira, 1987). Other scholars, however, have long acknowledged that risky decisions are not based exclusively on rational calculations but are also affected by individual predispositions toward risk (Bromiley & Curley, 1992). Thus, a stream of research suggests that risk-taking is predispositional rather than simply situational (Jackson, Hourany, & Vidmar, 1972; Plax & Rosenfeld, 1976) and that this risk propensity influences the effects of situational characteristics on risky decision-making behavior (cf. Sitkin & Weingart, 1995). This position is consistent with Big Five personality theory, which suggests that risk propensity is a facet of the trait of extraversion (Mount & Barrick, 1995). Such thought has been applied to the study of emerging organizations and the decision of whether to choose an entrepreneurial career in which one assumes ownership of an organization versus more typical *contractual* employment (Kihlstrom & Laffont, 1979). From this theoretical underpinning, predictions about risk propensity differences between entrepreneurs and managers diverge.

Theoretical Positions

[4]The literature is most often grounded in one of two theoretical positions. The first is that entrepreneurs have a higher risk propensity. Although the tasks of the entrepreneur and the manager both entail taking risks, entrepreneurs are generally believed to take more risks than do managers because the entrepreneurial function entails coping with a less structured, more uncertain set of possibilities (Bearse, 1982) and bearing the ultimate responsibility for the decision (Gasse, 1982; Kilby, 1971; Knight, 1921). Accordingly, more risk-tolerant individuals are likely to "self-select" into entrepreneurial careers, whereas more risk-averse individuals choose contractual employment (e.g., Ahmed, 1985; Begley & Boyd, 1987; J. W. Carland, III, M. Carland, Carland, & Pearce, 1995; Hull, Bosley, & Udell, 1980; Stewart, Watson, Carland, & Carland, 1999). This theoretical position suggests that the literature will show a marked risk propensity difference between entrepreneurs and managers.

[5]The second, competing, theoretical position is grounded in classic motivation theory (cf. Atkinson, 1957; Atkinson, Bastian, Earl, & Litwin, 1960; McClelland, 1961), where the focus is achievement motivation and the concomitant fear of failure or desire for success. Persons high in need for achievement set challenging goals of moderate difficulty, accomplish these goals through effort and skill, take personal responsibil-

ity for decisions (McClelland, 1961), and are moderate risk takers (Atkinson, 1957). Because entrepreneurs and managers are both high in achievement motivation (Perry, 1990; Sexton & Bowman, 1985), the precepts of motivation theory suggest that entrepreneurs do not differ from managers in their dispositions toward risk (e.g., Brockhaus, 1980; Masters & Meier, 1988; Meyer, Walker, & Litwin, 1961; Ray, 1982; Richard, 1989; Robbins, 1986). Therefore, there should be small or no differences in the risk propensities of entrepreneurs and managers.

Methodological Considerations

[6]A number of key issues in the entrepreneurial risk propensity research are problematic from both theoretical and methodological viewpoints and contribute to the confusion in the entrepreneurial risk propensity literature.

The Definitional Dilemma

[7]Research definitions of "entrepreneur" have spanned a range of economic actors. Early research often focused on entrepreneurial managers (Meyer et al., 1961), salespeople (McClelland, 1961), and decentralized branch bank managers (Litzinger, 1963). More recently, research definitions of entrepreneurs have focused on founders of new ventures (e.g., Ahmed, 1985; Begley & Boyd, 1987; Gartner, 1985) or owners of small businesses (e.g., Masters & Meier, 1988; Schwer & Yucelt, 1984), although some researchers also have used growth aspirations as a definitional criterion (e.g., Carland et al., 1984; Smith & Miner, 1983; Stewart et al., 1999). Researchers have sometimes used choice of college major as a surrogate for potential entrepreneurs and potential managers (e.g., Sexton & Bowman, 1983, 1984, 1986).

[8]This range of operational definitions has complicated the accurate discernment of the role of entrepreneurial risk propensity and requires great care in interpretation. We suggest two approaches to minimize definitional difficulties. First, we explicitly focus on the research question: Do entrepreneurs have higher levels of risk propensity than do managers? This allows us to focus on the most widely used definition of an entrepreneur, namely, an individual who independently owns and actively manages a small business (J. W. Carland et al., 1984), thereby excluding branch bank managers, salespeople, and so forth. Second, there may be different categories of entrepreneurs. In the most frequently cited typology of owner—managers, J. W. Carland et al. (1984) provided a distinction between two types, based

primarily on the individual's purpose for the business. J. W. Carland et al. (1984) proposed a distinction between entrepreneurs, owners who primarily focus on profit and growth, and small business owners, those who focus on producing family income. In keeping with the typology of J. W. Carland et al. (1984), we posit that there may be marked risk propensity differences between growth-oriented entrepreneurs and income-oriented entrepreneurs.

[9]Explicitly drawing on such a typology of entrepreneurs has several advantages. First, it allows empirical investigation of these groups to determine if they differ in risk propensity. Second, the empirical analysis of risk propensity differences facilitates the examination of within-cell variance in the extant entrepreneurial risk propensity research. That is, entrepreneurs who focus on growth and those who focus on income could be two different groups in terms of risk propensity, but both are often classified as entrepreneurs in the lexicon of the literature. If two such groups are combined within the same cell in a given study, risk propensity differences with managers would likely be minimized because of a depressed mean level of risk propensity in the entrepreneurial group (depending on the operational definition) and increased variance within the group. As a result, the statistical differences between entrepreneurs and managers could be doubly biased downward.

Sample Issues

[10]Most studies of entrepreneurial psychology have used small samples (Greenberger & Sexton, 1988), a condition evident in studies of entrepreneurial risk propensity. Small sample sizes may be a major source of confusion in narrative reviews because researchers see many insignificant results due to low power (Schmidt, 1996) and substantial variation in results that may be largely due to sampling error (Hunter & Schmidt, 1990). Given the large percentage of risk propensity studies that have used small samples, we would expect to see a sizable portion of across-study variance in risk propensity differences due to sampling error.

Instrumentation

[11]Measurement issues also have exacerbated the discord concerning entrepreneurial risk propensity. Two risk propensity instruments have been predominant, and each is purported to measure a generalized predisposition toward taking risk. The Kogan–Wallach Choice Dilemmas Questionnaire (CDQ) measures a generalized consistently cautious or risky outlook affecting a person's judgments in a variety of situations (Kogan &

Wallach, 1964; Wallach & Kogan, 1959, 1961). The CDQ contains 12 scenarios that describe a person who is faced with a choice of pursuing a risky course of action with high return or pursuing a less risky decision where the return is less. In each case, the respondent is asked to advise the person in the scenario by indicating what probability of success (1, 3, 5, 7, or 9 in 10) would be sufficient to warrant the choice of the risky alternative. Although scoring guidelines are not explicitly provided, most researchers have summed the scores across the scenarios to derive a risk propensity measure.

[12]Notably, the CDQ has been criticized for its reliance on projected assessments of risk (Ray, 1986; Shaver & Scott, 1991), which differ from actual behavior on tasks (Highbee, 1971), and for its failure to measure a unitary disposition (Cartwright, 1971; Plax & Rosenfeld, 1976), as evidenced by its factor structure (Stewart, Carland, & Carland, 1998). Other researchers have discovered that the CDQ has low reliability (Stewart et al., 1998), which would suppress covariance estimates between risk propensity and entrepreneurial status.

[13]The second primary instrument is drawn from the Jackson Personality Inventory (JPI; Jackson, 1976). The JPI is a structured inventory of 16 personality variables that is most appropriate for studies that investigate the personality correlates of occupations (Jackson, 1976). The Risk Taking scale of the JPI was designed to assess the willingness to commit to a decision that could lead to success or failure and the corresponding outcomes. Thus, the instrumentation addresses risk taking as a variable of personality in which exposure to uncertain outcomes is a key consideration (Jackson, 1978). It contains components of social, physical, monetary, and ethical risk taking but weights monetary risk taking most heavily (Jackson, 1976). Jackson (1976) attained the hypothesized factor structure, and several studies have reported acceptable reliability and validity results for the Risk Taking scale (cf. Stewart, 1996). Higher reliability results in less suppression of the measures of covariance between risk propensity and entrepreneurial status. Based on sound construction principles and demonstrated measurement properties, we expect higher levels of covariance between entrepreneurial status and risk propensity, as measured with the JPI.

Meta-Analysis

[14]In contrast to a traditional narrative review, meta-analysis is a method for mathematically cumulating the results of previous studies (Hunter & Schmidt, 1990). Although many readers of this journal are very familiar

with this analytic technique, we briefly highlight its advantages for summarizing the entrepreneurial risk propensity literature. First, meta-analysis is more replicable and accurate because it allows mathematical combination of effect sizes on differences between groups. In this case, we use *d,* where the numerator consists of the difference between the means of the two groups (entrepreneurs vs. managers) over the denominator of the pooled standard deviation of the two groups. The denominator's standard deviation is calculated by averaging the standard deviations of the entrepreneurial and managerial groups by their respective sample sizes. Therefore, *d* is independent of sample size (Hunter & Schmidt, 1990). Cumulating the effects across studies, and weighting effect sizes by sample sizes, enables greater precision in examining risk propensity differences between entrepreneurs and managers.

[15]Second, meta-analysis allows for the mathematical correction of certain types of methodological factors and design flaws (Hunter & Schmidt, 1990; Mitchell, 1985) that have obscured important relationships. Meta-analysis facilitates the examination of sampling error, overcomes many power concerns, provides a means for correcting measurement reliability, and enables the quantitative examination of the impact of moderator variables on the results (cf. Hunter & Schmidt, 1990). Thus, given the aforementioned methodological issues in the entrepreneurial risk propensity literature, we suggest that meta-analysis offers great promise in cumulating the literature on risk propensity differences between entrepreneurs and managers.

Method

Study Identification and Screening Criteria

[16]To facilitate a comprehensive meta-analytic review, we systematically searched the *ABI–INFORM, Business and Management Practices, UnCover, Dissertation Abstracts Online, Expanded Academic ASAP, General BusinessFile, Management Contents, PsycINFO, Sociological Abstracts,* and *Social SciSearch* databases. The primary criterion for inclusion was that a study must make a risk propensity comparison of a clearly defined entrepreneurial group to a managerial group of adults. The definition of the entrepreneur must have met the generally recognized minimum criterion—independent ownership and active management of the firm—or the expressed intention, via college major, to do so. The samples of Litzinger (1963, 1965) and Meyer et al. (1961) did not meet this criterion, and DeLeo (1982) and Phillips (1991) did not provide definitions that were clear enough to make a determination. Second,

the study must also have provided sufficient information on statistical relationships to calculate *d*: the means and standard deviations for each group, *F*s or *t*s. The studies by Hull et al., (1980), McGrath, MacMillan, and Scheinberg (1992), Schwer and Yucelt (1984), and Sexton and Bowman (1984) did not report the statistical information required for the calculation of *d*. Also, we were unable to acquire the study by Dewan (1982). Table 1 chronologically presents the studies of entrepreneurial risk propensity, the nature of the samples used, instrumentation, the obtained results, and the *d* scores. Notably, all of the studies used correlational designs.

Coding Procedure

[17]We independently coded all of the included studies. Empirical results, such as *t*s and correlations, were converted into *d*s to provide a common metric for analysis (Huffcutt & Roth, 1998; Hunter & Schmidt, 1990). In cases where authors made multiple comparisons in a study that would facilitate analysis of within-entrepreneur cell variance, we calculated a *d* for each of the comparisons. For example, Stewart et al. (1999), using the J. W. Carland et al. (1984) definitions, compared the risk propensities of growth-oriented entrepreneurs, current income-oriented entrepreneurs, and managers, resulting in three *d*s. In such cases, we combined the two types of entrepreneurs to derive a single group for comparison in the overall analysis. We also coded information concerning type of instrument used in the study (e.g., CDQ, JPI), reported evidence of measurement reliability, and the medium of the study, that is, journal, conference proceedings, or dissertation.

Meta-Analytic Approach

[18]We used the Schmidt-Hunter approach to meta-analysis (Hunter & Schmidt, 1990). This method includes computing sample-size-weighted mean effect sizes, correcting for research artifacts, and analyzing the proportion of variance in effect sizes due to research artifacts. To clarify our analysis, we note several selected aspects of our approach. All studies assessing the relationship between entrepreneurial status and risk propensity were combined into an overall analysis. The sample-weighted mean effect size was then corrected for unreliability, and the confidence intervals were placed around the corrected effect size. Finally, we computed the percentage of variance in effect sizes across studies attributable to sampling error and measurement error in risk propensity. We added these factors together to show how much of the variability in effect sizes was due to research artifacts, and we conducted moderator analysis.

Table 1

Sample Studies of Entrepreneurial Risk-Taking Propensity

Researcher(s)	Sample	Measure	Results
Brockhaus (1980)	New founders (n = 31, M = 71.00, SD = 11.94), newly hired managers (n = 31, M = 72 52, SD = 12.19), newly promoted managers (n = 31, M = 66.97, SD = 10.84)	CDQ	No significant differences (d = −.11)[a]
Ray (1982)	Owners (n = 53, M = 11.28, SD = 4.12), managers (n = 74, M = 9 68, SD = 3.32)	Harm Avoidance	No significant difference (d = − 44)
Sexton and Bowman (1983)	Entrepreneurship majors (n = 50, M = 64.36, SD = 15.52), nonbusiness majors (n = 107, M = 68.89, SD = 63.74)	JPI, PRF-E, CDQ	Entrepreneurship majors had higher RP (d = 32)
Ahmed (1985)	Immigrant founders (n = 71, M = 1 02, SD = 027), immigrant nonentrepreneurs (n = 62, M = 0 86, SD = 0 28)	RTPS	Entrepreneurs had higher RP (d = .59)
Begley and Boyd (1987)	Founders (n = 147, M = 29.08, SD = 4.35), small business managers (n = 92, M = 27 00, SD = 4.86)	JPI	Entrepreneurs had higher RP (d = 46)
Masters and Meier (1988)	Owners or owner–managers (M = 68 50), small business managers (M = 73.55), (N = 50, SD = 14.80)[b]	CDQ	No significant difference (d = 34)
Richard (1989)	Founders (n = 40), managers (n = 41)[c]	JPI	No significant difference (d = .16)
J C Carland and Carland (1991)	Entrepreneurs (n = 52)[c], small business owners (n = 152), managers (n = 174)	JPI	Entrepreneurs had higher RP than managers (d = 74) and small business owners (d = .70); no significant difference between small business owners and managers (d = .11)
J. W. Carland, III, Carland, Carland, and Pearce (1995)	Entrepreneurs (n = 114, M = 12 76, SD = 4.84), small business owners (n = 347, M = 9.71, SD = 5 31), managers (n = 387, M = 9.24, SD = 5 08)	JPI	Entrepreneurs had higher RP than managers (d = .70) and small business owners (d = .59); no significant difference in small business owners and managers (d = 09)
Palich and Bagby (1995)	Growth-oriented founders (n = 35), nonentrepreneurs (n = 57)[c]	RPS	No significant difference (d = .08)
Seth and Sen (1995)	Founders (n = 20, M = 17.95, SD = 6 19), mid-level managers (n = 20, M = 22 85, SD = 7 90)	CDQ	Founders had higher RP (d = 69)
Stewart, Watson, Carland, and Carland (1999)	Entrepreneurs (n = 101, M = 12.66, SD = 4.90), small business owners (n = 324, M = 9 73, SD = 5 34), managers (n = 342, M = 8 93, SD = 4.87)	JPI	Entrepreneurs had higher RP than managers (d = .76) and small business owners (d = .56), small business owners had higher RP than managers (d = .16)

Note. CDQ = Choice Dilemmas Questionnaire; Harm Avoidance = Harm Avoidance Scale from Personality Research Form; JPI = Risk Taking Scale from Jackson Personality Inventory, PRF-E = Personality Research Form E; RP = risk propensity; RPS = Risk Propensity Scale; RTPS = Risk Taking Propensity Scale

[a]We computed two *d*s for Brockhaus (1980). One *d* compared the first group of managers with entrepreneurs, and the second *d* compared the second group of managers with entrepreneurs. We averaged the resulting two *d*s and weighted the average by the total sample size (N = 93) for the analysis. Analyzing two separate *d*s would have overweighted the impact of this study and would be contrary to the tenets of sample size weighting (Hunter & Schmidt, 1990) [b]Individual–group standard deviations were not available. Overall standard deviation for both groups was used to compute a conservative d. [c]Means and standard deviations were not available. Effect size was computed from an *F* or a *t*.

Results

Outlier Analysis

[19]Analysis for outliers is an important part of meta-analysis because outliers can markedly distort meta-analytic results (Hunter & Schmidt, 1990). Accordingly, outlier analysis is routinely used in meta-analyses that examine individual differences (e.g., Huffcutt & Roth, 1998; Vinchur, Schippmann, Switzer, & Roth, 1998). The sample-adjusted meta-analytic deviancy (SAMD) statistic was designed to detect outliers in the effect size distribution in meta-analyses (Huffcutt & Arthur, 1995). The application of the SAMD statistic in Figure 1 illus-trates that the study by Ray (1982) is an outlier. The originators of the SAMD statistic encourage researchers to examine the individual studies to determine why they were outliers (Huffcutt & Arthur, 1995). In this case, Ray (1982) used the Harm Avoidance Scale of the Personality Research Form (PRF) rather than the Risk Taking Scale of the JPI to measure risk propensity—potentially a problem of conceptual equivalency and construct validity. The Harm Avoidance Scale focuses primarily on physical risk and personal safety, whereas the Risk Taking Scale of the JPI is a more comprehensive measure of risk propensity and emphasizes mone-

tary risk, which we believe is more germane to the entrepreneurial experience because of the entrepreneur's responsibility for the finances of the venture. The differences in the constructs assessed by the two scales highlight the importance of careful analysis and construct equivalence. On the basis of the SAMD statistic, we omitted Ray (1982) from the analysis.

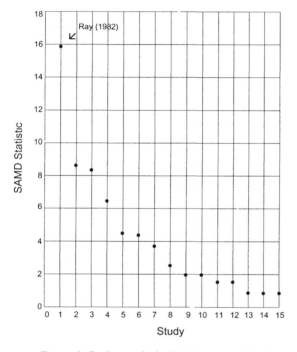

Figure 1. Outlier analysis (SAMD = sample-adjusted meta-analytic deviancy).

Coding Reliability

[20]Following outlier analysis, we examined the coding reliability for the studies in our data set. The coding of categorical variables used in the analysis, such as publication status and instrumentation, yielded complete agreement. Coding for effect size (*d*) and study sample size was nearly perfect, because the two codings correlated at $r = .99$.

Meta-Analysis Results Overall Analysis

[21]The primary focus of our analysis was to contrast the risk propensities of entrepreneurs and managers. Table 2 contains the overall observed *d* of 0.30, suggesting that the literature indicates that the entrepreneurs have a somewhat higher risk propensity than do managers. Yet, the observed effect size was downwardly biased due to the imperfect measurement reliability (Hunter & Schmidt, 1990) of risk propensity. We corrected the observed *d*s using the interitem reliability dis-

tribution (alphas) of the risk propensity instruments of the studies in our data set. The reliability-corrected overall *d* increased to 0.36. This correction for reliability was conservative, because interitem reliability indices do not contain variance in responses due to alternative forms or time, which often affect the reliability of measurement instruments (Hunter & Schmidt, 1990). We return to this issue later.

Table 2
Overall Results of the Meta-Analysis

Study	*d*	*d* rel	CI[a]	*K*	*N*	PVA
All	.30	36	30–44	14	3,338	100
Moderator analysis for instrumentation						
All using JPI	.31	36	30–.42	9	2,940	100
All Using CDQ	.25	—[b]	–.04–.51	4	340	79
All others	37	—[b]	.08–.58	2	225	59

Note d = average observed effect size, *d* rel = average effect size corrected for reliability of the measure of risk, CI = confidence interval, *K* = number of studies, PVA = percentage of variance accounted for by sampling error and measurement error, JPI = Jackson Personality Inventory, CDQ = Choice Dilemmas Questionnaire.

[a]Where applicable, confidence intervals are reported for measurement reliability-corrected *d* scores [b]No correction was made for the *d* statistic given the lack of reliability coefficients reported in this cell

[22]One hundred percent of the variance in all of the studies in the data set was simply a function of sampling error and variance in the reliability of measures used in the studies. Measurement error accounted for only 4.9% of the total variance (although our measures of reliability were quite conservative), and the remaining study variance was attributable to sampling error. Some meta-analysts would conclude that no more analyses directed at determining effect sizes were needed, given that analyses of all nonoutliers showed that all variance was a result of research artifacts. We continued *only* with analysis of measurement instruments because we had strong *a priori* reasons for examining this issue.

Moderator Analysis

[23]If one assumes that additional analysis is warranted, we found that the type of measurement instrument used to assess risk propensity was a moderator of study results concerning risk propensity differences between entrepreneurs and managers. Table 2 shows that the observed *d* for studies using the JPI measure of risk propensity, or an adaptation thereof (Sexton & Bowman, 1983, 1986) was 0.31, contrasted with a *d* of 0.25 for studies using the CDQ measure of risk propensity. Although we caution readers that the *K* and *N* for studies using the CDQ and other measures of risk propensity

were quite small and unstable, the cell using just the JPI measures of risk propensity deserved further attention.

[24]We corrected the JPI instrument-observed d using interitem reliability (alpha). The result was a measurement reliability corrected d of 0.36. As previously indicated, this correction was quite conservative.

Within-Cell Variance

[25]Earlier, we discussed how most studies of entrepreneurial risk propensity had used a definition of the entrepreneur that included both people oriented toward profit and growth and those seeking current income. However, previous conceptual work suggested that these two groups might differ substantially in their risk propensities (J. W. Carland et al., 1984). Further, we cautioned that inclusion of both groups in one cell might lead to a conceptually heterogeneous cell that would result in downward biases on primary study statistical significance. Therefore, we thought it important to investigate the impact of within-cell heterogeneity.

[26]We examined all studies that reported risk propensity differences in entrepreneurs on the basis of the J. W. Carland et al. (1984) typology. Only three studies (J. C. Carland & Carland, 1991; J. W. Carland, III et al., 1995; and Stewart et al., 1999) reported the necessary statistics to separate growth-oriented entrepreneurs from income-oriented entrepreneurs. The difference in risk propensity between the two types of entrepreneurs in these studies yielded an observed $d = 0.60$ ($K = 3$, $N = 1,093$). Correcting the observed d for measurement reliability (alpha of .76 reported in Stewart et al., 1999) increased the estimated d to 0.69. These studies suggested that income-oriented entrepreneurs had substantially lower levels of risk propensity than did those with growth aspirations. We also compared income-oriented entrepreneurs with managers and found the observed d to be 0.11 ($K = 3$, $N = 1,428$), suggesting that small business owners had a slightly higher risk propensity than did managers (corrected $d = 0.13$). Finally, we compared the growth-oriented entrepreneurs with managers and discovered an observed d of 0.73 ($K = 3$, $N = 1,148$), which rose to 0.84 when conservatively corrected for measurement reliability. Although the number of studies and sample sizes were small and precluded completely definitive conclusions, these standardized differences suggested that entrepreneurs with growth aspirations had the highest risk propensity, which was markedly higher than that of owners with a current income focus and a great deal higher than that of managers. The results also suggested that including both growth-oriented and income-oriented entrepreneurs in

the same group would result in a very heterogeneous cell.

Discussion

[27]The interest in how entrepreneurs differ from managers is longstanding. In the case of risk propensity, decades of investigation appear to show conflicting evidence of differences between entrepreneurs and managers, and many researchers interpret the evidence as indicative of small, if any, differences. Our results suggest that there is a difference, and that the magnitude of the difference depends on one's definition of the entrepreneur. Assuming that the term *entrepreneur* includes owners with variation in goals for the business, the meta-analysis indicates that entrepreneurs have a somewhat higher risk propensity than do managers (observed $d = 0.30$, corrected $d = 0.36$). Yet this analysis ignores extremely large within-cell variance. If we focus on entrepreneurs with growth aspirations versus managers, the differences in risk propensity become very large indeed (observed $d = 0.73$, corrected $d = 0.84$). These results seem to suggest that we are examining three different populations of individuals, as per the J. W. Carland et al. (1984) conceptualization, but we caution that these comparisons are based on only three studies and 1,148 individuals. Thus, a very relevant question for future research may be how the three groups differ.

[28]Given the role of sampling error in explaining variance across the studies, we undertook moderator analyses with caution. It appears that variants of the Risk Taking Scale of the JPI are associated with larger covariance with measures of entrepreneurial status.

[29]The implication of our analyses for theory is fairly straightforward. The achievement motivation theory position that predicts small or no differences in risk propensity between entrepreneurs and managers was not supported (even if entrepreneurs with and without growth aspirations are in the same cell). Alternatively, the effect sizes provide more support for the theoretical position that entrepreneurs have a higher risk propensity. Relative to managers, entrepreneurs appear predisposed toward taking more risks. If the entrepreneur's principle purpose is profit and growth, then the individual's propensity for risk taking appears markedly higher than those who are more current income-oriented, and strongly higher than that of managers.

[30]We also have asserted that traditional narrative reviews are restricted by human information-processing limitations. One such limitation is that narrative reviewers may draw conclusions from a study, or group of studies, that is unrepresentative of the literature (Hunter

& Schmidt, 1990). The results of the study by Brock-haus (1980), indicating no risk propensity differences between entrepreneurs and managers ($d = -0.11$), is representative of this tendency. The Brockhaus study is one of the most frequently cited studies, possibly because it was published in one of the preeminent management journals, and is often used as the primary basis for a conclusion about entrepreneurial risk propensity. Interestingly, the results for the field as a whole seem to differ greatly from those of Brockhaus.

Limitations

[31]There are three potential limitations to this meta-analysis. The first is due to a relatively small number of studies available to meta-analyze. Direct comparisons between entrepreneurs and managers are limited (Greenberger & Sexton, 1988), and the amount of data available for meta-analysis is small compared to some other meta-analytic efforts. Yet our set of studies shows that sampling error is primarily responsible for any observed differences in the extant literature. Thus, we are not sure that merely adding new studies to the database that do not possess some unique characteristics would markedly change the results.

[32]Second, due to difficulties in sampling failed entrepreneurs, and to the fact that many of the samples may have included entrepreneurs who had been in business for some time, there may be a bias toward successful entrepreneurs in the literature and, thus, in this study. Nonetheless, we believe that a systematic loss of either successful or unsuccessful entrepreneurs may lead to a conservative bias in our results. Such individuals might include highly successful entrepreneurs who sold their businesses, or entrepreneurs who failed. To the extent that entrepreneurial success is correlated with risk propensity, we would expect indirect range restriction and downwardly biased estimates of covariance (Hunter & Schmidt, 1990).

[33]The third limitation involves other reasons why our estimate of d is conservative. Frankly, we believe that a corrected d of 0.36 is downwardly biased for two reasons. First, as previously noted, the use of internal consistency measures of reliability provides overly optimistic estimates of reliability (Hunter & Schmidt, 1990). Such estimates lead to corrections that underestimate true effect sizes. Second, any unreliability in categorizing individuals into various classes (entrepreneur vs. manager or growth-oriented entrepreneurs vs. income-oriented entrepreneurs) in the primary studies downwardly biases d because of an overestimate of the denominator of d in many of the studies.

Future Research

[34]We proffer several suggestions for research methodology and theory building from the results of this study. In terms of methodology, four concerns are important. First, risk propensity has often been poorly conceptualized and measured (Sitkin & Weingart, 1995). Researchers should be very precise and explicit in their theoretical definitions and careful in their choice of instrumentation. Although the JPI and CDQ appear to measure the same phenomenon, there are no thorough direct comparisons of the two instruments, a consideration for future research. Given a choice of the two primary existing instruments, we recommend the Risk Taking Scale of the JPI for assessing risk propensity because of the relative attractiveness of its measurement properties. Second, we express renewed concern over sample size in entrepreneurship research in general. A concern over power applies to the results of any single study, and to many small-sample studies that can obfuscate an effect across multiple studies, thereby inhibiting the cumulation of knowledge. Third, researchers must also be careful to manage within-cell variance concerns. That is, we propose that growth-oriented entrepreneurs and income-oriented entrepreneurs may be different populations on the risk propensity variable, although more research is needed on this subject. Even if researchers disagree with us on definitional issues, and advocate some other typology of entrepreneurs, care in study design is indispensable. Studies should be designed so that different types of entrepreneurs are clearly identified and placed in appropriate cells. Finally, longitudinal research is needed to determine the effects of survivor bias. We take the first step toward clarifying the relationship between entrepreneurship and risk propensity by summarizing the existing literature, but more carefully designed studies are needed to track entrepreneurs through the venture life cycle. Such research could benefit the risk propensity literature by empirically examining any sort of survivor biases.

[35]The results also have a number of implications for refining and extending theory by examining risk propensity in a broader entrepreneurial decision-making framework. Risk propensity dominates the actual and perceived characteristics of the decision-making situation in influencing risk behavior, and it influences risk perception (Sitkin & Pablo, 1992). For example, a risk-averse individual may weight negative outcomes more heavily than positive ones (Schneider & Lopes, 1986). In turn, risk propensity and risk perception mediate the influences of organizational and problem characteristics

on risk behavior (Sitkin & Pablo, 1992; Sitkin & Weingart, 1995), such as previous experiences (Osborn & Jackson, 1988; Thaler & Johnson, 1990), problem framing (Highhouse & Yuce, 1996; Kahneman & Tversky, 1979), belief in risk-taking competency (Krueger & Dickson, 1994), time constraints (Ordonez & Benson, 1997), and outcome potential (Kahneman & Tversky, 1979). Thus, risk propensity appears to lie at the crux of a constellation of constructs that form an interconnected situation–trait rubric of entrepreneurial risk behavior. This nomological set, developed in studies of managers, needs examination and elaboration in entrepreneurial contexts. Although more research is needed, the entrepreneur's risk propensity, and its role in decision making in the pursuit of opportunity, may ultimately prove a vital component of a robust model of the process of entrepreneurship.

References

* Ahmed, S U (1985). nAch, risk-taking propensity, locus of control and entrepreneurship. *Personality and Individual Differences, 6*, 781–782.

Atkinson, J W. (1957). Motivational determinants of risk-taking behavior. *Psychological Review, 64*, 359–372

Atkinson, J W , Bastian, J. R., Earl, R W., & Litwin, G. H (1960) The achievement motive, goal-setting, and probability preferences. *Journal of Abnormal and Social Psychology, 60*, 27–36.

Barrick, M., & Mount, M. (1991) The Big Five personality dimensions and job performance. A meta-analysis *Personnel Psychology, 44*, 1–26.

Bearse, P J (1982). A study of entrepreneurship by region and SMSA size In K Vesper (Ed), *Frontiers of entrepreneurship research* (pp 78–112) Wellesley, MA Babson College

* Begley, T., & Boyd, D. (1987) A comparison of entrepreneurs and managers of small business firms. *Journal of Management, 13*, 99–108

* Brockhaus, R H (1980). Risk taking propensity of entrepreneurs *Academy of Management Journal, 23*, 509–520

Brockhaus, R H., & Horwitz, P S (1986) The psychology of the entrepreneur In D. Sexton & R. Smilor (Eds.), *The art and science of entrepreneurship* (pp. 25–48) Cambridge, MA Ballinger

Bromiley, P., & Curley, S (1992) Individual differences in risk taking In J Yates (Ed.), *Risk taking behavior* (pp. 87–132) New York: Wiley.

* Carland, J. C , & Carland, J W (1991) An empirical investigation into the distinctions between male and female entrepreneurs and managers *International Small Business Journal, 9*, 62–72

Carland, J W , Hoy, F , Boulton, W R , & Carland, J C. (1984). Differentiating small business owners from entrepreneurs *Academy of Management Review, 9*, 354–359.

* Carland, J W., Carland, J W , Carland, J C., & Pearce, J W (1995) Risk taking propensity among entrepreneurs, small business owners, and managers *Journal of Business and Entrepreneurship, 7*, 15–23

Cartwright, D (1971). Risk taking by individuals and groups An assessment of research employing choice dilemmas *Journal of Personality and Social Psychology, 20*, 361–378.

Chell, E. (1985) The entrepreneurial personality A few ghosts laid to rest? *International Small Business Journal, 3*, 43–54

DeLeo, J. G (1982). *To determine the difference in need for achievement and risk propensity between mountaineers and entrepreneurs* (Unpublished doctoral dissertation, Boston University)

Dewan, S (1982) *Personality characteristics of entrepreneurs* (Unpublished doctoral dissertation, Institute of Technology, Delhi, India)

Gartner, W. B. (1985) A conceptual framework for describing the phenomenon of new venture creation. *Academy of Management Review, 10*, 696–706.

Gasse, Y. (1982) Elaborations on the psychology of the entrepreneur. In C. Kent, D. Sexton, & K. Vesper (Eds), *Encyclopedia of entrepreneurship* (pp. 57–71). Englewood Cliffs, NJ Prentice-Hall

Greenberger, D B , & Sexton, D L (1988) An interactive model of new venture initiation *Journal of Small Business Management, 26*, 1–7.

Highbee, K (1971) The expression of "Walter Mitty-ness" in actual behavior *Journal of Personality and Social Psychology, 20*, 416–422

Highhouse, S , & Yuce, P (1996) Perspectives, perceptions, and risk taking behavior *Organizational Behavior & Human Decision Processes, 65*, 159–168

Hough, L , Eaton, N., Dunnette, M., Kamp, J., & McCloy, R (1990). Criterion-related validities of personality constructs and the effect of response distortion on those validities. *Journal of Applied Psychology, 75*, 581–595.

Huffcutt, A. I., & Arthur, W. A (1995). Development of a new outlier statistic for meta-analytic data *Journal of Applied Psychology, 80*, 327–334.

Huffcutt, A. I , & Roth, P L. (1998) Racial group differences in employment interview evaluations *Journal of Applied Psychology, 83*, 179–189

Hull, D , Bosley, J., & Udell, G (1980). Reviewing the heffalump. Identifying potential entrepreneurs by personality characteristics *Journal of Small Business Management, 18*, 11–18.

Hunter, J. E , & Schmidt, F. L. (1990) *Methods of meta-analysis Correcting error and bias in research findings* Newbury Park, CA Sage

Jackson, D. N. (1976) *Personality inventory manual* Goshen, NY Research Psychologists Press

Jackson, D. N (1978) Interpreter's guide to the Jackson Personality Inventory In P McReynolds (Ed), *Advances in psychological assessment* (Vol 4, pp. 56–102) San Francisco Jossey-Bass.

Jackson, D N , Hourany, L., & Vidmar, N. J. (1972) A four-dimensional interpretation of risk taking. *Journal of Personality, 40*, 433–501

Johnson, B. (1990) Toward a multidimensional model of entrepreneurship. The case of achievement motivation and the entrepreneur *Entrepreneurship Theory & Practice, 14*, 39–54

Kahneman, D , & Tversky, A (1979). Prospect theory An analysis of decision under risk *Econometrica, 47*, 263–291.

Kihlstrom, R. E & Laffont, J. J (1979). A general equilibrium entrepreneurship theory of firm formation based on risk aversion *Journal of Political Economy, 87*, 719–748

Kilby, P (1971). *Entrepreneurship and economic development* New York. Free Press.

Knight, F. H (1921) *Risk, uncertainty, and profit* New York Houghton Mifflin

Kogan, N , & Wallach, M. A (1964) *Risk taking* New York. Holt, Rinehart & Winston.

Krueger, N , & Dickson, P R. (1994) How believing in ourselves increases risk taking. Perceived self-efficacy and opportunity recognition. *Decision Sciences, 23*, 385–401.

Litzinger, W (1963) Entrepreneurial prototype in bank management A comparative study of branch bank managers *Academy of Management Journal, 6*, 36–45.

Litzinger, W. (1965) The motel entrepreneur and the motel manager *Academy of Management Journal, 8*, 268–281

March, J. G , & Shapira, Z. (1987) Managerial perspectives on risk and risk taking *Management Science, 33*, 1404–1418.

* Masters, R. & Meier, R. (1988) Sex differences and risk taking propensity of entrepreneurs *Journal of Small Business Management, 26*, 31–35

McClelland, D. C. (1961) *The achieving society* Princeton, NY Van Nostrand

McGrath, R. G , MacMillan, I. C., & Scheinberg, S (1992) Elitists, risk-takers, and rugged individualists? An exploratory analysis of cultural differences between entrepreneurs and non-entrepreneurs. *Journal of Business Venturing, 7*, 115–135.

Meyer, H , Walker, W , & Litwin, G (1961) Motive patterns and risk preferences associated with entrepreneurship *Journal of Abnormal and Social Psychology, 63*, 570–574

Mitchell, T. R (1985) An evaluation of the validity of correlational research conducted in organizations. *Academy of Management Review, 10*, 192–205

Mount, M K , & Barrick, M R. (1995). The Big Five personality dimensions Implications for research and practice in human resources management *Research in Personnel and Human Resources Management, 13*, 153–200

Ordonez, L., & Benson, L (1997) Decisions under time pressure How time constraints affects risky decision making. *Organizational Behavior & Human Decision Processes, 7*, 121–141

Osborn, R. N., & Jackson, D. H (1988) Leaders, riverboat gamblers, or purposeful unintended consequences in the management of complex dangerous technologies *Academy of Management Journal, 31*, 924–947

* Palich, L. E , & Bagby, D R (1995). Using cognitive theory to explain entrepreneurial risk-taking. Challenging conventional wisdom. *Journal of Business Venturing, 10*, 425–438

Perry, C. (1990) After further sightings of the heffalump *Journal of Managerial Psychology, 5*, 22–31.

Phillips, B K (1991). *Entrepreneurship Interpretation of autobiographies (responsivity)* (Unpublished doctoral dissertation, The Union Institute for Experimenting Colleges and Universities, Saratoga Springs, New York)

Plax, T , & Rosenfeld, L. (1976) Correlates of risky decision making *Journal of Personality Assessment, 40*, 413–418

Ray, D. M. (1982) *An empirical examination of the characteristics and attributes of entrepreneurs, franchise owners and managers engaged in retail ventures* (Unpublished doctoral dissertation, University of South Carolina, Columbia)

Ray, D M (1986) Perceptions of risk and new enterprise formation in Singapore: An exploratory study. In R. Ronstadt, J Hornaday, R. Peterson, & K. Vesper (Eds.), *Frontiers of entrepreneurship research* (pp 119–145) Wellesley, MA Babson College

Richard, J. C (1989) *A comparison of the social characteristics, personalities, and managerial styles of managers and entrepreneurs* (Unpublished doctoral dissertation, University of Windsor, Windsor, Ontario, Canada.)

Robbins, N E (1986). *Entrepreneurial assessment Characteristics which differentiate entrepreneurs, intrapreneurs, and managers* (Unpublished doctoral dissertation, University of Minnesota, St Paul)

Schmidt, F. L. (1996) Statistical significance testing and cumulative knowledge in psychology: Implications for the training of researchers *Psychological Methods, 1*, 115–129

Schneider, S L., & Lopes, L L (1986) Reflection in preferences under risk Who and when may suggest why. *Journal of Experimental Psychology Human Perception and Performance, 12*, 535–548

Schwer, K , & Yucelt, U (1984) A study of risk-taking propensities among small business entrepreneurs and managers An empirical evaluation *American Journal of Small Business, 8*, 31–40.

* Seth, S , & Sen, A (1995) Behavioral characteristics of women entrepreneur executives vis-à-vis their male counterparts: An empirical study. *Social Science International, 11*, 18–33

* Sexton, D L , & Bowman, N B (1983) Comparative entrepreneurship characteristics of students: Preliminary results In J Hornaday, J. Timmons, & K. Vesper (Eds), *Frontiers of entrepreneurship research* (pp. 213–225). Wellesley, MA: Babson College.

Sexton, D L , & Bowman, N B (1984). Personality inventory for potential entrepreneurs. Evaluation of a modified JPI/PRF–E test instrument In J. Hornaday, F Tarpley, J Timmons, & K Vesper (Eds), *Frontiers of entrepreneurship research* (pp 513–528) Wellesley, MA: Babson College

Sexton, D L , & Bowman, N B. (1985) The entrepreneur. A capable executive and more. *Journal of Business Venturing, 1*, 129–140.

* Sexton, D. L & Bowman, N. B. (1986). Validation of a personality index Comparative psychological characteristics analysis of female entrepreneurs, managers, entrepreneurship students and business students In R Ronstadt, J Hornaday, R Peterson, & K Vesper (Eds), *Frontiers of entrepreneurship research* (pp 40–57) Wellesley, MA Babson College

Shaver, K G , & Scott, L. R (1991) Person, process, choice. The psychology of new venture creation *Entrepreneurship Theory & Practice, 16*, 23–45

Sitkin, S B , & Pablo, A. L (1992). Reconceptualizing the determinants of risk behavior. *Academy of Management Review, 17*, 9–38

Sitkin, S B , & Weingart, L R. (1995) Determinants of risky decision-making behavior A test of the mediating role of risk perceptions and propensity *Academy of Management Journal, 38*, 1573–1592.

Smith, N R , & Miner, J. B (1983) Type of entrepreneur, type of firm, and managerial motivation: Implications for organizational life cycle theory *Strategic Management Journal, 4*, 325–340.

Stewart, W. H (1996) *Psychological correlates of entrepreneurship* New York Garland

Stewart, W H., Carland, J C., & Carland, J W (1998) Is risk taking an attribute of entrepreneurship? A comparative analysis of instrumentation *Proceedings of the Association for Small Business & Entrepreneurship*, 51–56

* Stewart, W. H., Watson, W. E., Carland, J. C., & Carland, J. W. (1999). A proclivity for entrepreneurship: A comparison of entrepreneurs, small business owners, and corporate managers *Journal of Business Venturing, 14*, 189–214

Thaler, R H , & Johnson, E. J (1990) Gambling with house money and trying to break even The effects of prior outcomes on risky choice *Management Science, 36*, 643–660.

Vinchur, A J , Schippmann, J. S , Switzer, F. S , & Roth, P L (1998). A meta-analytic review of predictors of job performance for salespeople *Journal of Applied Psychology, 83*, 586–597

Wallach, M. A., & Kogan, N (1959) Sex differences and judgment processes *Journal of Personality, 27*, 555–564

Wallach, M A , & Kogan, N. (1961) Aspects of judgment and decision making: Interrelationships and changes with age. *Behavioral Science, 6*, 23–36.

Address correspondence to. Wayne H. Stewart, Department of Management, Clemson University, 101 Sirrine Hall, Clemson, SC 29634–1305. E-mail: waynes@clemson.edu

From *Journal of Applied Psychology, 86*, 145–153. Copyright © 2001 by the American Psychological Association Reprinted with permission.

Discussion Questions for Model Literature Review 7

Editorial Note: All the model literature reviews in this book are presented as strong models. However, there are differences of opinion on the effectiveness of any particular piece of writing, even among experts. While answering the following questions, consider the guidelines in this book (as *only* guidelines, not principles) as well as your own standards for effective writing.

1. Briefly comment on the adequacy of the title of the review.

2. Comment on the adequacy of the Abstract. Does it effectively summarize the essence of the review given that abstracts are restricted to 120 words or less in the journal in which this review article appeared?

3. Does the review have a strong beginning? Does it get straight to the point? If not, have the authors used some other effective technique to begin the review?

4. Have the authors made a strong case for reviewing the topic(s) they cover? Have they shown that the topic(s) are important?

5. Is the material presented in a logical sequence? Are the headings (and subheadings, if any) appropriate and helpful?

6. Are key variables adequately defined? Are they defined at appropriate points? Explain.

7. Are there points where the references are not well integrated with each other (i.e., simply described as an annotated list)? Explain.

8. Are the strengths and weaknesses of some of the cited research described? If yes, name at least one section where this is done using paragraph numbers.

9. Have the authors made it clear what material is theirs and what is being summarized/paraphrased from other sources? Explain.

10. Are any portions of the review unclear to you? If so, identify them by paragraph number(s).

11. Are the individual paragraphs straightforward and to the point? Explain. If yes, identify one by number

that you think is especially good. If no, identify one that is weak.

12. Is the conclusion/discussion at the end of the review appropriate in light of the material covered earlier?

13. On a scale from 1 (very weak) to 10 (very strong), what is your overall evaluation of the literature review? Name one or two considerations that strongly influenced your evaluation.

14. Assume that you are on the editorial board of an academic journal and that the general topic of this review is within the scope of what the journal usually publishes. Which of the following would you recommend to the editor of the journal: publish as is, publish only after minor revisions, publish only after major revisions, *or* do not publish? Briefly defend your recommendation.

Table 1

Table of *Z*-Values for *r*

r	Z	r	Z	r	Z	r	Z	r	Z
.000	.000	.200	.203	.400	.424	.600	.693	.800	1.099
.005	.005	.205	.208	.405	.430	.605	.701	.805	1.113
.010	.010	.210	.213	.410	.436	.610	.709	.810	1.127
.015	.015	.215	.218	.415	.442	.615	.717	.815	1.142
.020	.020	.220	.224	.420	.448	.620	.725	.820	1.157
.025	.025	.225	.229	.425	.454	.625	.733	.825	1.172
.030	.030	.230	.234	.430	.460	.630	.741	.830	1.188
.035	.035	.235	.239	.435	.466	.635	.750	.835	1.204
.040	.040	.240	.245	.440	.472	.640	.758	.840	1.221
.045	.045	.245	.250	.445	.478	.645	.767	.845	1.238
.050	.050	.250	.255	.450	.485	.650	.775	.850	1.256
.055	.055	.255	.261	.455	.491	.655	.784	.855	1.274
.060	.060	.260	.266	.460	.497	.660	.793	.860	1.293
.065	.065	.265	.271	.465	.504	.665	.802	.865	1.313
.070	.070	.270	.277	.470	.510	.670	.811	.870	1.333
.075	.075	.275	.282	.475	.517	.675	.820	.875	1.354
.080	.080	.280	.288	.480	.523	.680	.829	.880	1.376
.085	.085	.285	.293	.485	.530	.685	.838	.885	1.398
.090	.090	.290	.299	.490	.536	.690	.848	.890	1.422
.095	.095	.295	.304	.495	.543	.695	.858	.895	1.447
.100	.100	.300	.310	.500	.549	.700	.867	.900	1.472
.105	.105	.305	.315	.505	.556	.705	.877	.905	1.499
.110	.110	.310	.321	.510	.563	.710	.887	.910	1.528
.115	.116	.315	.326	.515	.570	.715	.897	.915	1.557
.120	.121	.320	.332	.520	.576	.720	.908	.920	1.589
.125	.126	.325	.337	.525	.583	.725	.918	.925	1.623
.130	.131	.330	.343	.530	.590	.730	.929	.930	1.658
.135	.136	.335	.348	.535	.597	.735	.940	.935	1.697
.140	.141	.340	.354	.540	.604	.740	.950	.940	1.738
.145	.146	.345	.360	.545	.611	.745	.962	.945	1.783
.150	.151	.350	.365	.550	.618	.750	.973	.950	1.832
.155	.156	.355	.371	.555	.626	.755	.984	.955	1.886
.160	.161	.360	.377	.560	.633	.760	.996	.960	1.946
.165	.167	.365	.383	.565	.640	.765	1.008	.965	2.014
.170	.172	.370	.388	.570	.648	.770	1.020	.970	2.092
.175	.177	.375	.394	.575	.655	.775	1.033	.975	2.185
.180	.182	.380	.400	.580	.662	.780	1.045	.980	2.298
.185	.187	.385	.406	.585	.670	.785	1.058	.985	2.443
.190	.192	.390	.412	.590	.678	.790	1.071	.990	2.647
.195	.198	.395	.418	.595	.685	.795	1.085	.995	2.994

Notes: